A Better War Than Most

A Better War Than Most

A Novel of the Falklands War

Greg Willihnganz

The Wickfield Press

First published 2022
The Wickfield Press LLC
Cleveland, Ohio, USA
TheWickfieldPress@gmail.com

ISBN: 979-8-9864072-0-3 (paperback)
ISBN: 979-8-9864072-1-0 (e-book)

Book editing by Cindy Rinamen Marsch
Cover, interior design and formatting by Bea Reis Custodio

"No war is to be wished for, but if they have to be fought, this was a better one than most."

Patrick Bishop and John Witherow
The Winter War: The Falklands

DEDICATION

For Kit and Sara
Who give me joy and inspiration
And for Shirley
Their wonderful mother

CONTENTS

PART ONE

Argentina

Chapter One

February, 2022
Médanos, Entre Rios, Argentina

The nightmare raged within Reynaldo's mind, spreading throughout his body. His limbs ached in the darkness and the skin of his face pulled downward. He trembled and rolled to his side trying to free himself. He was back on the mountainside, flattened to the earth while the war passed over him. In the deep black night, he felt the thunder of the cannons in his chest and the palms of his hands. A wall of sound rolled over him, rattling machine guns, the crack of rifle fire, grenades bursting, missiles biting into the hillside. The deafening explosions sent geysers of peat and rock into the air digging holes that might have provided shelter if he could have reached them.

His rifle lay inches from his hand, but he dare not reach for it, touch it, or lift his head into the stream of bullets passing over him. The enemy was invisible in the night, relentless apparitions bent on tearing his flesh, blowing his limbs off, leaving his entrails to freeze onto these barren rocks. Then he heard the voice, heard it clearly, just as he had heard it so many times before.

"Run, Reynaldo. Run."

But he could not run. Frozen to the earth, he was powerless to drag himself out of this hell. The desperation and panic crushed his body, choking his throat closed, the pounding of his heart beating in his ears. From deep in his gut a sound slowly rose up his throat and into his mouth and left him in a raspy whisper.

"Marisol! Marisol!"

He ached for the touch of her, the shelter of her arms, the scent of her breath upon his neck. He cried in anguish, a wounded animal. Something was deeply, sadly missing. He tried to reach for it, grasp it, make it transcend this rolling horror of battle and night.

He came to his senses when he felt a dampened cloth and the hand of a woman upon his brow. He heard the soft spoken words. "Lie still, Rey. It was only a dream." Her touch was a caress, but he realized with a pang of loss that it was not Marisol. It was his sister Amalia. Faithful Amalia, loving Amalia, who asked for so little and gave so much. Four years younger than Reynaldo, she grew up worshipping him and worshipped him still. He would no more hurt her than cut into his own flesh.

And Marisol? She had been his wife for 27 years, the one love of his life, the only woman he would ever know in the intimate ways of husband and wife. Gone now, ten years in her grave from hemorrhagic fever, lying beneath the earth in a small graveyard outside Buenos Aires. She lived now only in his memory, but he felt her every day, her presence about and around him.

Rey rolled to his side keeping his eyes closed and fell into the blackness. The saving grace of his recurrent nightmare was its brevity. Once finished, he would sleep peacefully for the rest of the night. He did.

It was seven when he awoke, an hour past his usual waking time. But no one in the family would mind. His brother Mateo owned the ranch where Rey now lived and worked, but Mateo was very loose about hours and duties. Mateo was three years older than Rey and paid him only a small wage, but it was sufficient to Rey's needs and he was grateful to be out of the city.

Rey had left Buenos Aires in the summer of 2020, when the pandemic came to the city and began killing people indiscriminately. The virus moved like a cloud through the city driving people off the streets. The machine shop where Rey worked closed after two of the five workers died. He was grateful when Mateo called and offered shelter 200 miles from the city. Rey put his few possessions into storage and cancelled the lease on his apartment. He left the city in two days.

His sister Amalia came to the ranch four months later, after her husband Charro died of the virus. They had been living in the family house in Buenos Aires, caring for Rey's 83-year-old mother. Charro was asthmatic and the virus took him in only a week. Desperate to keep their mother safe, Amalia arranged a hasty funeral for her husband, packed up her mother and made the long trip out of the city to Mateo's ranch. Now the three children were reunited with their mother, living together as they had not done for nearly forty years.

Neither Rey nor Amalia had children, though both had longed for them. Now, in this most curious of years, they lived with their older brother who had six offspring ranging in age from five to fifteen. Mateo's noisy children filled the big house and the young ones were forced to share rooms when Mateo gave one large room at the end of the house to their grandmother.

There were no rooms left so Rey and Amalia took rooms in the *corbertiso,* an out building by the corrals, a combination barn, workshop, and dormitory. Two other workers bunked there as well and they all took their meals in the big house. Rey had a small room next to Amalia's, but it was actually not much smaller than the little flat he had rented in Buenos Aires. He was grateful he had any place to stay at all.

Rey dressed and washed his face feeling the stubble on his chin. It was too much trouble to shave and no one would care anyway. He looked at himself in the mirror. He was 58 years old, but looked older. Dark rings under his eyes and the sagging flesh of his face made him resemble his father. The old man had died many years ago, Rey could hardly remember when. After he gave up his work as a doctor, the life seemed to drain out of him.

Rey left the *corbertiso* and headed for the main house. He followed the path to the house and entered through the kitchen door. Juanita, the cook, was cleaning up from breakfast, but there was still food left out on the large dining table in the workers' hall. In better times, there had been twenty workers eating at this table each morning. Now it fed just Rey and Amalia, the children, and two field hands, Felipe and Alvaro. Mateo and his wife Lucia ate in the formal dining room deeper in the house. Grandmother Mariana ate dinner with them, but took breakfast in her room.

Now Reynaldo heard voices raised in the formal dining room. Even though it was a room and a hallway away from the kitchen, the sound carried. It was Mateo and Lucia arguing over money. Rey had heard this before and it filled him with guilt. He felt he must act and walked down the hall to enter the room with them.

"Forgive me," he began "I could not help hearing you. If my salary can help the finances, I will gladly give it up. I have savings and should really be paying you for the room and food you give me."

Mateo and Lucia stared guiltily at the floor. After a moment, Lucia raised her eyes to look at Rey. She was nearly crying. "I'm so sorry you heard this. Really, we squabble about money all the time. That's what married people do."

"And the little bit I'm paying you" Mateo added, "is nothing compared to the good you do for the ranch. None of the men could fix the tractor as you did or organize the workshop and barn. Please keep your salary. I would pay you more if I could."

"Well, I just wanted to offer..."

"No, no. There is no need. We have plenty of money. In fact, we're going to be spending a little this week on a celebration and we want you and Amalia to come."

Lucia brightened up, looking at Rey. "On Friday, we're having a grand dinner to celebrate our anniversary. We're going to dress up and eat by candle light and drink wine. It will be just the two of us and the two of you. And Grandmother Mariana, of course."

Rey studied their faces. "But, shouldn't this dinner be for just the two of you? It's your celebration. Wouldn't you rather have the evening to be a little more...intimate?"

Lucia looked at the two brothers. "After six children, we've had all the intimacy we need." They laughed together, breaking the tension.

On Friday, Amalia brought Rey his finest white shirt which she had carefully laundered and pressed. With straight black pants it looked very fine indeed, but Rey thought it lacked something. Rummaging through his drawers, he found a thin, silk scarf, red with no design on it, and tied this around his neck carefully pulling the ends down beneath his open collar. He fancied it made him look younger.

Amalia approved and sent him ahead while she fixed her hair for the celebration in the formal dining room up at the main house. The sun was just setting on a beautiful evening as Reynaldo leisurely walked up to the house, entering by the front door to honor the occasion. He was standing at the foot of the stairs when Mateo came down.

In an awkward moment, Mateo stopped dead and stared at Reynaldo's outfit. The smile dropped from his face and he pointed to the scarf. "Take that off immediately."

Rey was dumbfounded. He wasn't sure he had heard his brother correctly. It was a few seconds before he did anything.

"Take it off!" Mateo hissed. *"Do it NOW."*

Rey quickly untied the scarf and put it in his pocket, but his eyes never left Mateo who was more upset than he had seen him since he moved to the ranch. "Did I do something wrong?"

Mateo took Rey by the elbow and forcefully moved him down a hall, then into his private study. He brought him to the mantle and nodded toward a framed family photograph taken over forty years ago.

Reynaldo studied the picture and remembered the day they had gone to the studio in Buenos Aires to have it taken. There was his father, Dr. Emiliano Poralez, standing proudly, his hand resting on the shoulder of 10-year-old Amalia, so pretty in her pink dress. And Rey saw himself, at 14, smiling self-consciously, standing behind his mother, Mariana, the only one seated in the picture. Next to him stood 17-year-old Mateo, almost a head taller, looking like the confident young man he had been.

And there, on the right side of the family, taller than any of them, stood his other brother, Christobol. Handsome, proud, defiant Christobol, the eldest son at 21, who had come home from university for this photo. It was the last picture they had of him. His piercing eyes looked straight into the camera. He wore a white shirt with a red scarf tied round his neck.

Reynaldo sat down heavily, feeling like he had been struck in the chest.

"Have you forgotten him so easily?" Mateo said bitterly.

The shame of what he had done caught Rey fully and tears came to his eyes.

"Mother still prays for him every day" Mateo went on. "She lights candles in church for him. She believes he still lives."

Rey gripped the arm of the couch and turned from his brother. The pain washed up from deep within him. How could he have forgotten this picture? Forgotten this brother he worshipped as a child? The decades fell away and he felt himself looking up at him again, awed by his maturity, his intelligence and power. Christobol had been the hero of Reynaldo's childhood—and then he was gone.

Christobol Poralez was one of *los desaparecidos*, the disappeared ones. In the years between 1976 and 1982, the military leaders of Argentina threw out the elected government and began a reign of terror called *Guerra Sucia,* the Dirty War, during which they tortured and murdered 30,000 of their countrymen, suspecting them of being political opponents. There were no warrants or trials, people just disappeared, often based on rumor or hearsay. The military denied knowledge of the fate of these individuals, but they let the truth be known as a warning to any who opposed their rule.

Communists, union labor leaders, student activists, Peronist guerrillas, or anyone else who opposed the military junta, or was even suspected of opposing the junta, all were taken into custody, driven to one of three hundred and forty detention centers and never heard from again. Many were drugged and put onto death flights over the ocean where they were pushed out of cargo doors and dropped into the sea, their bodies never recovered.

Christobol had been active in the student protests against the military rulers. He had organized demonstrations and spoken against the junta. No one would ever tell the family what happened to him. He simply did not come home one night. Dr. Poralez was an influential man with many contacts in the military, but he hit a stone wall when he inquired about his son.

Mariana, his mother, was wild with grief. She refused to believe he was gone. She was certain he was being held somewhere, probably in the Navy School of Mechanics, down near the shore of the *Rio de La Plata*. Everyone spoke in whispers of this hellish detention center, the largest in Argentina, where thousands were tortured and died. People seen taken into the School of Mechanics rarely returned. The military denied they were even in custody.

As the months went on after Christobol's disappearance, Mariana inquired at every military and government office about her son, but could learn nothing. Finally, she joined the Mothers of the Plaza de Mayo. At first, she only marched with them, carrying a poster with Christobol's picture on it, wearing a white headscarf with his name and birthdate on it. But as the years went on, she became more active giving speeches and helping to organize the annual pilgrimage to Our Lady of Luján.

It caused great friction between Reynaldo's parents. There were bitter arguments about Mariana's involvement with the *Madres* and whether she was putting the family at risk. Dr. Poralez argued that when Mateo and Reynaldo had to serve their year of service in the army, they would be discriminated against, denied promotions, and given the worst assignments. Mariana didn't care. She hated the army and didn't want her sons serving in it for even a year.

All this seemed so far in the past, yet here it was with them still. The guilt at having forgotten his beloved brother for even an instant weighed heavily on Reynaldo. This was family and family was sacred. Some things we must never forget and this was one of them. He looked up guiltily at Mateo with tears still in his eyes.

"I'm sorry, Mateo. You're right, I should have remembered."

Incredibly, Mateo also had tears in his eyes and he sat down heavily on the couch next to Rey. "It's hard, so very hard. I know why Mother grieves and I grieve with her. He was so young and strong. I looked up to him. I thought he was invincible. It is still hard to believe he never came back."

They sat in silence for a minute or so longer, then rose and went to the dining room for the evening's celebration.

Chapter Two

The dream came again that night: Rey on the mountainside, pinned to the earth, the roar of battle around him, the smell of cordite filling the air. He stared across the ground at his rifle laying beside him, as useless as a balloon. He heard the voice again: *"Run, Reynaldo, run."* But he could not run, could not move, could only hold fast to the cold earth beneath him.

The dream was more than a recurrent nightmare. It was a shadowy recollection of his time on the islands, *las Islas Malvinas,* where he had fought his part in his country's brief little war forty years earlier. The dream captured his helplessness, his desperation, and the shame he bore being part of this national failure. There were darker memories he kept secret, scenes in his mind he never shared with anyone. He had secrets he would never acknowledge, could not even think of.

He awoke alone in his bed, grateful he had not cried out and woken Amalia. She had enough of her own sorrows without having to deal with his. Sometimes in the night, he heard her weeping softly, remembering her husband he guessed, but Rey did not know how to comfort her. He had been so devastated when Marisol died, he became a different person, a shadowy reflection of himself who went through the motions of living without understanding any purpose for it. He imagined Amalia felt the same. How could he help her? He could not even help himself.

A few days later, Reynaldo came in early from his work in the shop where he had been fixing a generator. He came into the kitchen and dining hall to find the usual after school chaos. Lucia and Amalia were organizing the children for afternoon chores, duties assigned according to their ages and capabilities. Juanita was preparing dinner, but she kept a pot of coffee going and Rey was grateful to get a cup and sit down to listen to the racket of children and adults negotiating on what needed to be done to clean the house and care for the livestock. After the years he had lived quietly alone in his apartment, Rey found it surprisingly enjoyable to be part of this thriving family.

After most of the children had dispersed to different parts of the house and ranch, Lucia and her eldest son, Marco, approached Rey sitting at the long dining table. Marco was 15 and strong for his age from years of working with his father on the ranch. He stood tall, but let his mother do the talking.

"Rey, Marco is writing a paper for school about the Malvinas War. He would like to interview you if you are willing to speak about your experience."

Rey looked at Marco whose grave eyes looked back at him steadily. He had been asked before about the war and his part in it, but he had always avoided speaking of that time, not wanting to call up those memories. But Marco was a fine young man, hard working and sincere and Rey felt great affection for him.

Amalia suddenly appeared, as if from nowhere, and put herself into the conversation.

"Marco, the war was a great many years ago and your Uncle Rey does not like to remember that period in our history. I'm sure there are many books in your school's library that can give you the information you need for your report."

Reynaldo smiled at Amalia, knowing she meant well. Dear Amalia was protecting her brother and standing up for him, as she always did. She knew what nightmares haunted his nights and feared bringing them into the daylight.

"But Uncle Rey was *THERE*" Marco said passionately. "He knows what really happened. He was part of it."

"He was wounded," Amalia replied, "in the service of his country and he has no need to dwell on that experience."

Marco was clearly getting upset and was about to speak again when Rey put up his hand to silence them both.

"Thank you, Amalia. I know you're trying to save me distress, but I think perhaps it has come time for me to speak about that war. Marco is right: there is much I can tell him that he will not find in books. I will share with him what I am comfortable sharing and leave the rest for others to speak of."

Amalia was unhappy with this, but Rey had made his choice and Lucia and Marco were pleased. It was arranged that in the evening after dinner, during the study hour, Marco and Rey would meet in Mateo's study where they could have quiet and privacy. Amalia offered to be with them, but Rey said it would be better if it was just the two of them. And so it was.

Marco came into the study carrying a lined notebook and two pens. He sat across from his uncle, in front of the fireplace where Rey had built a small fire. It was quiet in the house, the smaller children having already been bathed and put to bed, the older ones studying in their rooms. Marco shifted uneasily in his chair.

"I've never interviewed anyone, Uncle, so I'm not sure how to do this. I guess I should ask you questions and write down your answers. Maybe you could speak slowly so I could get the words down correctly."

Rey smiled feeling great affection for his nephew. "Why don't we just talk at first and then after you have a better feeling for the whole topic, you can write down notes."

Marco looked relieved. "Okay. Whatever is best. What can you tell me about these islands?"

Rey leaned back. "Well, they certainly weren't what I was expecting. You have to remember, this was forty years ago and I was just a boy of 18. I was pretty naïve. I thought the Malvinas were tropical islands, with sandy beaches and palm trees. I was very surprised when I discovered the real *Islas Malvinas*."

"What were they like?"

"Cold and barren. Rocks and peat and grass pastures as far as the eye can see. No trees grow on the islands and the wind never stops blowing. There are no roads to speak of, just a few in Puerto Argentino, but it is really just a small port and it is the only town on the islands. There were only two thousand British citizens living on all of the different islands. The English were spread out raising sheep on little ranches like this one."

"Weren't our people living there? Those are our islands, aren't they?"

"Well, they certainly *were* our islands, but that was almost two hundred years ago. When the English took possession of the islands, they shipped the Argentine settlers back to Argentina and replaced them with English settlers."

"So they stole our islands?"

"Yes, they did. But like you, I thought the people living on the Malvinas were Argentines. There were a few, but I never saw one. All I saw were the English."

"How did you get to the islands?"

"I was flown there after the navy and commandos took the islands and we captured the airport. It was not much of a fight. The English only had 80 soldiers on the islands. We had hundreds of soldiers and overcame all resistance in two days. By the time I arrived, on the third day, it was all over. I was a soldier and had just finished my year of mandatory service. I hadn't planned to stay in the army, but I was called back. I never learned we were going to the Malvinas until I was on the plane in the air."

"Were you scared?"

"Oh, no. We were thrilled. When they announced on the plane where we were going, everyone cheered and shouted in joy. We were going to be part of history. We were the great liberators going to free the islands and return them to Argentina. We all felt like heroes."

"But weren't you afraid that the British would come?"

"Oh, no. No one actually believed that. At least not at first. The English were 8,000 miles away at the other end of the ocean. And why would they come? To take back these desolate little islands and reclaim their sheep? It made no sense."

"Were the islanders happy to see you?"

"No, they weren't, but we tried to win them over. Our

commanders gave us very strict instructions. There was to be no looting or destruction of property. No abuse of the English in any way. We couldn't move into their houses or take their food, though we did occupy the police station and a couple other government buildings. But we listened to their complaints and tried to help them accept that they were now part of Argentina."

"How did they like that?"

"They didn't like it and some of the islanders were very angry. But mostly, they just scowled at us and looked on silently as we set up camp. A few were friendly, but none of them ever wanted us to stay. We hoped that as time wore on, they would come to accept us and accept the new government of the islands, but that didn't happen. It all ended much too quickly."

"How long were you on the Malvinas?"

"Ten weeks, though it seemed longer. When we arrived, we thought we would only be there a couple days. We would set up the new government and afterward we could go home. But then we learned the British were sending a big task force and everything changed. We had to defend the islands against attack and we were heavily reinforced and troops were sent all over the islands."

"Where were you sent?"

"When I got off the plane, I was taken to the docks where I helped unload the transport ships. We had few vehicles at first, so there was a lot of lifting and carrying. The town filled up very quickly and we had to set up tents in the fields. But the troops kept arriving and there was no room in the town. By the time the British arrived, there were 13,000 of us on those islands.

"It became so crowded, my whole company was moved out to the airfield. I was posted to the end of the peninsula and I had to live outdoors in a hole in the ground for nine weeks. It was the worst experience of my life. Then I was sent to Wireless Ridge, about three miles out of town. It was near the mountains, but it was really just a pile of rocks, 300 meters high. It overlooked the rolling fields below and was considered a good defensive position. I was only on the ridge for a few days before the war ended."

Marco was spellbound by what Reynaldo was telling him, but already Rey was having second thoughts about what he could share. Could he tell Marco about the actual conditions in that wretched little patrol post near the airfield? Should he talk about how the conscripts, like himself, were mistreated by the "real" soldiers, the *Buzo Tactico* and others? Could he tell him about Sergeant Cabruja? As if hearing his concerns, Marco spoke about something that had been troubling him.

"Uncle Rey, a boy in my class told me that his father saw an exhibition at the Military Museum in Buenos Aires many years ago that showed an Argentine soldier being tortured by his own officers. He said the exhibit had a manikin in an army uniform staked spread-eagle on the ground. Did you ever see anything like that when you were in the Malvinas?"

And there it was. The first of many questions he did not want to answer. And yet, it was forty years ago. Would his answers really matter? When Rey agreed to talk about the war with Marco, he had set a simple guideline: he would tell the truth or he would not speak about that particular subject. But this young man, who might face military service himself someday, needed to know these things. Rey could not gloss over his experience or make it pretty. He must share his knowledge of the military experience and hope Marco could understand.

"Yes, I saw men staked out and left in the cold for hours at a time, but such things were infrequent. You must understand, every army lives by its own justice, has its own courts and its own prisons. And if you desert the army or refuse orders or fail to fight the enemy, you can be imprisoned or even shot. Such things happen, but only to a very few soldiers. Most of us obey orders and survive."

"Uncle, did you ever kill anyone?"

Reynaldo felt himself pulled down into his chair as if gravity had suddenly increased. He looked at the serious young boy before him, so curious about what he might learn, so fearful of what he was asking. Did Rey have the right to bring the reality of war into this young man's thoughts? Was it kind to give him this knowledge, to share this bitter truth and hope he would somehow sort it out? What was moral behavior here? What was Rey's truth? Before he was clear himself, he felt the words spilling out.

"Yes, I killed a man. I am not proud of it and I pray to God it will never happen again. There is nothing noble or glorious about war, it is just what we must do when our time comes. You must be thankful you live in a time of peace. I can't say more now. In fact, I think we should probably end for this evening."

"But you haven't told me about the fighting, about how you were wounded."

Rey tried to smile at his nephew. "There will be time later. Your report isn't due for two weeks. We will talk again."

Marco was disappointed, but Rey was weary now and needed time to reflect, to gather his thoughts back together. He rose from his chair and left the study.

———•••———

It was all so long ago, another lifetime, and yet it was yesterday. How young he had been, how filled with ideals, and how naïve. They were going to free the islands and the happy islanders would welcome them, they were heroes. When the fighting approached, he thought he would be strong and courageous and stand tall against the British. He imagined concealing himself behind rocks, sighting his rifle on the enemy approaching. But when the dark night of war came, it was a hurricane of destruction, a roar of bombs exploding, star shells bursting, and machine guns rattling. In the blackness of their nighttime raids, he never saw a British soldier, only the flashes from their guns and cannon.

It was only after his surrender, when Rey was lined up with hundreds of other Argentine soldiers, prisoners like himself, that he actually saw the enemy. He realized with a shock how much older they looked. These were not conscripts like himself, these were professional soldiers who had fought for many years in many places around the world. And he saw how differently the officers related to their men. There was none of the arrogance or confrontation that was the rule in the Argentine army. It was always a struggle for power and control, but the British were much more casual and matter-of-fact when they talked. There was a respect between the officers and men that was curious in Rey's experience. It made him realize how young he had actually been and how limited his knowledge of the world.

Rey thought of the young man he had been, so excited, so full of hope. It was the last time he felt fully himself. So much changed so quickly, it recast his life. Though forty years, a lifetime in itself, had intervened, the course of his life was set during those months in 1982.

Chapter Three

February, 1982
Buenos Aires, Argentina

Reynaldo dressed quickly, getting ready for the evening. At 18, he was not tall, but he had a wiry athletic body that wore clothes well. Years spent playing soccer and lifting weights had paid off. He could feel his muscles beneath his shirt. His black wavy hair was slicked down with Brillantine and cut just right.

Rey was about to make his escape from the house when his brother Mateo entered his room, as usual, without knocking. Mateo, at 21, stood a full two inches taller than Rey and enjoyed teasing Rey by calling him Little Brother.

"Planning to step out, Little Brother?" Mateo waved his hand at the outfit Rey had put on for the night's adventure: tight black pants, a blood-red shirt and a yellow silk kerchief tied at his throat. Reynaldo already felt self-conscious about his choices and it didn't help that he was holding the black fedora Mateo always made fun of, insisting he looked like a miniature gaucho when he wore it.

"Don't you ever knock when you enter a room? And why shouldn't I go out? I'm an adult." Rey couldn't keep the bitterness out of his voice.

"Don't let father see you in that getup. He will not approve."

Rey looked away, knowing Mateo was right. "I'll take the back stairs. He won't even know I'm gone." The house they lived in, their parents' house, was one of the many things Reynaldo was grateful for. Their father, Dr. Emiliano Poralez, had done well in his career and they lived in a sprawling, three-story house at the edge of the medical district in Buenos Aires. As a child, growing up within these spacious rooms and winding halls, Rey had delighted in the endless places to hide while his sister Amalia would seek to find him.

Now, as Reynaldo felt his adulthood upon him, the house felt like a prison. The world at night lay just outside the door, dark and dangerous, but thrilling too. Buenos Aires was a nighttime city, rich with noisy cafes and throbbing dance halls. He was headed to one this evening in the company of his two best friends. It was always safer to travel in groups.

"Be careful" Mateo said to him seriously, "and don't let that hothead Sonny get you into any fights. Remember: *He is smart who runs away and lives to fight another day.*" This mangling of ancient wisdom, bestowed upon them by their Uncle Jorge in one of his drunken ramblings, struck Rey as funny and he couldn't help smiling.

"Okay, I'll do that. I'll do the running and let Sonny do the fighting."

"And don't stay out too late. Father won't notice, but mother will." This made Rey angry. "Enough already. I'll come home when I'm ready." He pushed past Mateo and left the house.

Rey met Sonny at the corner. Santana Dambolena, "Sonny" to his friends, was three inches taller than Rey and considerably broader in the chest. It was a powerful body fueled by a powerful temper that was easily set off. Girls adored him, though only those unconcerned with academic achievement. Sonny had no use for studying and barely scraped by in school. His advances toward the opposite sex were crude and unsubtle, but at times he could be very funny. Rey had met Sonny in school when they were both seven and they had been friends ever since. Sonny was intensely loyal and virtually fearless.

"How is your sister doing?" Rey asked. Carlita, Sonny's 10-year-old sister, had crashed her bicycle a few days earlier, leaving her screaming in the driveway of their home with a bloodied knee and a twisted ankle. Sonny had picked her up and carried her the two blocks between their houses, then asked if Rey's father, Dr. Poralez, could look at his sister. Dr. Poralez had a rule about never seeing patients in his home, but on this occasion, he broke that rule. Rey was proud of his father who was very gentle in dressing Carlita's wounds and wrapping her ankle.

Sonny's father, however, was not pleased when he heard of it. He swore at Sonny for begging the help of the rich Dr. Poralez and threatened to take a belt to him. But it was an idle threat. The old man was a drunk who had physically abused his wife and children for years until Sonny put an end to it after growing large enough to stand up to him. They had an odd relationship, in Rey's eyes, for Sonny loved his father and still respected him.

"Carlita's fine," Sonny said. "She's hardly limping anymore and she's back riding that stupid bicycle." He laughed.

The third member of their trio soon arrived. As far removed from Sonny as it was possible to be, Juraich Mitner, "Jury" to Rey and Sonny, was shorter than either of them, thin and pale, with the look of someone who spends too much time in the library. He was not quite ugly, but he had large eyes behind his glasses which gave him an owlish look. The females of this world paid him little heed.

Though Rey had only known Jury for three years, he considered him his best friend. Jury was the smartest person Rey had ever met. He excelled in every class and Rey believed he often knew more than the teachers who taught those classes. But what endeared Jury to Rey was his kindness, his genuine concern for others, and his uncanny ability to negotiate between people. He was a good person and Rey respected his counsel above all others. Rey did well in school, but he worked hard for it and never ascended to the level Jury attained effortlessly.

It was an odd group, this trio of friends, but Rey was proud to be part of it. There was no leader among them, but they seemed to easily make decisions together. They balanced each other. Jury could calm Sonny down when that was necessary, but Sonny's strength and confidence kept them safe from bullies and most of the dangers on the street. Rey was the binding force that gave them purpose and direction. He often initiated their activities, as he had this evening, suggesting they go to a notorious hotspot in the downtown district.

The three friends had registered for service together. All males in Argentina gave a year of service to the army after graduating from high school and, as they had hoped, they were posted to the same unit. It had been a rough year and they had been at the mercy of a sadistic sergeant who took every opportunity to torment them, but they had survived and helped each other get through it. They had been discharged together three weeks ago.

It took them two bus rides to get downtown and it was one of the seedier areas of the city. There were drug dealers and prostitutes walking the street and Rey shuddered to think what his father would say if he knew where he was. But this was adventure, excitement, a chance to get free of the routines that bored them all. The club they were headed for was *Toro Bailando,* The Dancing Bull, and everyone had heard of it.

They were on the street now and Sonny stopped them at a deserted park before they got to the club district. "All right, what have you brought for defense?"

Jury looked surprised and shook his head. Sonny smiled and brought out his "thumper," a metal contrivance he had made in his father's workshop. It was four steel rings welded together in a row, then filed and sanded smooth. It fit perfectly over the fingers of his right hand and the thick rings protruded well above his knuckles. He mimicked punching Jury in the forehead with it. Sonny was delighted when Jury instinctively jumped back.

"One punch to the forehead and it is lights out. What did you bring, Rey?"

Reynaldo looked around guiltily before reaching into his pocket. He brought out a beautifully curved folding knife with a white pearl handle that glistened in the streetlights. He held down a button at the end of the knife and with a flick of his hand, the five inch blade swung out and clicked into place. It was a move he had practiced many times at home.

"Mother of God!" Jury said. "What are you doing with that knife?"

Rey released the blade, folded the knife shut and put it back into his pocket. "Nothing" Rey said, "well...I don't think I will ever have to use it, but I thought I should bring something. It is Christobol's knife. I took it from his room."

Sonny and Jury looked at each other silently. They both knew, as did everyone who knew the Poralez family, about Rey's missing brother Christobol. He was probably dead after disappearing three years ago and Rey rarely spoke of him. It was shocking Rey would take this knife from Christobol's room which Rey's mother still kept clean and neat, hoping Christobol would return. They didn't want to say anything, out of respect, but Jury was upset.

"You can't take that knife into *Toro Bailando*. They have security guards. We will be searched. If they find any drugs or weapons, they will confiscate them and they won't give them back."

"How do you know that?" Rey asked.

"I've read about this place and made inquiries. I don't go anywhere that I don't know about and this is not a safe place. We need to stay together. But you should leave your knife here in the park. Hide it beneath a bench and we can pick it up on our way home."

"I can't do that" Rey protested. "I won't risk losing it."

"I put my thumper in a little pocket I sewed into my boot," Sonny said. He showed them how he concealed it. "Maybe you could hide the knife in you shoe."

"No. It's too large."

Jury looked at Rey thoughtfully. "What about your hat?" Rey took off his fedora and looked inside. "Tuck the knife into the lining on top and then put if firmly on you head. The guards will just pat us down, they won't look in your hat or Sonny's boots."

Rey followed this advice, but did not feel confident.

They could hear the sound of *Toro Bailando* half a block away. Reynaldo noticed how littered the streets were in this part of the city, how rundown the buildings and how many doorways were filled with idlers. It was not a place to linger. There was a line at the door stretching most of a block and they waited nervously for fifteen minutes before they got to the door. The huge security guard didn't bother searching them and just waved them inside.

The rock and roll blaring inside was nearly deafening. This was no upscale tango salon where the dancers wore classic costumes and swirled majestically across a beautiful parquet floor. The building was an old converted factory where the inside walls had been knocked down to make a giant dance floor that held hundreds of gyrating dancers while hundreds more watched from the sides. Sonny pointed across the room at a tightknit group of teenagers, mostly males wearing white tee shirts with purple bands sewn around their left sleeves.

"*Los locos del Lavalle*" Sonny said, "the worst street gang in the city. Don't mess with them. Bad business."

Jury grabbed Sonny's arm and pulled it down. "Don't point. We don't want to be noticed." But he was a moment too late. Two of the larger gang members had seen Sonny pointing and now marched toward them, their powerful arms swinging at their sides. Rey saw that several others in the group were now nodding toward them, watching the confrontation that was unfolding.

The first of the gang stepped to within a foot of Sonny and spoke straight into his face. "Who are you little *chiquitas* pointing at? Eh? You looking for trouble maybe?"

Jury stepped next to Sonny, but before he could speak, the gang member casually took hold of Jury's forehead and with a violent push sent Jury reeling, but his eyes never left Sonny.

"Stay out of this *pequeño*, I want this one!"

Sonny was not easily intimidated and he stared back into the angry face before him calmly, but even Sonny could see his position was hopeless. Even if he could subdue this *pandillero*, his companion standing behind him was even bigger. And the gang now watching them intently from across the room was unlikely to let this end in a fair fight.

Reynaldo also saw their position. He did not feel panic, but rather a resigned concern. They had miscalculated, believing that three of them together would keep them safe. But this was a different place than Rey had imagined and now a fight was about to erupt. He had been in fights before and he determined that whatever the outcome, he would give a good account of himself. Rey had a curious thought: he hoped Jury's glasses would not be broken.

As Rey stood looking at the two combatants before him, he felt an odd sensation, like someone had his arm around his shoulder and was pulling him close in an affectionate form of comradeship. It took a moment of adjusting to this sensation before he realized this was not his imagination: he was being drawn to someone on his right. That's when he heard the voice.

"Aliendo, these are my *comaradas*. Leave them. They are no threat to you."

In a moment of genuine horror, Rey recognized that voice. A brief glance to his right confirmed his worst fears. This was no rescuer, no savior coming to bring them out of the wilderness. This was Bartoli Cabruja, the man Rey feared above all others, the infamous Sergeant Cabruja of the military police, who had made Rey's year of service in the Argentine army a living hell. He stood a full six feet and three inches and his muscles bulged across his chest and down his arms. When Rey pulled away and looked at Sergeant Cabruja, towering behind him was his equally violent and dangerous *compañero,* Lobo Iturat.

Of all the people Reynaldo had met in his eighteen years of life, these two were the worst. Vicious, ruthless, and cruel by nature, they enjoyed inflicting pain and taking advantage of others. They lived to torment. And once in their web, as Rey and his friends now were, there was no escape. Since Rey, Sonny, and Jury had enlisted together, they were discharged together as well. Technically, they were no longer under Bart and Lobo's jurisdiction, but that would make no difference. To no one's surprise, the two gang members melted into the crowd and were quickly gone from sight.

"Well, now" Bartoli began, "it seems I have saved you from a bad beating. What do you think my reward should be?" The three friends standing before him were silent. With a deft sweep of his arm, Bart snatched the fedora off Rey's head. As he did so, the knife hidden inside fell out, landing at his feet. He picked it up, carefully inspecting the beautiful knife.

"Oh, my, look at this. A pearl-handled switchblade." Bart pushed the button to open it and admired the gleaming blade. "This is a fine knife for me to be carrying. Much better in my pocket than hidden away in this stupid hat." He threw the fedora at Rey.

"Give it back!" Rey demanded. "It's my knife. You cannot steal it."

"I'm not stealing it. I'm appropriating it to keep you safe. You're not allowed to have such weapons in this place, so I'm doing you a service. Think of me as one of the security guards."

"GIVE IT BACK."

At that moment, Jury stepped in front of Rey and boldly took Bart's elbow pulling him off the dance floor. "Sergeant Cabruja, let me talk to you for a moment. You have every right to take that knife, but there are a couple things you should know before you commit yourself to that act."

"Commit myself to what? What are you talking about?"

"Please, follow me." Jury led Bart and Rey to a small alcove off the dance floor where the noise was less. Sonny and Lobo stayed behind glaring at each other.

"The knife you're holding" Jury began, "belonged to Rey's brother Christobol. It was given to Christobol by his father, and by Christobol to Rey. It must remain in their family."

"Why?"

"Because it bears the mark of the curse. Look at the base of the blade. There is a small half moon with a cloud partly covering it. Whoever steals this knife is cursed and will die by the knife itself."

Bart looked closely at the knife and saw the mark Jury spoke of. "This is silly. It's just a mark."

"It is a mark cut into the steel blade itself. Feel how sharp the blade is. Now imagine how easily it will cut through the organs in your stomach. You can keep the knife, but I really don't think you want to."

"Do you think I'm stupid?"

"No. I think you are wise and I think you're devout. And that is why you must give the knife back to its rightful owner. The Virgin Mary will know you have done this and it will save you more grief than you can imagine."

Bart studied the knife for a moment, then pushed the button and folded it closed again. He handed it back to Rey. Rey put the knife in his pocket and tentatively held his hat out to Bart.

"Keep your damn hat! Now get out of here before I change my mind."

Outside, they ran for a full block before they slowed down, laughing nervously.

"My God, that was a close one," Sonny said. "Jury, how did you know there was a mark on the blade of that knife?"

"I saw it when Sgt. Cabruja opened the blade and held it up. Then I made up the story about the curse. Cabruja is a sadistic psycho, but he's curiously religious and superstitious. Rey, do you remember the night he had you caned?"

It was Rey's most bitter memory of the last year. He had made some offhand remark, trying to be funny, and the sergeant had taken it the wrong way. Bart dragged him into the washroom in the barracks and made him stand facing the wall for fifteen minutes while he sent Lobo back to his office for the special rattan canes he kept for just this purpose.

When Lobo returned, Rey was forced to drop his pants and his underwear and bend over. Rey was determined not give Bart the satisfaction of crying out, but the first stroke was so electrifying and agonizing he screamed out anyway. He screamed with every stroke. Lobo struck him again and again with all his force. When it was finally over, Rey was bleeding and his backside was covered in bright red welts. It was several weeks before he healed.

"It is not something I'm likely to forget."

"I heard him praying, later that night. A couple hours after lights out, he came to the end of your bed and asked the Virgin Mary to forgive him. I think he genuinely regretted having done it. Of course, that would not keep him from doing it again. He is a truly sick man."

"Sick or not," Sonny said, "he did save us tonight. And he even let you keep your hat."

Rey smiled and firmly planted the fedora back on his head.

Chapter Four

Six weeks later, Rey sat at a long dining table at one of the fanciest restaurants in Buenos Aires. His family were all dressed formally including Rey who, at his mother's insistence, was wearing his army dress uniform. He had been called back into service without notice and had been ordered to pack his combat gear and report to the airport the next morning. Jury and Sonny had also been called back. They had no idea where they were going to be sent or how long they would be gone.

The unexpected call-up came on the night the family was going out to celebrate Dr. Poralez's sixtieth birthday. They had been planning this party for months, a big celebration in a private dining room at *El Palacio de La Marimba,* The Marimba Palace, an expensive restaurant and tango hall in the north end of the city. It featured a 40-piece orchestra with two giant marimbas, playing before a beautiful hardwood dance floor where only the most talented tango dancers were allowed to perform. Competitions were frequently held here.

The dining areas were on two stories and formed in a U-shape looking down on the dance floor. The downstairs floor was for open dining, but upstairs there were several larger dining halls for bigger parties.

Dr. Poralez had spared no expense for this second floor room and invited his family to bring guests in addition to the numerous relatives in attendance. Rey's mother, Mariana, had asked Rey if he was bringing a girl to the party, but he shook his head and told her there was no one special he was seeing at the moment. He finally invited Jury to come with him just so he would have someone to talk with other than relatives.

There were over sixty people in the party. Rey had wisely chosen a seat far from the head of the table where he and Jury could easily get up and move about or leave the room. There was a large glass wall that looked out on the second floor balcony so diners could watch the dancers below. An arched opening into the room was big enough to allow several people or waiters with large platters of food to easily enter.

Along one wall, there was a long table covered in gifts for Dr. Poralez. After a full dinner of many courses, Dr. Poralez was making a great show of opening each present individually and exclaiming his pleasure at receiving it to the applause of those watching. Amid the clatter of the waiters clearing away dinner dishes, Rey and Jury slipped out onto the balcony unnoticed.

The wide balcony had small tables, each with two chairs, placed alongside the railing so guests coming out of the dining rooms could sit and watch the dancers below. Reynaldo looked along the balcony surrounding the dance floor until his eyes came to rest on one girl, sitting alone watching the dancers.

She was not the most beautiful girl he had ever seen, but there was something intriguing about her. Her large eyes seemed to miss nothing that was going on below and he could sense the intelligence behind those eyes. She wore a white dress with flowers embroidered into the neckline, and a knitted shawl of yellow lace. She was smiling as she looked at the dancers below.

"Look at that girl" Rey said to Jury.

"I know her," Jury said. "She was in my sister's class in school. She is the daughter of Vice-Comodoro Lantana and don't even think of talking to her."

Rey turned to his friend. "Why not?"

"To begin with, she is two years younger than you are. And the Vice-Comodoro is an important and influential man. But the real reason to stay clear of her is that she is the favorite niece of Captain Alfredo Astiz and he is highly protective of her. People who cross Astiz disappear very quickly and he has agents everywhere. Be smart, leave her alone."

Rey looked affectionately at Jury. "But that's the problem. I'm not very smart. And I need a little adventure." Before Jury could reply, Rey walked off leaving him shaking his head in dismay.

There were two chairs at the table on the balcony where she was sitting and Rey stood behind the empty chair and waited until she turned to look at him.

"Hello, my name is Reynaldo and I was wondering if I might sit down and watch the dancers with you."

She looked a little frightened. "I don't think that would be proper."

"I'm just a young person like yourself, enjoying the evening. The dancers are wonderful, but they would be so much better if I could just share them with you." It sounded a little odd, even to his own ears, but he thought he saw the hint of a smile come to her face. He could not be sure.

"My father would not approve."

Rey abruptly sat down across from her. "Then we won't ask your father to join us. I'll only stay for five minutes, I promise. Well...unless you ask me to stay of course."

She turned away from him, but he could see she was smiling.

"You are very forward," she said, "and it is not proper for me to be speaking with you."

"I'll only stay for a few minutes and I'll probably do most of the talking anyway so you won't really be speaking with me. Please let me stay. May I know your name?"

It was clear to Reynaldo he had caught her interest. Now if he could only maintain it. Looking into her eyes, he realized she was far prettier than when he had seen her at a distance. She seemed to radiate light and he wondered if possibly just a little of that might have come from his attention to her.

"My name is Marisol, but everyone calls me Marie."

"Well, if everyone calls you Marie, then I will call you Marisol.

It is a beautiful name. You should call me Rey. Everyone I care about calls me Rey. I'm here with my family; all of my family, cousins, aunts, uncles, they're all here. We're celebrating my father's sixtieth birthday..."

Thus began a conversation Rey knew he would remember the rest of his life. They spoke of their families and their friends, of school and Rey's military service. They talked about classes they had loved and classes they hated. They talked about books they'd read and movies they had seen. The only thing they didn't talk about was the dancers below them.

They spoke for almost an hour and the conversation flowed between them easily. There was never any hesitancy and their words carried an urgency neither really understood. It seemed impossible to bond in so short a time and yet they did. Rey could have spoken with Marisol for the whole night, but it ended without warning.

Marisol stood. "Father."

Rey also stood and turned to face the tall figure of Vice-Comodoro Lantana who was not smiling. "Marie, where have you *been?*"

"I've been right here, watching the dancers."

"And who is this young man?"

Rey spoke quickly to keep Marisol from any awkwardness. "Sir, I am your daughter's friend. I am Reynaldo Poralez, the son of Dr. Emiliano Poralez."

This last bit of information surprised the Vice-Comodoro. "You are the son of Dr. Poralez?"

"Yes, sir. We are celebrating his sixtieth birthday in the dining room over there." He pointed. Vice-Comodoro Lantana did not bother to look, but instead inspected Reynaldo.

"Your father is a good man. He has treated me."

"We are all very proud of him."

"Well, be that as it may, you are too old to be speaking with my daughter. You may leave us."

But Rey held his ground. "Sir, as you can see from my uniform, I am a soldier in the army of Argentina. I have completed my year of service, but have been called back into service. Tomorrow I will be shipped out, I don't know to where or for how long, but I believe it may be many months. I would like to write to your daughter while I am gone."

The Vice-Comodoro looked bemused by this request. "And why should I allow you to write to my daughter?"

"Sir, I am just a soldier looking at a long period of service ahead and thinking it would make my service easier if I could share my experience with someone back home other than just my family. I would not try to romance your daughter or treat her with anything but respect. You may read my letters to her if you wish."

The older man looked at the younger man for several moments without speaking. Then he turned to his daughter.

"Marie, do you wish to receive letters from this young man?"

Rey saw her smiling. In fact, she was beaming. "Yes, father, I do."

"All right then, I will permit this, but only under strict conditions. First, you will not try to 'romance her' as you put it, but will confine yourself to talking about your experiences in the army. And yes, I will read every letter you send her. You will not be having a relationship with her when you return from wherever you are going, but you may write letters while you are gone. I will read those letters before I give them to her, so you will send them to me."

The Vice-Comodoro took a small leather folder from within his jacket and pulled a card from it. On the card was a military address to his office and below it a series of random letters that appeared to be a code word.

"The army censors read soldier's letters, so when you send them to me, don't write your name in the return address corner. Instead, put this code. Then the censors will send the letters straight on to me without opening them. You may write freely about your unit, where you are stationed, your officers and how you're being treated—anything you wish to write. It won't matter, I'll be the only military person reading them. I'll also read Marie's letters to you."

Rey gratefully took the card. "Thank you, Vice-Comodoro. I will not violate your trust."

As they walked away from him, Marisol turned to look at him again. She was still smiling. He felt elated. He did not know where he was going, but he was taking a little bit of her with him.

Chapter Five

Though Rey didn't know his destination, Marisol's father, Vice-Comodoro Lantana, did. He had scheduled the flight Rey would be on. Lantana was in charge of Logistics and Planning for the Argentine Air Force and only that morning he had requisitioned dozens of civilian aircraft to carry conscripts and regular units down to the *Comodoro Rivadavia* Air Base in southern Argentina. From there, it was a four hundred mile flight to the *Islas Malvinas* and those flights were already scheduled. The invasion was definitely on and Lantana had been assigned a critical role in orchestrating it.

Allowing this young man to write to his daughter had nothing to do with promoting their friendship or providing comfort to a homesick soldier. The Vice-Comodoro was gathering information, that was all. He spent his days gathering information about any potential enemies of Argentina. But, more importantly, he compiled information about the enemies of the Argentine Air Force and that meant, specifically, the Argentine Army and Argentine Navy. Rey would tell him what was really happening on the ground, unlike the rosy reports he was certain he would receive from the Army high command.

The military junta that had ruled Argentina since 1976 was made up of an uneasy alliance of the three branches of the military. Though pledged to the greater good of the country, the services fought constantly over resources, funding, personnel, political influence, decision making, strategic goals, and a hundred other issues. After the start of the Dirty War, the infighting had become even more vicious and secretive.

Lantana did not trust the Army. The reports they gave his office, when they gave them at all, were full of boasts about their power and were often untrue. The Navy was even worse. It was hard to measure the treachery and manipulation within any of the service branches, but knowing and understanding it was his responsibility. Argentina had seen two different ruling juntas in the last six years and the current leader, President Galtieri, had only been in office for four months. He had already fallen under the spell of Admiral Anaya who was taking the nation into war.

Vice-Comodoro Lantana had no love for *el Presidente*. General of the Army Leopoldo Fortunato Galtieri was a vain, ruthless, dangerous manipulator who drank too much Scotch and knew more about engineering than economics or politics. Conditions in Argentina had steadily deteriorated since he took office and now there were protests and riots every week as inflation got worse. Thousands were marching in the streets.

Galtieri's "liberal reforms," allowing more freedom of speech and protests, had backfired and only made people more aware of how perilous their lives had become. Even the Dirty War could not control the communists and Peronists agitating in the cities. The people were rising up against the junta.

Galtieri was a graduate of the infamous School of the Americas, the CIA's training ground for counterinsurgency. Desperate to keep communism from spreading throughout the hemisphere, the United States had set up this terrorist school to teach South American politicians how to use torture, murder and intimidation to control their countries and keep out the Reds. President Jimmy Carter had limited aid to Argentina due to its human rights violations, but Ronald Reagan was willing to turn a blind eye to the Dirty War in Argentina, so long as it kept the communists at bay.

Vice-Comodoro Lantana opposed the Dirty War, but not on moral grounds. For him, politics was war and some people were bound to get killed. But he felt the Dirty War was ineffective and was creating more enemies for the junta than it was eliminating. The real problem was the economy. Inflation had jumped and was steadily getting worse. In a desperate move to stay in power, Galtieri started the war for the Malvinas, knowing it would be wildly popular. But Lantana saw a major problem with this strategy:

reclaiming the Malvinas actually meant taking the islands away from Great Britain and they would never stand for this.

In this belief, the Vice-Comodoro was alone among the leadership of the Argentine junta. Galtieri and the high command all believed the British would just accept the Argentine takeover of the islands. Or, at the worst, taking the islands by force would lead to some sort of UN takeover that would force the British to seriously negotiate the transfer of sovereignty back to Argentina.

Lantana knew this was folly. During college, he had studied for two years in England at both Sandhurst and at the Royal Air Force College at Cranwell. He understood the British and their armed forces as few in Argentina did. He was sure they would never simply give up those islands and move 1800 of their citizens back to the home islands.

But there was precedent. Argentina had very close ties with the United States and the U.S. had never supported Britain's colonial interests. In 1956, when Egypt took over the Suez Canal, Britain was ready to go to war, but the U.S. and the United Nations forced them to give up control of the Canal. Could it happen again in the South Atlantic?

That was a question for the diplomats, Costa Mendez and his gang. All that concerned Lantana was getting enough men and materiel to the Malvinas before the British could intervene. Once Argentina had secured possession of the islands with reinforced garrisons and air cover, there was no way the Brits could come down 8,000 miles of ocean and take the islands back.

Or was there? He wondered.

———•••———

April 1, 1982

Dear Marisol,
I thank your father, once again, for the privilege of writing to you about my time in the service of our country. I am honored to do so.

I write these words sitting on the floor of a giant airplane hangar at the Comodoro Rivadavia Air Base in Southern Argentina. Hundreds of us in my unit have been told to sit down and wait for further orders. We've been sitting and laying on our duffle bags for hours. It seems this is always the way with the army: hurry up and wait! We have no idea where we are going or what we will be doing once we get there. It is possible this is all some kind of huge war game or exercise. No one knows.

Of course, there are a lot of rumors. Many believe we are going to be shipped to the Chilean border to give them a show of force so they'll retreat from the Beagle Channel. I don't even know where they Beagle Channel is or why it is important. But they haven't issued us guns yet so I don't think we will be fighting any time soon.

The truth is in a year of service with the Army, I have only fired a rifle once and they just gave us a few shells to practice with. We spent a lot of time learning how to clean a rifle, and how to operate a machine gun (in theory, we never actually fired one). And we spent a lot of time digging fox holes and then filling them in. And we spent even more time marching— marching, marching, marching. Some days, that's all we did.

My friends Sonny and Jury are both with me, freezing their butts off just like I am sitting on this hard concrete floor. What we've seen sitting here is a lot more conscripts like ourselves arriving and being marched off to someplace else. We've also seen some planes unloading the Buzo Tactico, the elite rangers who are a different type of soldier altogether. They are bigger and look meaner than any soldiers I've ever seen. And we can tell from their attitude they don't respect us in the least. They don't talk to us and if you ask them a question, they pretend they don't hear and walk away like we are some kind of lower life form. Even so, if we ever got into a shooting war, these are the guys I would want on my side!

We haven't been fed for six hours and I'm hoping food will arrive soon. They probably have too many mouths to feed with all the troops arriving. And I have no idea where we are going to sleep tonight. We haven't been issued bed rolls or anything so I'm hoping we will be put in a barracks somewhere. So this is the glamorous life of a soldier! Wait and see, wait and see.

Sorry for complaining so much. I hope your activities at school are going well and I look forward to hearing from you.

Thank you again for letting me write to you.

Your friend,
Reynaldo

April 5, 1982

Dear Reynaldo,

I am so excited to be writing to one of the Malvinas Heroes. You cannot imagine what has happened in Buenos Aires since it was announced that we have taken back our islands. There are parades and celebrations all over, not just in Buenos Aires, but everywhere in the country. Last week people were demonstrating against the government, this week they are demonstrating for the government. People are waving flags and cheering everywhere you look. At school, the teachers try to follow their lesson plans, but all anyone wants to talk about are the wonderful Islas Malvinas.

In your first letter (the first of many, I hope) you did not know where you were going to be sent, but I am sure that you are one of the brave soldiers sent to the Malvinas. I can feel it! And I hope you will tell me all about your experiences there. Were the people there glad to see you? I know they have sent some of the British back to England (good riddance!), but are the islanders happy to be back with the government of Argentina? What are these islands like?

I have so many questions I can hardly put them into words. But I am sure you are busy doing important things so I will let you tell me what is happening whenever you can.

Thank you for what you are doing for Argentina. You are very brave.

Your good friend,
Marisol

PART TWO
Great Britain

Chapter Six

March, 1982
London, England

The third martini finally hit. He'd been waiting patiently—too patiently he thought irritably—for the lunch that took twenty-five minutes to arrive. During the wait, he hand-flagged the waiter twice to order drinks. Now it didn't matter, the third martini brought that little euphoric mellowing that came right out of the back of his head.

He was drinking too much. He knew that, had known it for some time, was ashamed of it, but felt powerless to stop. Three martini lunches and four martini dinners were frequent, his days without liquor less frequent. Though he didn't drink himself to sleep every night, once or twice a week was common. His stomach seemed reconciled to his consumption, probably even enjoyed the regular loosening of muscle tissue.

That was what middle age had brought Mike Ferrol, a loosening of muscle tissue, a gradual organic decline. He was 38, but felt ten years older even though his skin didn't hang. He had a small roll at his middle, ten or fifteen pounds he guessed, enough to push his waist out another inch after the inch he'd picked up during his divorce six years ago. Too many things like that in the past. Too much to think about. He finished his martini and nodded sagely as the waiter finally brought his lasagna.

It was surprising how the British made better lasagna here in London than the Italians did back in Detroit. Maybe it was just better gin. He took up his knife and fork.

Two hours later, Mike sat at his desk at the London Chronicle. It was a grey metal desk, identical to 35 other grey metal desks laid in six neat rows across the sprawling floor of the newsroom. His assigned desk was toward the far back corner, an indication of his place in the pecking order.

He reviewed his morning's work. It was a "local news" story, the bane of any serious reporter, but important for keeping the local residents reading about their neighbors. This was a story about Joel Esterhous, a four-year-old who won the Preschool Poets Competition in Twickenham. His poem read:

"Brave people fight Tigers. They chase them in circles until they turn into butter."

Mike called young Mr. Esterhous and interviewed him on the phone. Between Joel and his mother, Mike was able to cull out enough anecdotes and printable quotes to put together an entertaining little human interest story. He probably should have been a social worker. But he lacked the ideals and the patience.

Reuben Blake came down the aisle toward him. Blake was in his mid-sixties and had been on the staff before typewriters went electric. He wielded his modest powers as Metro News Editor with a lack of arrogance, refreshing in a newsroom. Like most newspaper men, like Mike himself, Reuben could be very charming. The difference was he did it as a matter of course, not just when it suited his purpose.

"Here's one for the International Page for you, Mike. Give it a bit of humor."

Mike smiled dubiously. "Can't promise that, Reuben. I don't get funny until midnight and it's not the sort of thing you want to print."

"Oh, stick it up your bustle, Yank. You're a great imported talent, an international journalist, famed on both sides of the water."

"And equally famous in the middle of it." Mike took the papers Reuben handed him. "I'll do what I can with it."

Reuben waved and moved away from Mike's desk.

It occurred to Mike as he looked across the newsroom that twenty years hence he was likely to be in this same room, five rows up and three desks across, sitting in Reuben's chair, waiting for retirement just as Blake was doing now. It made him shudder.

He looked at the papers that now lay on top of his desk. It was an AP wire, straight off the printer, describing an incident 8,000 miles away on the bottom of the globe. An Argentine scrap metal merchant, Constantino Davidoff, had landed a party of workman at Leith on South Georgia Island, a British possession next to Antarctica. But Davidoff failed to get permission from the British Government to clear the abandoned whaling station at Leith, even though he had negotiated a contract with a Scottish-based shipping firm. Too damn complicated, Mike thought. After landing the scrap metal workers, Davidoff raised the Argentine flag giving at least the appearance of a civilian invasion, though Leith was deserted.

It was the sort of action that could lead to a serious international incident, but Mike was hard pressed to find any humor in it. Maybe Reuben was pulling his leg. Mike wrestled with the story for over an hour and finally came up with an article titled "Argentine Invasion Turns Into the Pirates of Penzance." When he handed it in, Reuben was not very impressed.

"It's a bit thin" Reuben commented after reading it, "but I guess it will do."

Mike gave him a two-finger Cub Scout salute and headed for the door. He walked six blocks to Bellow's briskly. It wasn't much for exercise, he realized, but it gave his heart a chance to pump things through the system one more time before the alcohol came.

Mike enjoyed walking quickly. He imagined it made him look active, involved, a man with important things to do. In truth, it was easier to move quickly when heading toward a drink, but he still managed to do flights of stairs two at a time on occasion. He moved least on the cold, damp mornings when he woke with a headache.

Inside the front door of Bellow's, he had to elbow his way through the hot, smokey room past a loud group of lorry men, still in uniform. He got to the journalist's traditional section of the bar at the crook of the L. Mike waved to Patty to bring his gin and tonic over. Patty waved back and moved to his bottles. He was pouring before Mike found a stool.

The group tonight included three reporters, two columnists, a sports editor, and someone Mike had never seen before. Malcomb Hollister held the floor.

"Did you see my story on the blind axe murderer?"

"Old news, Malcomb."

"Get off it, I think you two are having us on."

"Where'd he do this here alleged murderin'?"

"Warburton, in Manchester" Malcomb said. "Did in his wife and daughter, both while they were sleeping, right in their own beds. While they were lying all peaceful, countin' lambies."

"Come on, Malcomb. A little respect for the dead. You wouldn't want someone hacking you up while you were lying about in one of your alcoholic stupors, now would you?"

Malcomb pulled at his coat lapels and frowned. "I take exception to that, sir."

"He takes exception to that" Johnny Lamb said. "He *would* want to be hacked up in one of his alcoholic stupors!"

They all laughed.

"My story on the pot-headed peer was better" Aidan Scoffield said. "Watch for The Great Cannabis Debate when Pulitzer time comes."

"You draw that one? Rather dull if you ask me. All talk and no action. The law remains the same."

"Well, the debate might have got dull toward the end" Aidan said, "but it was worth it just to hear the Marquess of Tweedale say he knew pot was harmless from personal experience. He's done himself in with that one."

"Naw, the beggars will cheer him on. As long as you're not talking any kind of temperance, they're all for you."

The banter went of for 25 minutes and another drink before someone mentioned dinner and headed for the door. It was then Mike realized he'd forgotten something. Tonight was dinner at Maddie's. Damn. It was stupid to put off thinking about things like that and he'd gotten himself in trouble this way before. Now he was half an hour late.

Maddie made a fine dinner, that wasn't the problem. She was as skillful in the kitchen as she was in the bedroom. In both areas, she was generous to a fault. They had been lovers for two years and Mike had nothing to complain of. Except these dinners with her husband.

Madeline's husband Ted was a Lieutenant Colonel in the Naval Intelligence Service. Mike had met him while writing a story on armaments expenditures. Ted impressed Mike as rather a prig, keen-eyed and tight-lipped, who said things too carefully. He was never rude, but he didn't give you anything printable unless he wanted it printed.

So it surprised Mike when he met Ted a week later in a pub and found him quite open. Out of the office, Ted was a different man. They got very drunk that night and at the end of the evening, Ted invited Mike to dinner with his family.

That was how Mike met Madeline. Madge, as Ted called her, was a striking woman. Auburn-haired with thin, delicate legs, she had full breasts just a little too large for her sleek figure. Those breasts drew men's attention immediately and Mike was no exception. It wasn't until later that he realized she colored her hair.

Madeline had been awkward as a child, you could see it in the way she held herself now. She was not quite sure of her beauty and that alone gave her a vulnerability Mike found attractive. Indeed, it was hard to keep his eyes off her during the first dinner at their house. Having seen her, he wondered how she had connected with the dour Ted Tomlinson.

After an hour, he began to get the feel of the marriage. They were not a happy couple. It was clear in the way they moved around each other, in the lack of touch, in the guarded way they brought up topics and the dullness of their replies. Here was a lonely woman getting lonelier. He knew this spelled trouble for anyone fool enough to get involved and he made a mental note to stay as far away as possible.

But London was lonely for Mike too and when he met Madeline, two months later, drinking alone in a pub in the afternoon, he couldn't resist sitting down for a quick drink. Ted, it turned out, was out of town. Out of the country in fact; in Tunisia, doing God-knew-what for the Intelligence Service. Their 11-year-old daughter, Edith, was off to her cousin's in Chelsea. So Madeline was alone and Mike was alone and one thing led to another.

Now, two years later, the three of them were sitting down again, in what had become a bimonthly ritual based on the friendship between Mike and Ted. Mike suspected Ted's dinners were offered so he could casually pass him the information the Intelligence Service wanted spread without direct quotes, but it was a small price to pay for having an explainable relationship with Madeline.

The problem was Mike had come to like Ted Tomlinson. Once he got past Ted's professional reserve, he found Ted interesting and enjoyable company, a friend, something Mike hadn't found in the three years since he'd moved to England. Ted had a wealth of stories to tell about his military experiences and a storehouse of information Mike could frequently draw from for stories and background. He was surprisingly well-versed in current world politics and discussed them without the proselytizing conservatism of most military men.

Which made it awkward for Mike to continue with Madeline, but the simple fact was, he had fallen for her and could not imagine ending the affair. She was sweet and beguiling and the most sexually satisfying woman he had ever been with. But there was a darker edge to this relationship that he tried not to dwell on. Mike had achieved something rare in his experience: the privileges of the marriage bed without its responsibilities. From a quite cynical point of view, it was an arrangement Mike cherished.

Ted's marriage was the one thing Mike and Ted never discussed, nor did Madeline and Ted discuss it, but Madeline often spoke of it with Mike. It was far easier when Mike could just see them separately.

Once, as Ted went off on one of his trips, he suggested Mike might take Madeline out. It was possible Ted knew what happened while he was gone, but Mike doubted the Lieutenant Colonel would do anything about it, even if he knew. The distance between Ted and Maddie was already too great. He might leave her, but he wouldn't fight for her. A consoling thought since, even at six-foot-two, Mike was no match for the ruggedly built naval officer who had previously served with the Special Air Service. But Ted would have to contend with his own infidelity before he could confront Madeline with hers.

Maddie said she knew of at least two on-going affairs Ted had had in the past, one of which nearly broke the marriage. She was certain he found women in whatever part of the world he travelled through. The bitterness this caused in the early years had distanced them in a permanent way, now their relationship was less a marriage than a convenience. They shared money, food, and their daughter, maintaining the façade of a family. Behind the façade was a couple who were polite without being intimate and a daughter who hardly knew her father.

Edith, despite her dowdy name, was an even greater beauty than her mother. Her 13-year-old figure had developed in the two years Mike had know her and now gave promise of a woman who would break hearts casually, without artifice, without trying. Her delicate features were set shyly on a face with the deepest brown eyes Mike had ever seen. Yes, Mike thought ruefully, they'll kill themselves over that one. It was easy to see the tensions that might arise between this daughter and her father. But that wasn't enough to explain their particular distance.

The sad fact was that Ted had no time for Edith and had never taken the time when it was needed. He was not a cruel man, but he was often insensitive to his daughter's needs, preoccupied with his work and unable to share any of it with her. There were security issues of course, but really it came down to the fact that he was just not the sort of man to share that part of himself. Mike had listened to many hours of Maddie discussing Ted and Edith. He felt a guarded sympathy for the girl, but mostly he felt relieved not to be caught in a similar situation. Hearing about it once a month was bad enough.

Tonight Edith was off to a friend's for the evening and that would make things easier. He apologized to Maddie at the door for being late, but she was all sweetness and light, handing him a martini before he sat down. Ted glanced briefly through some mail on the bureau, then threw it back into a pile. He took his own drink, scotch, and sat on the couch across from Mike.

"How's the media tonight?" Ted asked. "Any breaking stories I should know about?"

Mike speared his olive and stirred. "Just the routine things. A blind axe murderer in Manchester and a Peer who wants to smoke pot."

"I thought that issue died in the 60's" Ted said.

"Not for all of us."

"You a pot smoker?"

"No" Mike shook his head, "I've tried it, but that was a long time ago and it didn't agree with my system." In fact, Mike had only smoked marijuana twice with a roommate in college, in the dorm, before he'd even lost his virginity. He considered it a low thrill experience not worth the time or money. Alcohol was better and it was legal.

"I had an interesting story earlier" Mike said. "You might have heard of it. Seems some scrap metal merchant down in Argentina has decided to invade one of our islands."

"Invade? Is this an army expedition?"

"No, no. Strictly a commercial venture. But he raised the Argentine flag and didn't have permission to land on South Georgia in the first place."

"Hmmm..." Ted shook his head, "sounds like something for the Foreign Office to me. You'd better ask them how to deal with it."

"But isn't this the sort of thing that leads to diplomatic incidents? And don't diplomatic incidents lead to war?"

This was a familiar game between them, the "what if" scenario.

"No, Mike. You've got the wrong slant on this one. Listen, this guy is some sort of commercial operator, right?"

"Yes, a scrap metal merchant."

"So he's down there doing a job for a company. This is a civilian enterprise I take it."

"Right."

"Well, as a military planner, what I ask myself is: what is the strategic value of the position he is threatening? And the answer is: next to nothing. Then I ask myself what force is he exerting on the objective and how much force would be required to displace him. The answer: not much."

Mike nodded.

"Then I ask myself, what is the tactical value of this objective? This property is off in a corner of the world that is practically unpopulated, it is not a shipping or transportation choke point and it cannot be used to launch an attack. So, tactically, it is useless.

"Finally, I ask myself if this may portend a greater invasion. The answer is an unqualified no. I mean, did the Japanese send fishing boats ahead of them to Pearl Harbor? Hardly. This is just some Latino patriot trying to get his name in the paper."

Mike smiled. "Yes, I'm sure you're right. It didn't even make much of a story."

"And I didn't make much of a dinner" Madeline said as she entered from the kitchen, "but you're welcome to what we have. Now come along."

Madeline was always briskly efficient when serving. There was fresh linen and a sparkling service with crystal goblets for the wine. Tonight she served first an Italian salad with a light vinaigrette, then Cornish game hens with wild rice and creamed asparagus tips on the side. There was white wine and candied figs for dessert.

Maddie's cooking always pleased Mike, but he was aware of an irritation too. He was never comfortable with the fuss she made over his coming. She seemed to take such pleasure in bringing her "men" together. But Mike felt uneasy and used somehow. He was beginning to have doubts about this relationship.

Chapter Seven

Ted watched from the window as Mike drove away. He waited another five minutes, then made an excuse to Madge and left for the Ministry. He hoped he hadn't laid it on too thick with Mike, hadn't seemed too eager to discount the event or too knowledgeable about it. Actually, he had been following the incident at South Georgia since the moment it was reported, and though it was minor as he had said, there were too many signs in that part of the globe just now, too many indications that things might be headed out of control.

For the first time in many years, Ted was aware of his fear. Not fear of international tensions or nuclear holocaust; it was a simpler fear, less noble though no less awesome: he feared his personal destruction. He rarely articulated this fear to himself and never to others, but it was always with him.

Ted had been a professional soldier all his life, like his father before him and his grandfather before that. He'd grown up on tales of the Royal Marines and the Small Boat Squadron and the Parachute Regiment. His boyhood dreams turned to reality with surprising success. He was a bold and disciplined officer who had seen a wide variety of service and known action from the jungles of Malaya to the streets of Belfast. He'd joined the Special Air Service, the SAS, because they were the hardest trained and toughest fighting unit in the world.

But somewhere along the line something happened to Ted, something deep inside that he could not look at too closely. The danger no longer excited him or drove him to take chances. He wanted safety, predictability, and the assurance he wouldn't be called in the middle of the night and told to pack up his kit and head into battle. Then an opportunity arose to join the Naval Intelligence Service where his combat experience would help him in planning operations without ever having to actually take part in them. He accepted quickly. He'd done well for several years in Intelligence, but he was aware that planners are sometimes called into combat zones and this trivial incident down in the South Atlantic seemed to be drawing him toward it.

The situation was more serious than he could say to Mike. Indeed, his superior had strictly warned him not to "tell that newspaper chum of yours" anything about the energy and attention now being focused on the South Georgia incident. Negotiations with the Argentines were extremely delicate. The area of dispute was not South Georgia, but the Falkland Islands. That was the prize they were after.

The long neglected Falklands. What a useless piece of barren rock, Ted thought. Half a million sheep and 1800 British nationals, living together in a feudal economy at the end of the earth. Why did the Argentines want it? For pride, that was all. To puff themselves up, to forget about the hunger in their bellies and the unemployment on the streets. The military government of Argentina, the latest junta, was less than four months old and already it was tottering on the brink of collapse. They needed a war so the people would look the other way. The only question was: who would they fight? Britain or Chile?

Each country controlled territory Argentina had long claimed. But attacking Chile compromised South American stability, whereas ending British colonialism would likely draw world support. Britain could hardly defend a target from 8,000 miles away. The garrison posted on the islands, 40 Royal Marines, could offer only token resistance. The Argentine Army would sweep them away in a few hours. Retaking the islands, however just a cause, might not be possible. Argentina's economic chaos was due largely to their spending vast sums on the most advanced armaments available. By far, they had the most potent armed forces in South America.

Ted smoked a cigarette as he drove to the Ministry. He was smoking more lately, a filthy habit bred of anxiety. He parked in the deserted lot and went up to the fourth floor where the lights were still shining. He found Burke and Wingate already at work at their desks.

"Hello, Ted" Burke said. "All set for the war with Argentina?"

"Yes, I suppose so. What's the game tonight?"

"We're doing a third phase contingency plot. Leach wants to know not just the numbers, but the specific ships: in drydock, in port, and at sea. And time projections for mounting an amphibious assault on the Falklands assuming a full Argentine defense."

Wingate looked up from his desk. "And he wants to know the results of course."

"Right" Ted said laying his briefcase down. "Whether we'll win. We'd better. I suppose he wants this by morning."

"Oh, no" Burke said, "he wants the initial report by eleven."

"Eleven? How's he expect that?"

"You know Leach. He just does."

Admiral Sir Henry Leach, First Sealord of the Admiralty, was in the delicate position of working with the Admiral of the Fleet to explain the Royal Navy's position to the Cabinet. This critical interface of the permanent military establishment and the temporary civilian government was the juncture at which all major decisions were made. These decisions had implications not just for the people of England, but for humanity as a whole. As a nuclear power, Britain could launch the war that would truly end all wars.

Leach was expected to know the safety of the entire Commonwealth at any given moment. Contingency plots, drawn up by the intelligence staff over months and years, tried to anticipate any eventuality world politics might cast upon them. Plans were drawn up so that Britain might continue her NATO commitments and still fight the war. That, of course, would depend on the support of the United States, but in an invasion situation, there was no question of America supporting Britain. That, at least, was one worry they did not have.

Ted enjoyed working with Larry Burke and Tom Wingate. They were capable, steady men who handled themselves well in a crisis. They had been together almost six years now, in this same office.

All of them had the highest security clearance and there were no international secrets within this room.

The plan they drew up that night was similar to the reports drawn up in each of the defense posts around Britain and around the globe. The difference was that here, all the information was brought together at once, so the possible functioning of the entire system could be plotted. The system went far beyond military craft and personnel. The British fleet included every merchantman under British registry and all commercial shipping facilities; docks, storage, and crews. In time of crisis any of these could be, and would be, used.

The trick now was to assess what resources were available at this moment, not only in the military sphere, but from the Merchant Marine as well. Then to look at how these resources would need to be changed to be suitable for use in a South Atlantic conflict. Finally, by some leap of imagination, to guess the probable effect of this force: whether they could win.

This last factor was the least reliable. Ministers tended to look only at numbers and consequently got a distorted view of the real picture. How should you weigh the technological advantage Britain enjoyed over Argentina? What did experience count for, since Britain had fought well so often and Argentina had never fought at all? How could you measure support of Britain by the United States, the ultimate power on the globe?

Britain had a full missile force capable of being deployed anywhere in the world. But was she strong enough for a non-nuclear confrontation? That was an acute question since beef-rich Argentina had been taken over by the military who invested in high tech armaments, many purchased from Britain.

Later that night, Ted wrote the summary paragraph for the report:

The outcome of a conflict in the South Atlantic between Britain and Argentina is uncertain at best. The Argentine forces are well-armed, well-trained, and will be fighting for a cause they

*passionately believe in. Assuming a full Argentine resistance, once
a takeover of the islands has been effected, there is no guarantee
we could retake the islands even in the best of circumstances.*

Ted read the paragraph to his colleagues. "What do you think?"

Larry chewed on his pen and looked off thoughtfully. Tom shrugged and looked at his watch. "All our research justifies what you've written, but I keep wondering if we're being too pessimistic."

"I'd rather err on the side of caution" Ted replied. A messenger arrived and Ted hastily typed up a cover sheet for the report.

"I'll take this directly to the Admiral's office," the messenger said, "and Major Brockton would like to see you, sir."

"Me?" Ted asked. How had Brockton even known he was in the building?

"Yes, sir."

"All right, I'll be along directly." Major Brockton was Leach's personal aide and a very influential man. He was a tall Etonian, usually charming, but he could be ruthless and aggressive without warning. Ted was always careful around this man.

Ted waited fifteen minutes outside Brockton's office before he was ushered in. The Major waved him into a chair and pointed to the mountain or reports and dispatches littering his desk.

"Everything is in a rush now. Sir Henry wants it all done by midnight and we'll probably be here half the night. Anyway, good evening. Sit down. I've seen that report you did yesterday and it's quite good. Thank you. We've had some news from the Foreign Office. Do you know the status of things down there?"

"I gather the Argentines haven't left."

"Damn right they haven't left. In fact, they're putting supplies ashore. Not a military buildup yet, but it's some kind of buildup. If they decide to overrun those islands, either at South Georgia or in the Falklands, we're powerless to stop them."

"I realize we can't physically defend the islands" Ted said, "and won't have any military options until after the fact, but if we could make some sort of minor concession..."

"Dammit, man, the minor concessions have all been made. We've been conceding in the United Nations for the past 17 years. The Argentines just aren't having any more of it. We're going to blows down there, I can feel it in my bones, and I want to be sure we're ready for it when it happens."

"I'm wondering if we may precipitate action by the Argentines if we make any moves which might be considered aggressive."

"What's aggressive if we're defending our own islands?"

"The problem is they believe they are Argentine islands."

"Well, they're wrong about that, aren't they? Damned right! And they're going to stay wrong about it for a long time. Tomorrow we'd like your section to re-evaluate your report."

"Actually, I've just sent the Admiral an updated Sit Summary..."

"Very good, but we'll need you to expand and augment it in depth. Make full use of the fleet around Gibraltar on Operation Springtrain. I want estimates of the time to launch them ship by ship and how quickly we can move a force in earnest down to the Falklands. We may be in a situation where days matter, so get the most complete information available. Limited options are not going to be possible.

"We'll have to assume the Americans go with us on this one and are willing to cover NATO without us. Every ship, every man, every plane we can spare will have to go south in the event of an emergency. There's no sense in going down there to have the Argies slap our faces and send us home. We're going to win or we're not going at all."

"Yes, sir." Ted was surprised by the major's emphatic tone which was extreme even for Brockton.

"Oh, one other thing. Don't be afraid to put the negative aspects of your proposed campaign into the reports. It'll help convince the PM we need a full task force. Of course, they'll call us doom-sayers, but maybe they'll try to understand what we're up against."

"Very good, sir." Ted saluted and left.

As he went downstairs, he wondered what the point was in telling the government we might lose. They'll never believe it, he thought. Not unless it happens and by then it won't matter what they believe.

The next week was the longest in Ted's life. First, they received intelligence reports that Argentine ships were moving toward the Falklands. While the Royal Navy was on maneuvers off the coast of Spain, the Argentine navy was holding joint maneuvers with the Uruguayan navy. The monitoring of radio signals at sea showed increased activity in the South Atlantic, but this did not clearly point to the Falklands.

On Saturday, March 27, a disturbing number of factors came together. Two Argentine missile corvettes broke away from their fleet and headed for the Falklands. In addition, army leaves were cancelled all over Argentina. The army seemed to be gearing up for action. On the Falklands themselves, observers reported increased over-flights by Argentine Hercules aircraft, which could be either harassment or intelligence gathering. At the same time, in Argentine embassies all over the world, Easter leaves were cancelled and the staffs told to stand by and await further developments.

What kind of developments? Would the Argentines take over all or part of South Georgia and leave their claim at that? It was possible that might satisfy them, but Britain could hardly accept the situation and allow that precedent to be set. Some retaliation was called for and it seemed inconceivable that the Argentines would not understand this.

On Monday, a report came to Ted that an Argentine submarine was headed for the Falklands. There was also further evidence of Argentine ships moving into the area and substantial troop activities on the mainland. He later learned that that morning the Prime Minister, Margaret Thatcher, and Lord Carrington had flown to Brussels for a Common Market meeting. They discussed the situation on the plane and decided to send three nuclear submarines immediately. They phoned the Defense Minister, John Nott, from the airport and he notified Fleet Headquarters at Northwood.

This changed the whole complexion of the crisis. Now it was no longer a local event, to be guided and negotiated from afar, with the diplomats in charge. Now forces were being moved into the area and lines drawn. Planning became paramount, as though a jolt of electricity had gone through the entire building Ted worked in.

The Times reported that five Argentine vessels were in the South Georgia area, but the country hardly took notice. Only Ted and the other planners knew that a show of force was in the offing, on the Argentine side if not on the British. How should they respond to this challenge? It was playing out in the time honored progression of wars down through the ages: claims were met with counter-claims, threats met with counter-threats, and finally military action. Nothing of consequence had yet happened, but the direction of movement was clear.

That day Sir Henry Leach called his staff together at Whitehall for a major planning session. Ted looked around the large briefing hall and noted that intelligence, operations, logistics, and supply staff were all present. Only a crisis of sufficient stature could require such an assemblage and the hushed silence and attentive faces carried an unmistakable message: there was danger about and each of them would be affected.

Major Brockton opened the meeting. His look was grave. "You all know the situation down in the Falklands. The Argentines seem headed for a major showdown and there isn't much we can do about it. The question is just whether it will be a diplomatic show or a military one. All along we've felt we might have a breathing space of months or even a year before Argentina's usual belligerence turns critical. Now we're reassessing that.

"Argentina may try to pressure us in a variety of ways. There may be harassment of third party foreign trawlers that use Port Stanley or they may try private landings on some of the islands. They've already given support to the landing in South Georgia, but they may also try to occupy uninhabited islands. Beyond this, of course, there is the possibility Argentina may launch headlong into a full scale takeover of the Falklands. This is the eventuality we need to consider today.

"The three submarines we are now sending south may deter the Argentine navy after they arrive, but it will take us close to three weeks to get them down there. *Spartan* is on maneuvers near Gibraltar, but *Splendid* and *Conqueror* will have to be brought down from Faslane in Scotland. If an invasion comes sooner, we have no way of stopping it at all."

He paused to clean his glasses with a handkerchief. Ted wondered if he really needed to clean his glasses of if this was just a theatrical way to punctuate what he was saying.

Brockton continued: "Argentina has a formidable navy with surface, underwater, and air capability. At least six of their ships have the Exocet sea-skimming missiles, also our principal surface weapon. Two of their subs have full anti-sonar electronics and it will be the devil to find them.

"Their air force is quite modern with Skyhawks, Mirages and Super Ètendards. They have over two hundred planes, most of them the effective Pucara attack planes which would work well in a land conflict in the Falklands. I'm afraid we'll be fighting our own technology, in many cases the weapons we've sold them.

"What we're facing is a modern army that will be well entrenched long before we arrive. We're looking at an island assault launched from 8,000 miles away with no local support bases and only floating platforms from which to launch an attack. By the time we get down there we could easily be facing a force of five or ten thousand men.

"We can rule out, then, any plan which does not embrace all the resources we have available. We will need carriers, subs and an amphibious assault element in full strength. Before we look at what specifically we will need on our side, let's consider what the enemy's going to be shooting back at us."

Brockton went on to list the various canon and mortars the Argentines possessed and the German anti-aircraft guns that used the Skyguard radar system. He spoke about the French Roland and British Tigercat missiles they possessed, the British Blowpipe man-portable system, the Westinghouse Mobile Radar valued at millions of pounds, and finally the French Exocet anti-ship missiles, perhaps the greatest threat to the British Navy.

"I want to emphasize to you the difficulties we're going to be facing in an operation of this size." He paused a moment, looking around the room. "The logistic considerations alone are staggering. Men, machines, ammunition, food, fuel, and spare parts will need to arrive at the dockside at the right time and in the right order for correct operational loading. There will be loading schedules with tens of thousands of items. The list of what we shall need is practically endless"

Brockton shuffled through his papers to find a list. "Harrier jets, helicopters, tanks, guns, lorries, Land Rovers, armed recovery vehicles, combat engineer tractors, field engineering stores, earth movers, electronic warfare equipment, missiles of all types, bombs, ground attack rockets, anti-tank rounds, grenades, thousands of shells, millions of rounds of small arms ammunition, medical supplies of every type, tents, clothing, boots, ration packs, and, of course, several thousand gallons of beer."

Muted laughter followed, but Ted could feel the tightening across his back, gripping him so tightly it pulled his shoulders up. He consciously pushed them down and forward, stretching the muscles, forcing his body to relax. He eased his shoulders again and let his spine settle back into the seat. He was able to focus more easily when Brockton continued.

"Every ounce we transport those eight thousand miles to the South Atlantic will cost many times its value, but it will be useless to us if it is buried somewhere in the hold of a ship where we don't know about it or cannot get to it when we need it.

"In all your computations, remember the two dominating factors: fuel and spare parts. If our parts list fails us, we will lose; it is as simple as that. And if our fuel supply falters, we shall lose even the dignity of sailing back to England defeated and be forced to surrender on the spot. I trust you will appreciate the Admiralty's desire to avoid that circumstance.

"Now in a moment, we'll go over the communications and electronic warfare equipment list, but first the Admiral will address you."

Admiral Sir Henry Leach stepped up to the podium taking several seconds to look over the men assembled before him. "We should be clear from the outset" he said, "that this will be a Royal Navy show from start to finish. The Prime Minister, the Cabinet and the other services are in agreement with that view. We may expect the full cooperation of the other services in supporting our efforts, but naval considerations shall, of necessity, take priority in all circumstances.

"We must at the same time maintain the best possible relations between the various branches of our armed forces and put aside the peacetime rivalries which sometimes come between us. Each branch, each unit and each soldier will be assigned tasks for which they are the appropriate choice. The job at hand is much too large for any of us to attempt without the aid of others. All of us need to work together in this thing and do what needs to be done.

"I don't think we're going to have nearly as easy a time as many of you seem to think we'll have. The Argentines are quite capable of hurting us and if we don't take them seriously right now, we're going to pay the cost later.

"I've read your Contingency Planning Reports with great care. I appreciate the thoroughness with which they were done and I trust you will continue and increase your input as we move into the crisis. As we pass our reports on to the Cabinet with a clear statement that we stand a good chance of losing in a guns-up showdown, we need to keep in mind that following an Argentine invasion, it's very unlikely any British government could stay in power unless they responded in kind, regardless whether we could win.

"You should keep in mind too that the Argentine government, once committed, cannot falter either. The military junta will fall unless they can take and keep the islands. We must expect a full armed resistance at the maximum level they are capable of delivering. Based on the figuring we've done so far we know that will be a force of significant potency.

"Now let's get to business and talk about how we're going to beat them."

On April 1, the decision was made to launch a full task force, capable of recovering the Falklands after an Argentine takeover. This was a day before any Argentine soldiers actually landed on the islands.

As units were recalled, stores assembled, and ships launched, Ted was aware of his fear returning. Just when he was enjoying himself, just when he'd gotten back to the thrill of battle preparation, it would steal up on him like a beggar in the park.

He knew that death in battle came through lack of planning or skill, or from mistakes. But it was equally true it came by chance; cruel random chance leading to impersonal, statistical death.

Ted was not a man prone to gambling. Certainly not with his own life.

Chapter Eight

They were fighting again.

After brief sex and the barest exchange of pleasantries, suddenly they were fighting. Mike had seen it before, watched her well up into anger so quickly he couldn't quite believe it. Early in their relationship, he'd learned to write off some of her behavior to "moods," but more and more lately, her flashes seemed to spring up from some great well within her, some generalized anger toward life and men.

Madeline's complaint was always the same: Ted neglected his daughter. He did so at a time when she needed his approval and attention desperately. Madeline could talk for hours about the situation and she ignored Mike's pointed statements that he would prefer not to take part, even vicariously, in her family's life. She drew him in whether he wished it or not.

"It's not that he's cruel" she said, "or thoughtless, even. I think he means well, but he's doing terrible damage to Edie and I won't sit by and see it happen."

"What damage is he doing?" Mike asked warily.

"She has fears. Fears of men, fears of adults and other children. She's a thirteen-year-old girl who should be getting out, being involved in sports, clubs and activities. We all know she's rather beautiful. But she doesn't know it at all. And he doesn't help her know it."

"Maddie, must we discuss this now?"

"I don't see why we shouldn't, it's happening now, isn't it?"

"Look, I don't see how there's a lot I can do about the way Ted treats Edith."

"I didn't say you should. I just wanted you to understand what I'm going through, what it's like living with the two of them. Perhaps my feelings are of no consequence, but they're important to me."

"I just don't see what I can do for Edie or Ted."

"Well, you might try and be more aware of her. Let her know she's an intelligent, attractive girl. You could come a little early and talk with her about school and whatnot. Why you might even take her out on a Saturday, shopping or something."

"Madeline, I don't feel right trying to fit into Ted's shoes that way."

"But she needs someone, can't you see it? She needs affection and approval. Acknowledgment that she has something to give the world."

"But I can't give her all that."

"You could talk to Ted about it, couldn't you? Make him see..."

"Maddie, I'm not going to DO THAT" he shouted at her.

"Why not?" she said sharply.

"Because I don't want to be his therapist or his conscience. We don't talk about you and Edie. We talk about guns and war and the world. It would be out of place for me to say things like that."

She was hurt now, defensive. Feeling used by him. But he could not be drawn into this, he wasn't part of her family. He was an outsider and though he cared deeply for her, this was an area of her life he could not share. And she was right, he didn't concern himself about her feelings, they were often of little consequence to him. He felt like a cad, but he realized he was being used by her just as she was being used by him.

The sheet slipped from under her arm revealing the silken breast beneath it. He followed the familiar curve to her nipple. Amazing how even her nipples became erect when she argued. Madeline covered herself again, folding her arms tightly around the sheet.

They were silent for several minutes. Mike got up from the bed, lit a cigarette, and opened the window a crack to take out the smoke. He sat across from her in a chair by the bureau and made no attempt to cover his nakedness.

Moments like these had nearly wrecked this place for him. It was sad, they'd been so happy when they found it. The house was hidden off a winding little road twelve kilometers north of

London. There were three rooms in the old house and an equally old, partially deaf widow who rented them out indifferently. She waved away Mike's carefully prepared story for why they had to meet in the afternoon and reached for his money.

No one else seemed to occupy any of the rooms. Mike had heard of the house with rooms to let at a party and had written down the information without comment. He'd never again seen the man who referred him to this place.

The building was a battered old stone house, two stories high, with wood ticking stuffed in along the steep roofline. The ground floor room they took had a door leading to a patio. This fronted on a meadow with a small creek running through where cows grazed. There was a huge fireplace in the room, a small table for dining and a massive bed. The bed was made of hewn oak, with lashing beneath to hold up the mattress which was thick and soft. The bed was really too soft for sleeping, but that was not something they did together anyway.

The first time they came, the sheets were not as clean as Madeline demanded and she spoke to the old woman to get better linen. Maddie began touching up the room almost as soon as they finished making love the first time in it. At first, she just straightened things up, dusted, picked up a few things, straightened the paintings on the walls. Then she began bringing things in, in a small bag she carried with her: some flowers and a table runner, a couple ashtrays and a small bowl of fruit.

During the first six months they'd come here, they came to this room every week, sometimes two or three times. They spent weekends here, while Ted was away and Edie could go to her cousin's. It had been a room of great joy then, great joy and great lust. He'd listened to her eagerly then, falling in love and felt an honest remorse when she left him to return to her husband.

In those days, they shared a fantasy existence, a pretense of marriage. When they went out at night, to a bar or a movie or a restaurant, they touched in special ways, a sort of casual intimacy that spoke of a familiar liaison several years old.

But when they were alone, in that room, it was as though chains had dropped from their limbs. They wrestled and grappled and pawed each other with furious abandon, sometimes tearing their clothes. At the start, they would make love three or four times in an afternoon, and afterward they kept touching, rubbing each other playfully. Sometimes Madeline would thrust her breasts into him from behind while he was trying to light a cigarette.

They were very gay in the beginning. Once he served himself to her on a bun with lettuce on the side and she laughed until her sides ached and she curled up into a ball. She was naked and the sight so excited him he fell upon her straightaway. It had been easy to love her then, easy to take all she offered without worry or hesitation. Now being together with one another carried a price in frustration and demands, a price he was not sure he could pay.

The illusion that their time together isolated them and took them out of their normal lives was beginning to collapse. Though he still loved her, Mike felt he was sliding down an incline toward some barrier he could not see.

After he dropped Maddie at her car, Mike stopped at a tavern for a few rounds. Drinking alone was not healthy, he realized, but it certainly beat not drinking at all. He got to the newspaper office a quarter hour late. He was no sooner through the door than Reuben signaled him to join a group at his desk. Malcomb, Johnny, and Aidan all stood silently. They weren't talking rugby today.

"Mike, you're just in time. We're putting a rush on this Falkland's thing. We need to divvy it up right away."

"What Falkland's thing are we divvying up?" Mike asked.

"We're not sure of that yet. There's a lot of activity at Whitehall and the defense boys seem to be gearing up. We don't know what's going on, but we need to cover all bases. Johnny, I want you at the Admiralty. Malcomb, I want you to get into the Foreign Office and find out what's happening diplomatically. You've got to get past the secretaries; we can't wait for appointments.

"Aidan, you will approach the Argentine embassy directly. See if they have any sort of statement to make. I doubt they will, but we need to keep checking with them in case something develops. After that, I want you to follow a lead we have through the War Armaments Institute at the University of London. They apparently can give us some sort of factual estimation of the Argentine army, air force, and navy; things we might need to know later on.

"Mike, I want you to cover the historical development of the conflict, from the time the islands were first sighted down to the present."

"History? You want me to research the history? Don't we have all that in the files?"

"It's sketchy and we need to know each of the various circumstances surrounding the treaty agreements down through the years."

Mike's spirits sank quickly as he imagined sitting at a library desk, wading through treaties 200 years old. "Couldn't we better use my time at Westminster or the Admiralty? If things are really moving in a military direction..."

"Can it, Mike. I know what you're asking. Right now, we need history."

"But we can pick that stuff up anytime."

"I want it now. Now. Understand?"

It was futile. "Right."

"I've arranged for you to meet Professor Clive Cranson-Hyde at London University's History Department in one hour. You'd better get moving."

Mike raised his hand as if to speak, but Reuben shook his head disdainfully. "Don't be a rebel, Yank. I'll give you a shot at the glory later."

An hour later, he was ushered into a tiny, book-lined office that smelled of cherry tobacco. A small, grey-haired, grey-suited man sat hunched over his desk. "Mr. Ferrol?" he said smiling.

"Yes, Mike Ferrol, just call me Mike." Cranson-Hyde did not get up from his desk but extended his hand for a brief, dry handshake. Mike sat in the only chair.

"Professor, I'm looking for information regarding the Falkland Islands."

"Yes, a specialty area of mine. I've studied them for 20 years or more. Wrote my thesis on the International treaties we had to break to take over those islands."

"Take over? You mean they weren't British?"

"Of course not. It was an act of outright piracy. The Americans are the ones who took them of course. We just claimed the spoils. The Spanish insulted the wrong American captain and he gave them a lesson in gunboat diplomacy that has lasted 150 years. That's the long and the short of it."

"Professor, you obviously know a good deal more of the history than I do. Perhaps you'd be good enough to give it to me in a short form."

The professor leaned back in his chair and drew open a drawer on the right side. He withdrew a curved-stem pipe and laboriously filled and lit it. "I can talk for an hour or six hours. How much would you like to hear?"

"For starters, why don't you just briefly sketch the history of the place. Give me five minutes worth, then I'll pick areas for clarification. What I mostly want to know is how the islands came to be British."

"Okay. How the islands came to be British. We'll take it chronologically. The islands were first sighted in the 1500's and over the next two hundred years they were claimed by the French, the Spanish, and the English. The islands were nothing but a wind-blown outcropping of rock with a horde of penguins living on it. No trees, just small grasses and no large game at all. It was cold, wet, and inhospitable and no one came there.

"In 1764, a French nobleman finally claimed the islands with a full plan to take and settle them. But that same year, 1764, the British landed on West Falkland and founded their settlement, Port Egmont. They had no idea the French were also on the islands.

"A year later, Captain John McBride was sent to consolidate the British holdings and eject any other settlers. That's when the British discovered the French settlement. But McBride had only a couple dozen men and there were 250 French settlers, so a stalemate developed.

"In 1767, the French ceded their interest in the islands to the Spanish and two years later, the Spanish moved the British off the islands. The British ministers weren't happy, but we eventually abandoned the islands altogether.

"Britain and Spain signed the Nootka Sound Convention in 1790 by which Britain formally renounced any colonial ambitions in South America 'and the islands adjacent.' After we signed that, the Spanish occupied the islands as a colony for 40 years, right up until the collapse of Spain's New World empire.

"But the Spanish didn't maintain occupancy of the islands. In 1810, when Argentina started stirring for independence, the colonial authorities moved all the Spanish settlers from Puerto Soledad, that's Port Stanley to us, back to the mainland. The Falklands went through a period of years when they were ignored except for sealing and whaling vessels and any captain in the area was a law unto himself.

"In 1820, Argentina sent a frigate to claim the Falklands as part of a colonial legacy from Spain. The commander of that vessel told the various hunting and fishing ships moored at the islands they were now under his jurisdiction, but no one took him seriously. It was a pretty anarchic community.

"In 1823, the government in Buenos Aires appointed its first governor and restored order for the next decade. They imposed restrictions on the indiscriminate slaughter of the seal population and controlled the port completely. But the second governor of the islands, Louis Vernet, ran into real trouble when he tried to control an American ship, *Harriet,* and confiscated some of her property.

"Vernet sailed with the ship into Buenos Aires and put her captain on trial. The Americans, of course, got very upset and unfortunately happened to have an American warship, the *USS*

Lexington, in port. They sent it to Puerto Soledad to secure restitution of property, mostly sealskins, that Vernet had confiscated.

"And that's when the real trouble started. The captain of the *Lexington* was a mean old rapscallion who was a law unto himself. He didn't just recover the confiscated sealskins, he also spiked the Argentine guns, blew up their powder, sacked the settlement buildings and arrested everyone except convicts whom he turned loose as the new inhabitants. He then declared the islands "free of all government" and left.

"Now that was piracy, pure and simple. No way around it. The Argentines sent another governor to the islands, but the convicts who were left promptly murdered him.

"The British Admiralty, having been alerted to the vulnerability of the islands, sent two warships, under the command of Captain James Onslow. He ousted the Argentine government that remained and established himself as the new law, though it was law without order. It took another six months before they hunted down all the vagrant gauchos who refused to accept British rule."

The professor watched silently as Mike frantically wrote down dates and names.

"Anyway, that's the story in a nutshell. We've held the islands now since 1833, a hundred and fifty years, and the Argentines have been protesting the whole time. We've negotiated back and forth during the past twenty years, the UN's been involved in it, but the situation is basically that it's a British island, British held, British run, and British populated, and we're not giving it up for love or money, much less for diplomatic pressure."

The professor leaned back in his chair and reloaded his pipe.

"Professor, what do you think is going to happen in the current situation?"

"I'm not really up on what's happening right now. I don't read the newspapers much, unless something's brewing. But I can tell you what's going to happen in the next year."

"All right then, what's going to happen in the next year?"

"War. We're going to war with Argentina."

Mike put down his pen and looked up. "Are you serious?"

"Quite serious. It's been a hundred and fifty years and the Argentines take anniversaries very seriously. There will be an invasion of the islands and a subsequent war between Great Britain and Argentina within the next year. It's inevitable due to one overriding factor in Argentine life."

"Nationalism?"

"Inflation. The inflation rate in Argentina is now over 100% and it's rising. Do you know what that kind of inflation means? It means you can't keep a dollar in your pocket. You buy all the meat you can today because it will cost a lot more before it can spoil. When you go to work in the morning, you pay 35 pesos at the toll booth, but it's 50 pesos when you return that night because the value of money is taking a permanent nosedive.

"They're facing economic chaos down there. The basic medium of exchange, money, is too unstable to permit commerce to continue. We're not just looking at unemployment, we're talking starvation, riots, and revolution. The military junta is only as strong as the economy it can provide and this one is in serious trouble."

"So they'll go to war just to get the people's minds off their pockets?"

"Exactly. Once the junta launches a war for the Malvinas Islands, the whole country will rally around them. They can impose any restrictions they like if they can get those islands back, even for a short time. It gives them carte-blanche."

"Who do you think will win this war?"

"I can't imagine we'll lose" the professor said with a shrug. "But I'm not really qualified to say. You need a military analyst, not an historian."

Mike was writing again and as he put the words down, he realized they were starting to slant to the right, the way they did when his hand moved quickly. He was onto something here, this was a good story.

"Professor, what sort of confrontation do you see leading up to the actual war itself?"

"Oh, I'd think the usual progression would take place. The breaking off of negotiations, withdrawing diplomatic missions, imposing economic sanctions. We'll probably freeze their assets. They have extensive holdings in this country, billions I'm sure. I imagine the Treasury will attach those as soon as the first military moves are made. It's always nice to have a down payment on reparations."

The professor was smiling again, but Mike didn't notice as his pen flashed across the page. He was pretty certain he'd hooked into something big. He stayed with the professor another half hour to flesh out the details, then headed back to the newsroom.

"No, Mike, we can't use it."

"Can't use it? What are you talking about?"

"Now don't get your knickers in a twist. The boys upstairs think we'll just be stirring something up based on the speculations of one man. Right now, we can't use any of this."

"What about the history? Don't you think people should know why the Argentines think they own the islands?"

"I'm not disputing the history, Mike. I'm just not sure this is the appropriate time to bring it up. The writing's fine, we just want to hold the material for background later. Tell you what, why don't you head over to Military Intelligence and round up that colonel of yours, see if maybe he can tell you anything."

Mike shook his head and fought with himself to keep from commenting on the idiocy of senior editors. He managed to give Reuben a weak smile. "Thanks." He headed for the door.

At least now they were being smart. He should have been talking with Ted that morning, though he still thought the story he gave them was pretty good. A professor predicting war was certainly news. The senior editors just wanted to play it politically.

That was the trouble with publishers and editors, they sold themselves for a little influence, a little slice of the pie. Mike realized it was exactly this attitude of his that had gotten him into serious trouble back in Detroit, gotten him fired from one of the best newspapers in the city. He gave a shrug and tried his best to forget about it.

It took him half an hour to get to Ted's office. The outer secretary protected an inner secretary who protected Ted. He saw immediately that things were busy. The couriers in the hall were moving quicker than usual and the secretaries were sitting up straighter. He could hear the crispness in everyone's voice and there was palpable tension: something was up.

"I want to see Colonel Tomlinson."

"I'm sorry, sir, he's in a meeting right now. It just began, we don't expect him back this afternoon."

"I'll wait. He might return."

"If I could take your name, I'd give you a call."

"I have to see him now."

"Why don't you give me your name and if he calls in I can tell him you're here."

"All right, it's Ferrol, Mike Ferrol."

"Oh, Mr. Ferrol, yes, I have a message for you."

"What did the colonel say?"

"It isn't from the colonel, it's from Mrs. Tomlinson. She wants you to call her at home. She left the number."

She handed him a slip of paper, dialed a number on her phone and gave him the receiver. Suddenly, here was Madeline.

"Hello?"

"It's Mike Ferrol. I got a message at Ted's office..."

"Can you talk?"

"No" Ted smiled at the secretary who was waiting for him to finish his call, "not really."

"Then I'll do the talking. Look, I'm sorry about this afternoon. I had no right to ask you to get involved. I won't bother you about this again." A faint hope, Mike thought dismally.

"Now I think I have a lead for you. There's some kind of buzz on down at the Ministry and Ted's very keyed up about it. Says it's all hush hush. He's working late tonight and may not be home at all. He gave me a story to tell you about going to his mother's for a few days if you should call. I thought you'd want to know."

Mike realized he should be grateful for the information Madeline gave him, but he felt irritated instead. Why did she always pit him against Ted? She never missed an opportunity to show him that she was more faithful to her lover than her husband. As though they were in some sort of competition.

When he had started seeing her, Mike had thought of Maddie as a lonely woman he could make happy, someone who could make him happy in return. But that was too thin a pretext for Madeline. She had to cast herself as the victim of a cruel fate, a prisoner trapped in a loveless marriage who remained only for the sake of her daughter. And Mike was the knight who secretly saved her, even though he couldn't take her away.

It was all becoming too much for Mike. It started as just a physical affair, then he found himself in love. But now he felt mired down, tangled in a situation he hadn't imagined. At moments like this he wondered if it would be best to just end it.

"Thank you, Mrs. Tomlinson. That's good to hear."

"Ted's very busy. Could we have lunch together? Could we?"

Another irritating habit, repeating her questions. "I'll have to check with my editor about that. I'll let you know later."

"Yes" she said, pausing a moment. "Of course. I understand. You can't talk right now. Well, bye then." The line went dead.

Mike smiled at the secretary as though she had done him a great favor and gave her the phone back. He sat down to wait for Ted.

Damn all women and their petty soap operas, Mike thought. It wasn't enough that he had to lie and sneak around the back of Ted, who might have been his friend; there was all this emotional baggage he had to carry as well.

The secretary across from him returned to her typewriter and began pounding furiously. Mike moved to the other side of the room for an ashtray and noticed that as he passed the desk, she covered what she was working on. He began thumbing through a magazine, hoping this wouldn't take more than an hour.

Two hours later, the secretary rose and covered her typewriter with a plastic case. "I'm sorry Mr. Ferrol, it's 5:30 and you'll have to go, we're closing the office."

"So there's no chance he'll be back before dinner?"

"I don't believe so, sir."

"Who has he been meeting with the last two hours?"

She was immediately offended. "I'm sure I don't know. It's not my business to know such things." But it was and she did, and Mike cursed himself for making her lie.

"Sorry. It's really none of my business either. Well, I guess I'll come back in the morning."

"That would be fine." She picked up her purse and moved him toward the door. After he'd left, she locked it.

It's never smart to offend secretaries, he reflected. Too often they wield more power than their bosses. Mike made a mental note to try and woo that one the next time he saw her. He left the Ministry of Defense and made his way three blocks to where he found a phone.

"London Chronicle" a voice said into Mike's ear.

"Aidan Scoffield, please."

"Just a moment." A minute later, the operator returned. "I'm sorry, Mr. Scoffield is not in the office. Would you care to speak with Mr. Blake?"

Aidan was working on Argentine armaments and Mike needed to know about them to talk intelligently with Ted. If he ever found Ted. "Thanks anyway, I'll call back later."

It occurred to Mike that much of this information might be public record, so he hailed a cab and went to the main library. He was just heading up the stairs to the Research Section when he met Madeline and Edith coming down the stairs. For a wild moment, he wondered how Maddie had engineered this encounter, but then realized that was impossible since he had not known himself he would be here half an hour ago.

"Hello, Mr. Ferrol," Edith said. She had seen him many times when he came to the house for dinners with Ted and Madeline, and easily recognized him. Edith usually ate before Mike arrived, preferring to leave the adults to talk among themselves, but she always greeted Mike when he came to the house.

"Hello" Mike said, nodding a greeting to Maddie. "Have you been doing research upstairs?"

Edie brightened at once. "Oh, yes. I'm going to be competing in the horse show at Trillingham Park on Saturday. We doing dressage and I'll be riding Marvel, a black mare from the stables where I usually ride."

Madeline smiled at her daughter. "Edie is a fine rider and it should be a very pleasant afternoon. We'll probably go early and have lunch at the clubhouse. You could join us if you wanted to."

Mike was caught off guard by the invitation. He stalled for time, addressing himself to Edith rather than Madeline. "I don't want to intrude on a family outing. I'm sure your father will be going." He hoped Edie would give him a way out, but he was quickly disappointed.

"Oh, Daddy always says he'll come, but he never does," Edith said. "If you come, you might see me win a prize. Please—do come."

Mike looked at Maddie who had a bemused expression. She'd put him on the spot and she knew it, now she was clearly enjoying seeing how he would handle it. And here was Edith, all innocent and sincere, wanting only this little bit of validation.

"All right," Mike said, "I'll come."

Maddie was clearly surprised and obviously pleased. *Well,* Mike thought, *it isn't just to please you, dear, sometimes I can do the right thing.* And Edie's delight was so heartfelt, he was certain he had made the right decision.

But on the day before the horse show, the war began and Mike, like her father, forgot about Edith completely.

PART THREE

The Islands

Chapter Nine

They lie deep in the South Atlantic, closer to the South Pole than the equator, 780 small islands and two large ones: East Falkland and West Falkland. The islands span 4,700 square miles, roughly the size of Wales or the State of Connecticut. In Great Britain, the population density is 600 people per square mile, but in this British protectorate, there is less than one person per square mile. Two thirds of the population live in the port city of Stanley while the other third are out in the camp, on the rural sheep farms that can only be reached by sea or by air. There are no roads across the jagged rock outcroppings of these islands.

The islanders raise sheep on the vast open grasslands that roll over the islands. They birth, shear, and slaughter them in endless cycle. But the grass grows so sparsely, it takes two acres to support a single sheep, so the farms are spread far apart and trips to Stanley are a rare indulgence.

Eighteen hundred people and half a million sheep, living together in a one-company town at the end of the earth.

———•••———

Jenny Corbyn was a fourth generation Falklander, married to the foreman of a shearing gang who worked the sheep all over the islands. She lay on a blanket watching the clouds move above her. It was one of those rare, precious days when the wind was warm and the sun shone brightly on the waves in the bay.

She was three months pregnant. It would be their second child. Jenny's son Darrell was six years old and she hadn't been sure they would have another. She was glad now they would. She wanted a second child.

Today she was having a picnic alone, on a blanket on the north shore of the bay, across from the town of Stanley. Darrell was in school and her mother would pick him up so Jenny had the afternoon free. Her husband Grant sailed her across the bay in their 19-foot dayboat, then dropped her on the shoreline while he continued his sail all the way down to Whalebone Cove. She could have persuaded him to join her for the picnic, but he loved sailing so much, she hated to deny him time on the water and today was a perfect day for sailing. Lots of sun and wind. He would pick her up on his way back. She was actually grateful for the time alone.

She was rarely alone anymore, working by day at the shop and home at night with Grant and Darrell. It was luxurious to just lay back with nothing but her thoughts and the baby inside for company. She was certain it was a girl and though she couldn't feel her yet, she knew she was there, part of her body, part of her future.

She did not fear the birth experience at all. Of course, she trusted the staff at King Edward Hospital to take care of her, but she surprised herself by looking forward to the birth process and felt a little giddy. It would be so good to have a warm baby to hold in her arms again just at the time when Darrell was beginning to resist any prolonged cuddling.

Grant would be pleased too. Jenny's husband loved children though he was usually too rough with them. Grant was sometimes short-tempered and he tended to think of himself first, but he was also generous and fun. He loved the craft of the sea as much as any man could. He thought nothing of putting to sea in their small dayboat with nothing but a canvas dodger to keep out the waves. The over-sized sail bent the mast like a hoop. He actually liked bad weather. They lived in Stanley so he could sail, not, as he contended, so her mother could torture him with her cooking. Grant needed his weekly sail like a drug. He was off work today while the crew was between shearings, plying the waves with two sails set. He might have taken Darrell with him, pulling him out of class, but she'd asked him not to. Darrell wasn't doing well in school and needed to focus his attention.

Jenny looked at the fading sunlight as it played across the town of Stanley across from her. The crown jewel of the Falklands, she thought, laughing to herself. The town was only half a mile long and a quarter mile wide, but it looked as pretty as any postcard from a resort in Margate or Weymouth. Distinctly British, it was a village of clean streets, well kept lawns, and pretty houses. The tall spire from the Cathedral cast a long shadow in the twilight. Jenny breathed in the clean, crisp air and was grateful there was no pollution on the islands.

With a sigh, she realized it was getting late. She hastily packed her things. Standing at the end of an old stone jetty, she waved a handkerchief until Grant caught sight of her and brought the boat over. He was grinning, as she knew he would be.

"Perfect day for a sail, eh, my love? Wind's just right, sun's so warm you can sail in your shirtsleeves."

She pulled at his cotton jacket. "Doesn't seem to be what you're doing." She carefully climbed into the boat.

"Now, if we lived in Australia" he said, casting off from the jetty, "we'd have this weather all the time."

"Oh, get off with you. It's not *that* wonderful, and you'd only get bored with it."

He stood with the tiller held to his side. "Oh, yes. Fat chance of that." It worried her when he stood in the pitching boat as it rolled through the chop in the bay. She worried he might fall overboard leaving her to turn the boat around and save him. But Grant was perfectly fearless and explained that she needn't rescue him at all. Even if he went over the side, the boat would point up into the wind naturally and stop. He could then pull himself up over the stern and get aboard again. She needn't do anything. It was scant reassurance in her eyes.

"Sit down and mind your course" she said. "You need to get me back as quickly as possible. I'm a little late."

"Old Feather-biddy going to give you a hard time?"

"Mrs. Featherstone treats me very well and I've nothing to complain of, but she needs me this afternoon and I'm closing the shop."

Evangeline Featherstone had come to the islands forty years ago, following her marriage in England to a man from the Falklands who persuaded her to move there. Shortly after arriving, she had entered the West Store, the only store on the islands at that time, and asked the manager, Gaven McKendrew, for a darning needle. McKendrew shook his head sadly and said: "Aye, there's none such as that on these islands, Missy."

"That's Mrs. Featherstone, my good man, and we shall have to remedy that." She then began making a list of things she could easily purchase in England, but were unavailable in the Falklands. Six months later, Mrs. F. and her husband opened a store to supply these items to the islanders and named their shop *The None Such Shoppe*. Over the door, beneath the name of the store, she painted the words McKendrew had said to her:

*"There's none such as that on
these islands, Missy"*

Far from being offended, McKendrew was delighted and helped Mrs. Featherstone in any way he could. He gave her the names of his suppliers, information on the most reliable shipping firms, and which vendors she should avoid. Mrs. F.'s relatives back in London also helped her source materials and the store prospered. After McKendrew retired, she established the same cooperative relationship with his successor.

Now Mrs. Featherstone was widowed and getting on in years and was moving more of the work to Jenny. They had spoken of Jenny some day taking over the store, but Jenny hoped to put this off until the children were older. Mrs. F. never had children.

Grant carefully guided the boat up to a dock downtown where Jenny could easily alight.

"I could walk you over there if you like."

"No" she said, trying to sound casual, "that's not necessary. Go ahead, finish your sail."

The truth was she had no intention of returning to work, had the day off in fact and had errands to run which Grant could not know about. Not just yet anyway.

Half an hour later she stepped into the Post Office and sighed at the line. There were three ahead of her and old Mr. Fanwick at the counter was casually polishing his glasses, oblivious to anyone in a hurry. She was almost beside herself at the end of twenty minutes when she could finally speak with him.

"Have I had any special deliveries?"

"Don't know" he said slowly, "have to check." He pushed himself off his stool and ambled to the back before disappearing among the shelves. A few minutes later, he returned holding a small box and some letters.

"This is for you. One of 'em was a special delivery. Even says to hold for you at the Post Office. Never heard of that one before."

"It's a surprise for my husband. His birthday. Let me have them please."

"Here, just sign this." He gave her a slip of paper which she hastily filled out. "Got something else for you too."

"What?"

"Unstamped letter. Delivered right here, no address, just your name. You'll have to sign for it and pay the postage." He got back off his stool again and shuffled off to the back of the building. It was making her crazy. If he knew about the letter, why hadn't he picked it up when he got her other mail?

She took a moment to examine the box in her hand. It was from a marine fittings company in England, part of Grant's birthday present. This was the biggest present she'd ever given him, a surprise she'd saved six months to afford. It was a new mast and sail for Grant's boat. The mast and sail had already arrived and were hidden at Mr. Jamison's boat yard. This box just held the last of the fittings. She should have had everything sent directly to the boat yard, but she hadn't thought of it when ordering.

Mr. Fanwick at last reappeared and gave her another form. She signed and left a few coins, taking the envelop which bore only her name written a little crookedly across the front of it. She hastily tore it open and unfolded a single sheet of paper. The three words that appeared took her completely by surprise: *Hello Beautiful Lady.*

She looked up and her eyes met the smiling face of Judson Muran. He was ancient and when he smiled, his tongue showed through the spot where his front teeth had been. His whiskery wrinkled face looked like a hound to her.

Jenny shuddered and left the building immediately. She couldn't believe it. Old Jud Muran leaving a note like that for her, then waiting around to watch her open it. It was worse than crude, it was an affront to a happily married woman. However crazy his family had always been, he had no right to subject her to this sort of thing.

Jud Muran was at least 70 years old and had been a crazy, drunken fool for as long as anyone on the islands had known him. His family all drank too much, though he was said to have given it up in the last year or so. Jenny had never spoken a word to him in the 25 years of her life. A month back, Jud had taken a job working for that peculiar Mrs. Wallborn, the widow trying to run a fish shop down at the market. Her shop was nothing more than a canvas covered booth, but she greeted each ship that came into Stanley and bought exotic fish the market wouldn't handle.

To augment her income, she'd started raising flowers which she also sold, putting a sign up on her booth *Fish and Flowers.*

"Can you imagine what her hands must smell like at night?" Jenny's mother commented.

Most people thought old Mrs. Wallborn was as crazy as Jud himself, but they bought her fish all the same, especially after Jud started delivering about town on his bicycle. He was quite a sight, a 70-year-old man crookedly bumping along on his bike with a basket full of fish on the front. Jenny never bought food that way, she inspected every bit of food before it was purchased and she could imagine the sad fare left by Jud Muran for those poor old folks who couldn't afford better.

She thought about the hunched over little man standing off to the side in the Post Office, with his shabby coat turned up around his collar the way he always wore it. She gave another shudder. It was too horrid to think about. She wouldn't tell Grant, it would only anger him, then there would have to be an apology. It was better to just forget the whole thing.

She made her way to Jamison's Boat Works as quickly as she could. Mr. Jamison was in the back shop with two mechanics who were overhauling an engine. He wiped his hands on his filthy pants and waved a greeting as she approached.

"Got the sail yesterday, just like the agent said I would. She fits the mast with plenty of room to spare. She's an absolute beauty."

A wave of relief swept over Jenny and she followed him to a corner of the front room where a large box lay open with the sail spilling out. The sail was sheer white Dacron, with a bolt rope sewed in just as she had specified and Grant's initials, GC, printed in large letters at the peak above the number 100.

It was magnificent. She felt faint for a moment and couldn't touch it. Mr. Jamison stood back respectfully, but he was as proud as though he'd made it himself.

"She's a beauty all right" he said, "and if you'll just give me that downhaul fitting, I'll have it put on tonight and we'll be all set to step her as soon as you're ready. Pity you couldn't get a new boom too."

"Afraid not." Jenny was smiling. "In November, I'm getting my sewing machine and after that Christmas is coming." Jenny left Jamison's and headed for the center of town. She still had a couple things to take care of and everything had to be wrapped. She'd bought two little gifts for Darrell, just small things, but something so he wasn't left out.

When she got to the corner of Dean and Fitzroy, she ran into Grant's brother, Colin. Two years younger than Grant, Colin was steadfastly unattached. He was cuter than Grant, but in a boyish way. Colin treated her like a younger sister and liked to tease her about dumping "ole Grant" and running off with him.

"Hello Jenny. Everything set for tonight?"

"I think so. I baked a cake this morning and I'll ice it just before dinner, then wrap a few things and we should be ready to go downtown about eight o'clock. Does that give you enough time?"

"Yes, Jamison and I can have the job done by then."

"He put up a little fuss about your not coming to dinner you know."

"Did he?"

"Well, you have come the last three years running."

"He'll appreciate me all the more when he finds out where I've been."

Colin was very good with tools and as much a sailor as Grant. He and Mr. Jamison, along with a mechanic they'd recruited, planned to sneak the boat into Jamison's yard after Grant had left it moored and gone home. In the yard, they'd rig her with the new fittings, step the mast and run up the sail so Grant could see her in all her glory. He wouldn't have to do anything but sail her and if she knew Grant, he'd probably do that immediately even in the dark. But she must make sure he took Colin and not Darrell. Sailing the bay at night was no place for a six-year-old.

"We only need to drill six holes" Colin said, "the chainplates she already has are perfectly fine for our purposes."

"Where will you work on her?"

"In a stand in the yard. We've already set up lights and we've got a string of lights for when he comes later."

"That's wonderful, Colin. He'll be so thrilled when he sees it."

"I've got it all arranged. We're running one of Jamison's yard lights up the mast and we'll have lights coming down the forestay and the backstay, just like a Christmas tree."

"Oh, what fun! This will be wonderful."

"I'll wait until you've got the truck parked and brought him round the side. Then, as soon as he's around the corner, I'll hit the switch. You'd better have tissue ready. You're going to see a grown man cry."

"Get on with you, Colin. You're always full of the devil."

"I'll call about 8:00 and propose a drink at the Globe. See that he's ready and pack Darrell along as well."

"We couldn't leave him behind. He'll be more excited than Grant. But call at 7:30 instead or he'll be up the whole night."

Colin gave her arm a squeeze and her hair a sniff. "Don't forget your perfume, dear. Corbyn men need a good scent in the air." He winked and was gone.

Jenny watched him walk away. Colin was very cute, it was a wonder some young girl hadn't snapped him up. He was even a good relative and friend, though he did play an occasional trick as though she was one of the men at work. He worked at the freight office down at the wharves and seemed to enjoy the rough seamen he encountered there.

Jenny turned and for the second time that day, her eyes met those of old Judson Muran. He was only a dozen feet from her, wearing his shabby overcoat with his faded cap pulled down over his ears, the old wool the same color as his whiskery beard.

"Afternoon, m'lady" he said with a toothless grin.

Before she could reply, he pushed off from the curbstone and pedaled his way down the street weaving from side to side with two small parcels bouncing in the basket in front of him. He smelled of the fish at his workplace and Jenny shuddered again. What an awful little man. He'd followed her just so he could leer at her and ride away. Where did he get the nerve to act like that?

Jud Muran was a complete stranger to Jenny and she had no intention of acting toward him otherwise. It was infuriating, intolerable. If it happened again, she'd have to tell Grant, though she regretted turning his considerable wrath against anyone. It was Jud's own fault, he'd have to take the consequences.

Jenny focused on what she must do for Grant's birthday. There were a million details to attend to. There would be canned ham for dinner, a favorite of Grant's since it was practically the only relief from their continuous diet of lamb and fish. She'd fixed the ham with pineapple slices and brown sugar, just the way he liked it. Her mother was bringing a salad, "picked from my own garden with these hands" she told Jenny over the phone. But Jenny still needed the sour cream and butter for the cake icing.

She stopped first at the grocery, then at the West Store for a card for Grant and a punchout book for Darrell. She was spending too much on the boy again she realized, but she couldn't help it.

Grant was home when she arrived with her packages and she made a big to do about not letting him see what was inside. Darrell loved secrecy of any sort and patrolled the kitchen entrance to keep his father away. Grant set to work behind their house fixing a stone fence they used to keep stray dogs and such away from their garden. Jenny worked quickly and by six o'clock, when her mother arrived, she was quite prepared for the evening.

It was as Jenny was closing the front door behind her mother that she saw the figure approaching down the road. She was unsure who would be out riding at the dinner hour and it took her a moment to realize who it was. It was old Jud Muran, pedaling himself toward her, a large bouquet filling his basket.

Jenny turned with a start before he could see her.

Could this be happening? The old fool was paying her court like some adolescent, even at the house of her husband. He must be insane. But he must also be stopped. For a moment, she felt a tightness in her chest and tears at the corners of her eyes. She hated scenes of this sort and was terrified what might happen if Grant lost his temper. Now she was frightened.

"Are you all right?" Grant asked, suddenly next to her in the hall.

"Oh, Grant, it's terrible. I'm sorry. You must make him go away, leave me alone."

"Make who go away?" He was very concerned. She heard it in his voice.

"That old man. He's been following me all day, passing me notes, trying to talk with me. Now he's coming here with flowers. You must get him away."

Grant glanced out the window and looked back at his wife. "It's Jud Muran."

"Yes, old Jud Muran. And he's bringing those flowers to *me!*"

"Of course" Grant said, shaking his head. "I ordered them from him, paid him for them too."

"But this morning he left a note for me at the Post Office and stood there gaping while I read it."

"What sort of note?"

"Here. This..." she reached into her coat and pulled out the note.

Grant glanced at the paper, then back at his wife. "Darling, I wrote this note to you. I left it at the Post Office as a surprise for you. I thought you'd know it was from me."

"But it isn't your handwriting."

He held up a bandaged finger. "Couldn't grip the pen very well."

"You mean he hasn't done any of those things?"

"No. I paid him for the flowers on Wednesday, so he's known all week he was going to bring them to you. He just saw you today and smiled, that's all."

Jenny's composure collapsed. She began crying. "I'm such a fool. I thought such evil things about that poor old man and all he's guilty of is bringing me flowers from you. I've misjudged him so badly. I must apologize."

Grant was smiling now, his arm around her shoulders. "No, my love. You needn't apologize to him, he hasn't taken offense. He hasn't even known of it. Just dry your eyes and go out on the porch and get your flowers. Here..." He gave her a bill, "give him this and wish him a good day."

"Yes" she said, pulling a tissue from a box in the hall. She was just straightening her blouse when he knocked at the door.

The celebration that night went even better than Jenny had hoped. Darrell was delighted with the meager gifts she'd been able to pick up for him and Grant seemed content with the sweater her mother had knit him and the expensive soap and cologne set she'd bought to confuse him until he saw the boat. He was such a gentleman, he'd never think to complain about what he was given and Jenny was nearly giddy by the time they got down to Jamison's boat yard.

Grant was wonderfully confounded when she stopped the car at Jamison's and marched around the building in the dark without a word of explanation. Darrell knew the truth, of course, but he kept his secret as she knew he would. When Colin finally threw the light switch, the gasp that Grant gave out might as easily have come if he'd taken the shock directly. He was speechless and disbelieving and couldn't take his eyes off it for the first half hour.

Then, of course, he wanted to take her out in the bay, darkness be damned he said, and see how she caught the wind. Despite Jenny's protests, he took both Colin and Darrell, all of them wearing life preservers, with an electric lantern burning at the bow.

She could have gone with them, but a bouncing ride in the cold night air was nothing she looked forward to, not while she was three months pregnant. There would be plenty of time for a ride in the boat later when the sun was out and Grant could talk to her for hours about how the new sail handled and what other things he planned for her.

Besides, she didn't want to interfere with the men launching their boat together. She couldn't deny her fear for Darrell, but she knew Grant and Colin would look after him and she felt great pride as they cast off.

"Good night for a sail, wouldn't you say Grant?" Colin said as he pushed them off from the jetty.

"Well, it does beat shearing sheep" Grant replied.

"Enjoy the sheep while you can, mate. When the Argies get here, we'll all be raising cattle. Ever shear a cow?"

The brothers laughed together.

Chapter Ten

April 1, 1982

They were sharing a pot of tea, listening to music on the radio, when the announcer, Mike Smallwood, said that Rex Hunt, Governor of the Falkland Islands, was about to make an announcement. It was 8:15 pm and Darrell was already sleeping. It had been a quiet evening and Jenny wondered what could be happening.

Looking at the radio, Grant said: "What do you suppose this is about?" Before Jenny could reply, the voice of Governor Hunt came over the radio.

"Good evening. I have an important announcement to make about the state of affairs between the British and Argentine governments over the Falkland Islands dispute. I now have evidence that the Argentines are preparing to take the Falklands by force. An invasion is imminent, possibly at dawn tomorrow. I have alerted the Royal Marines and I now ask for all serving and active members of the Falkland Islands Defense Force to report to the drill hall as soon as possible. If the United Nations Security Council's urging to keep the peace is not heeded by the Argentine government, I expect to have to declare a State of Emergency, possibly before dawn tomorrow. I would urge you all to keep calm and keep off the streets."

Mike Smallwood came back on the air and said the station would continue broadcasting all night and promised to broadcast any further information as it became available. He added: "Don't panic, folks – we will now continue with *Record Requests.*" Incredibly, the music resumed as if it were a normal evening broadcast.

"Bloody fucking hell" Grant said. Jenny winced as if she'd been slapped and sat motionless in her chair. She was terrified and despite the reassuring voice on the radio, she felt herself beginning to panic. Grant rarely swore and the vehemence of his profanity surprised her. The news itself was nearly incomprehensible. The Argentines were invading? How was that even possible? Could they simply march in and take over her homeland? There must be some mistake. There must be something...

"Grant, can this be happening? I can't believe this is real."

"Oh, it's real, I'm pretty sure. That was Rex Hunt's voice on the radio and he wouldn't kid about something like this. But maybe the Argies won't land. Maybe they'll just form some kind of blockade around the islands and declare them Argentine. Maybe this is just some kind of diplomatic move and not really a military invasion."

"Do you think so?"

"No, not really. The Argies aren't clever enough for that. They're too hot blooded. They'll want to make the grand gesture, march their troops into Stanley and tear down our flag. It's been a long time coming, but I think maybe this is the real thing."

"What can we do?"

Grant shook his head and looked at the floor. "I don't know if there is anything we can do. Stay inside. Stay safe. Hope there isn't any shooting."

Just then there was a loud knock on the door and Colin entered without waiting to be invited in. He was wearing the combat outfit of the Falklands Defense Force and he was carrying a rifle.

"Jesus, Colin, how did you get here so fast?"

"I heard a rumor before Hunt went on the air. Half the boys are already down at the hall. Even though you aren't a regular, I thought you might want to come with me to find out what's happening."

Grant thought about this a moment before replying. "No, I'll stay with my family. But let me know anything you learn. Is that rifle loaded?"

"Damn right it's loaded. These are our islands. We're not giving them up."

Grant stepped closer to his brother. "Colin, stop and think for a moment. Is it really wise to carry a loaded rifle into town tonight? There are going to be thirty or more of you out on the streets, looking for Argies around every corner. If you're all carrying loaded weapons, somebody is going to get hurt. This isn't a mobilization, it's a meeting. Please, just leave the rifle here. You can pick it up again after the meeting."

"What if they order us to take defensive positions or go on patrols?"

"They won't. I'll tell you exactly what is going to happen at this meeting. They're going to tell you that if any fighting needs to be done, it will be the Royal Marines who will do it. They have the training, the discipline, and the equipment. Bringing in a bunch of gun-toting civilians can only muck it up. Go to the meeting, but please, leave the rifle here."

Colin thought hard about what his brother had said. His blood was up, but he could hear the logic in Grant's thinking. "All right. I'll leave my rifle, but I don't want any grief when I come back for it."

"I promise I'll hand it right back to you after the meeting. But in the meantime, I'm going to remove the bullets. I don't want any loaded weapons in a house with a six-year-old."

"All right, then. I'll see you later." And he was gone before Jenny had said a word to him. The phone rang and Grant answered, quickly handing the receiver to Jenny. It was her mother who had been listening to the radio and knew what was happening. "It's all too ridiculous" she said, "and I don't believe any of this talk of invasion. The Argentines have been threatening that for years. It's just posturing. I'm taking the phone off the hook and going to bed. You can come over and wake me when the war is over."

Jenny had to smile despite her concern for all of them. Her mother was made of stern stuff and had managed to make a life for herself after the death of her husband while Jenny was still a teenager. Whatever the outcome of this night, Jenny was sure her mother would carry on as she always did.

Colin returned an hour later to report that the invasion appeared to be on and the Falkland Islands forces were preparing to make a stand at Government House. He had been recruited to help bury government documents to keep them from the Argentines. He asked for a couple sandwiches and a thermos of tea. He said he wouldn't need his rifle back just yet, but he would appreciate a shovel.

It was a long night of waiting and listening and wondering. Jenny poured endless cups of tea for Grant and herself. Neither could sleep. On the radio, Dave Emsley took over from Mike Smallwood and continued playing music while they waited for further news. Jenny went out on the front porch to sit in the fresh evening air. It was a magnificent night: warm, cloudless, no wind, with thousands of stars shining above. It was hard to believe anything could break this perfect tranquility.

At half past midnight, the Governor reported that Argentina had not responded to demands that their ships be recalled. Then at 4:30 am, he announced that the President of the United States, Ronald Reagan, had spoken to President Galtieri on the phone, but Galtieri refused to let the US mediate the issue. When it became clear the invaders were not going to turn back, Governor Hunt finally declared a state of emergency. At 5:15, he announced that Argentine landing craft were entering the Narrows. His rueful comment was: "It looks as though the silly buggers mean it."

Jenny heard the first gunshots at 5:45 am. There was small arms fire, then what sounded like grenades, and finally the clump of mortars. The sound filled her with dread. It seemed to come from both ends of the town. She woke Darrell and took him down into the dugout cellar beneath the house. They had worked hard and saved for two years to afford this stone house and Jenny was grateful for the shelter it offered. She brought blankets so Darrell could sleep more if he needed to, but he was up and full of questions about what was happening. Jenny had few answers.

Grant came down into the cellar a few minutes later bringing some toys and books for Darrell along with the radio. There was a light in the cellar, but no electrical outlet so he had to run an extension cord down to power the radio.

"I saw a patrol of Royal Marines heading up King Street, keeping low going past the Fire Station. Then they vaulted the fence into St. Mary's Paddock and started firing further up King Street. I could hear return fire from the Argentines. We'd better stay below for the time being."

"I hope Colin is staying out of it."

"I didn't see any civilians with the Marines. And we still have his rifle so I expect he's staying clear."

Patrick Watts took over at the broadcasting studio and began issuing reports from residents who were calling in. Alistair Greeves called to say that he and his family had to stay lying on the floor most of the time, but he could see at least seven armored personnel carriers coming down the road from the airport. He also reported there were helicopters overhead and the Argentines appeared to have taken the airport.

Other townspeople called in to report that their houses were being hit by shrapnel and canon fire. There was a report that the armored personnel carriers had opened fire. Ally Greeves called back to report from beneath his table. He said something big had just gone through the roof of the Ionospheric Station.

At 9 am, Governor Hunt phoned the radio station saying that there was heavy fighting at Government House and they were receiving fire from all sides, but were holding out. As the sounds of the battle increased, Darrell became frightened and Jenny did her best to calm him by reading some of his favorite stories and calling his attention to the pictures. Curiously, Jenny found it calmed her down too.

Shortly after the Governor's call was broadcast, they heard a loud banging on the front door upstairs. Grant went up to investigate. A few moments later, he came back down to the cellar with Jenny's mother. Incredibly, she had been crying. Jenny had only seen her cry twice before and the sight unnerved her.

Jenny's mother, Millicent Varnay, had been born on the islands, just as Jenny had. She was a strong woman who had made her way farming the land with her husband Tom. Millicent gave birth to a son early in their marriage, but the boy had died as a child. Jenny came several years after that. When Tom died suddenly of heart failure, Millie had carried on with farming for another seven years, but finally the work became too great for her and she moved to Stanley to be nearer her grandson. Now she maintained a small clapboard house with a garden in the front and worked in the green grocer section of the West Store.

"They attacked my house" Millie sobbed. "The bullets have shattered the windows and come through the walls. One of their shells landed on the roof and burst my water supply tank. There's water everywhere. It's ruined. My house is ruined." She cried in earnest again and Jenny hugged her, patting her gently on the back.

"It's okay, mum. We'll fix your house. I promise. But for now you'd better stay down here with the rest of us. We'll keep you safe."

Grant was about to say something when the Governor's voice came over the radio. "I'm sorry to report to you that our forces defending Government House are now facing insurmountable fire from the Argentine army. To preserve life and property, I feel the only responsible thing to do is to seek a truce and begin discussion with the Argentine forces. We shall proceed on that course. God save the Queen."

Grant, Jenny, and her mother sat in stunned silence. The gunfire soon ceased, but they could hear shouting in Spanish out in the streets and laughter as hundreds of Argentine soldiers poured into the town. Then they listened in horrified fascination as the enemy took over their radio station. Patrick Watts, desperately tired after a night of broadcasting, was heard saying:

"Just a minute—just wait there—No, I won't do anything until you take that gun out of my back—We have been taken over as expected by the Argentines. They have given me some tapes they want me to play..."

Soon the Argentine national anthem was played over the radio and they realized the end had actually come.

The Falklands Radio was the heart of the islands. It was a small, informal, friendly station that broadcast local information and community news as well as old radio programs, comedies, quiz shows, and BBC programs. To the wider, scattered community across the islands, it was the vital link that kept the outlying farms in touch with Stanley and with Great Britain beyond. It was the voice of the people of the islands. Now it was silenced.

Within an hour, the Argentines broadcast four Communiques that had obviously been prepared well before the invasion. Each was read, first in Spanish and then in English, then they played the national anthem. Grant commented that the Argentine anthem seemed to go on forever; every time you thought it had finished, they would start up again with a few more verses. "Perhaps they pause so the musicians can regain their breath" he said.

In the first Communique, the Argentines asserted their sovereignty and asked for the islander's cooperation "to facilitate the normal life of the entire population."

Communique No. 2 stated that they were sending the colonial and military authorities, and their families, back to Britain. It further asserted Argentine control of South Georgia and the Sandwich Islands.

No. 3 said that "all people are to remain at their homes until further notice," and warned that "military troops shall arrest all people found outside their homes." They closed all schools, shops, and stores, but if the residents had problems, they could place a white piece of cloth outside their homes and military patrols would visit them.

In the final Communique, they said that "the population is exhorted to continue normally with their activities in an atmosphere of peace, order, and harmony."

As the last of the Communiques was read, Colin came down the stairs into the cellar.

"Heavens, Colin" Jenny said, "have you been out on the streets?"

"Yes, it's a bit dodgy out there right now, but I hid behind fences and came down the alley ways. The Argies don't have a clue about how this town is laid out and they don't know much about patrolling either. Mostly, they're just standing around, talking up a storm in Spanish, congratulating themselves I expect."

"Have there been any casualties?" Grant asked.

"I don't believe so. I saw one Argie lying face down in front of Government House. I'm pretty sure he was dead. But I don't think any of our lads were hit."

"Thank God" Jenny said.

Her mother stood up and walked a few steps to speak with Colin. They had known each other for many years and Colin had done work on her house.

"Hello, Millie. Glad you found shelter here below ground."

"They've shot up my house" she replied. "Fired through my windows and put holes in the walls. One shot went right through my headboard while I was lying under the bed."

"Sorry to hear it. How did you get here?"

"I ran. They don't shoot old women on the run, apparently."

"Well, that's a blessing isn't it?"

"But they blasted the water supply tank on my roof and now there's water everywhere. Now I'll need you and Grant to help me put it all back together."

Colin looked at Grant. "Sure, Millie, but let's wait until they let us out of the house."

"Don't wait!" she demanded. "Put a white flag out the front door and tell them you have to stop the damage to my house. Go on. Do it now."

Grant nodded and said "All right. Let's give this a try." He led Colin upstairs and they hung a white pillowcase on the front door. The stream of Argentine soldiers passing down the street paid no attention. Finally, Grant stepped out the front door and waved the pillowcase in the air to catch their attention. Several of the soldiers saw the pillowcase and waved back. Clearly, they thought it was just a greeting.

"Bugger this" Grant said, "we need to push on. Let's go out into the street and see what happens." He led the way and Colin followed.

Grant carried the pillowcase above his head, waving it gently, but none of the Argentine soldiers paid it any mind and there was no effort to stop him or Colin. As they walked up the street, they were shocked to see what had happened to the town. First, there were the soldiers, hundreds of them, walking casually up and down the streets, taking pictures, standing in groups smoking cigarettes and talking constantly. Then there were the armored personnel carriers, a dozen or more of them, pulled up on the main street, breaking through the pavement as they moved. The roads in Stanley were never designed to support this kind of weight.

Most unnerving of all was the huge Argentine flag that now hung from the flagpole in front of Government House. As Grant looked beyond it, he saw the hundreds of bullet holes in Government House itself. They had put up quite a fight, these Royal Marines, and he felt a surge of pride in the hopeless resistance they had offered.

"Look there" Colin said, pointing back to the airport. Huge American-built Hercules C-130s were landing and taking off, bringing hundreds and ultimately thousands of Argentine soldiers to these formerly peaceful islands.

It was the saddest sight Grant had ever seen.

In addition to the armored personnel carriers, there were armored cars and amphibious landing vehicles, noisily grinding up and down the streets. The armored vehicles were lined up from one end of John street to the other and St. Mary's Walk was filled with them. Islanders carrying white flags were forced to move out of the way of this random traffic. No one appeared to be in control. The islanders waved their flags in greeting to each other. The soldiers looked on curiously, wondering what it was all about.

Grant noticed that there were two distinct groups of soldiers: the common conscripts, who appeared to be mostly teenagers, and the Argentine special forces, the *Buzos Tacticos*. The latter were clearly the professionals, taller, better equipped, and a bit surly. Unfortunately, it was the teenagers who were driving the vehicles and Grant watched in horror as one of them tore down a fence in front of a house. He also noted that all of the Argentine vehicles appeared to be new.

As he was considering this, he was greeted by John Smith who was out walking with his son Thyssen. They had quietly been taking an inventory of all the Argentine equipment they had seen and where it came from: the Land-Rover type vehicles were made by Mercedes, Panhard armored cars were from Belgium, armored personnel carriers and helicopters from the USA, other helicopters that were French, and out in the bay, Type 42 destroyers from England. Ironically, the Argentine aircraft carrier was the former *HMS Venerable* of the Royal Navy.

None of it was made in Argentina.

Grant and Colin walked on noting how many Stanley residents were also walking about, holding their white flags. Apparently no one had told the Argentine soldiers that the townspeople were required to stay in their homes. As they passed the Upland Goose Hotel, they saw Vice-Comodoro Carlos Bloomer-Reeve, who had been in charge of the Argentine airline office in Stanley a few years back. He crossed the street to speak with them. He had not been on the islands for some time, but Grant remembered him well and had spoken with him many times.

"Hello, sir" Grant said.

It was a tense moment as this Argentine soldier tried to reestablish contact with islanders he had known in better times.

"It was Carlos before, Grant. I'd like to keep it that way."

Colin spoke before Grant could reply. "Maybe we're not comfortable talking with soldiers who have invaded our country."

Grant felt embarrassed and he could see that Carlos felt the same way. Grant said: "I'm sorry, feelings are running high today. We're all trying to understand what has happened."

Carlos shook his head. "It's unfortunate that this transition has taken place this way. It would have been better to have negotiated this change in government. I know it's confusing."

"It's NOT confusing..." Colin said a little too loudly, but Grant raised his hand to stop his brother before he could continue.

"This is our home" Grant said. "We were born here. Our parents were born here, and our grandparents before them. These islands have been British for 150 years."

Carlos looked pained. "I know this is hard. I'm sorry. I was stationed in Germany until a few days ago. My family is still there. I was ordered back here and appointed as *Secretario General.* I will be the liaison between the civilian population and the military authorities. If there is any way in which I can help you or anyone you know, please don't hesitate to contact me. I will do whatever I can for you."

"Thank you, Carlos."

Grant and Colin walked away down the next street toward Millicent's house. Grant could tell Colin was fuming.

"Why are you kissing up to that bastard?"

"He's just a soldier doing what he is told to do. He didn't plan this invasion, probably didn't even know of it."

"He was probably spying for them the whole time he was here."

Grant stopped them in the middle of the block and turned to look at his brother. "Look, insulting them won't make them go back to Argentina. They're here now and they won't be going home any time soon. We don't know how this is going to play out and that man may be important to us, important to the whole island. Let's not burn any bridges."

"I'm leaving" Colin said, as he looked out on the harbor, now filled with Argentine ships.

"Where are you going?"

"I have good friends in Fox Bay. They'll put me up. I can't stay in this town as long as they are here."

"Well...all right, maybe that's the best thing. But, Colin, please don't do anything foolish. When you leave, don't try to take any guns with you."

"Not very likely. I may be angry, but I'm not stupid."

Colin walked away alone, heading toward Millicent's house.

PART FOUR

Convergence

Chapter Eleven

The Argentine government had expected the British to accept the loss of the Falkland Islands with good grace. They would protest, certainly, but there was little they could do from 8,000 miles away and world opinion would coalesce against this last relic of colonialism. The full weight of Argentina's overwhelming commitment to recovering the islands would preclude any possible British response.

They could not have been more wrong.

World opinion immediately turned against them. The day after the invasion, the United Nations Security Council passed the strongest possible resolution against Argentina's actions and demanded they withdraw their forces. Their fellow South American countries gave them verbal support, but that was all the support the Argentines received. Most important of all, the United States, a staunch Argentine ally, strongly opposed the invasion and gave aid to the British.

The assumption that Britain would take no military action also proved wildly incorrect.

Within days, Great Britain sent two aircraft-carriers, twenty-four destroyers and frigates, and three nuclear-powered submarines. In addition, there were fuel tankers, troop ships, hospital ships, tugs and repair vessels. In total, 127 ships of all kinds sailed, manned by 25,000 sailors, soldiers and airmen of the Task Force. It was the greatest military force Britain had launched against an enemy since World War II and the country supported it one hundred percent.

But for President Leopoldo Galtieri and the Argentine government, there was no way back. Once having set foot on the Malvinas, they could not withdraw or their government would fall. This was equally true for Margaret Thatcher and the British government. Both sides were now fully committed.

———•••———

April 3, 1982

Dear Marisol,

It is with humble pride that I tell you I am part of the glorious 25th Regiment, the main occupying force on the Islas Malvinas. It is a great honor to serve with this unit and to play such an important role in our country's history. Every day I am grateful to have been chosen for this honor. Unlike other regiments, our unit has been drawn from the best soldiers all over Argentina and we symbolize the nation as a whole.

The islands are not what I expected. We are now occupying the only city and it is nothing more than a little town with only one main road! And there are no Argentines here. I had thought there would be crowds of them, cheering our arrival, but there are only English here and they are not happy to see us. They are sullen and act like they want to spit on the ground when we walk by. But we have been strictly warned not to take offense or mistreat them in any way. Looting and abuse of civilians is harshly punished.

The weather here is most peculiar. It is grey and cloudy most of the time and the wind never stops blowing. There are no trees! The grasslands beyond Puerto Argentina just roll on as far as you can see with rocks forming hills they call mountains, but they don't look like any mountains I have ever seen. Because there are so many rocks and the peat that grows everywhere is so soggy, there are no roads around the islands. I hope we will not have to do any marching around this place because it will not be fun! They say winter is coming on, but we will only be here for a few weeks until the regular Argentine civil government takes over.

Thank you for writing to me and being my friend. It is good to have someone I can tell about my great adventure. I have not heard from my family yet, but I expect sending mail through your father's office makes it get here a lot quicker.

We were not told where we were going until we were actually on the plane flying to the Malvinas. What a shock! Everyone cheered and we were very excited. Then, when we got off the plane, they lined us up and gave us green berets for our dress uniforms. Only our 25th Regiment gets to wear these berets and they look wonderful. There have been a lot of jokes about how we are now part of John Wayne's army since he made that movie about the US Army unit called the Green Berets.

That's all for now. Thank you for writing to me. I look forward to your next letter.

Your friend on the Islas Malvinas,
Rey

Vice-Comodoro Lantana sat at his desk in Buenos Aires. He read this letter and was struck again by the sincerity of this young man, his pride, and his dedication. Lantana hoped he would not be killed in the battles that might come, it would break Marie's heart. But Lantana knew the British and yesterday, April 5, they had sent an armada to the Southern Ocean. He hoped this soldier was prepared for what was ahead; he hoped Argentina was prepared.

What Private Reynaldo Poralez did not know as he wrote his letter was that another army unit also wore green berets: the 3rd Commando Brigade of the Royal Navy Marines, who would soon be headed to the South Atlantic. Lantana had trained with some of them during his two years in England. They were the most professional soldiers he had ever met. Unlike the conscripts in the newly formed Argentine 25th Regiment, the British Commandos of the 3rd Brigade were a seasoned, highly trained force and among the fittest and toughest troops Great Britain possessed. They were trained in arctic and mountain warfare and carried out regular winter exercises in Norway. It was the ideal training for fighting in the Falklands at the onset of winter. The only defense against them, Lantana felt sure, was to stop them from ever getting to the islands. The Argentine navy would never stand up to the firepower of the British navy. Only the Argentine Air Force could stop them.

The air force of Argentina vastly outnumbered any force the British could bring on their two carriers. With over two hundred planes, they had scores of Mirages, Daggers, and Skyhawks, faster and more maneuverable than the bulky Harriers the British would be bringing. The Matra missiles they carried should be a good match for the American-made Sidewinders the Royal Air Force used.

Though their pilot training was not as rigorous as the NATO-level training of the British flyers, Lantana knew the courage and dedication of the Argentine pilots was second to none. They would fight and die, if necessary, to defend their islands. The arrogant British would assume they were facing an inferior air force, but they would soon face the finest jet planes on the planet. The Argentine Air Force was easily the most formidable air force in South America and countless millions had been lavished on the latest technology.

Of course, what he really hoped was that the diplomats would somehow avoid a war. Maybe the British would back down, as they did in 1956, during the Suez Canal crisis. That would be the best outcome for everyone. They must accept that the islands belonged to Argentina and give up this foolish idea that they could somehow take them back.

His daughter was now writing to this soldier on the Islas Malvinas every day, but Lantana was sure this was just a phase she was passing through. She was sixteen and the letters she wrote showed her age and her limited maturity. She wrote about her classes, her participation in the girl's soccer team, her friends, and the school play she was trying out for. Why a soldier would want to read such drivel he could not imagine, but her letters had become so frequent, he had envelops addressed to the young man made up in batches of a dozen.

On the other hand, the letters she was receiving from Private Poralez were most informative. The army, it seemed, was taking the threat of a British counter-invasion seriously. They were digging in and preparing for a siege. Lantana was mostly concerned about the airport just two miles from Stanley. It must stay open. It was the lifeline into the islands.

Lantana knew that if negotiations failed and the British submarines began sinking Argentine supply ships, the navy would be forced to pull back into port. Then it would fall to the air force to keep the British task force from landing troops on the Malvinas. If they could hold them at sea until the middle of June, the arctic winter would set in and an invasion would become impossible.

A week later, Lantana opened another letter from Private Poralez.

April 11, 1982

Dear Marisol,

Thank you for all your letters and for telling me about your life at school. They are very cheering and make me think of my own days when I was in school. It was not so long ago, and yet, it seems like a lifetime. I'm sorry I cannot write to you as often as you write me, but, as you might expect, we are extremely busy. There are so many troops on the islands now that it has become a military encampment with rows of tents and huge food service areas. There is a lot of confusion about why the British are coming and what they will do when they get here. Many believe this is just a show of force so they can negotiate a better deal with the UN and they will never really try to land here. I hope this is true.

But we have to be prepared in case they actually want a fight. So when I am not helping unload planes, I am digging air raid trenches around the airport. These are very damp and uncomfortable and I pray we will never have to use them.

My best friends, Jury Mitner and Sonny Dambolena, are

both in the 25th Regiment with me, but they have been assigned to other units so I rarely see them. Still, it is wonderful to know they are also here on the islands. Sometimes we meet up when we line up for the food tent. We exchange stories about the duties we have to perform.

Mostly, we talk about the officers. The corporals and sergeants are always demanding and they boss us around and threaten us with various punishments, but mostly they seem like pretty good guys. But the commissioned officers are a different breed. These "career" officers are arrogant and talk to us, when they talk to us at all, as if we are children. They clearly think we are only here to serve their needs and do their bidding. They have their own food—better food than we get—and they get little liquor bottles as part of their supply packs!

The officers also seem to fight amongst themselves a lot and there is always a lot of haggling about how things should be set up and which units should do the work. I wonder if we actually get into a shooting war if all this squabbling will straighten itself out. We often seem confused as to what the plan is. During the invasion, they brought a whole lot of heavy Am Tracs and parked them on the streets of downtown Puerto Argentino. Then they turned them around, loaded them back on the ships and sent them back to the mainland. Who is deciding all this?

We had an embarrassing moment when the Argentine flag was blown over breaking the flagpole and bringing the flag down onto the ground. It was very windy that day (as it is every day!) and the flag was much bigger than the one the British had been flying, but still, it shouldn't have blown over. It was not a good sign. The officers were furious and there was a lot of shouting and name calling.

It does not look like we will be returning to Argentina any time soon. We will be the defending army on the Islas Malvinas until the British threat is neutralized and no one knows how long that will be. I'm hoping the British will just give up and go back home. None of us want to fight them, but if we have to, we will.

Thanks again for the letters. I look forward to them every day.

Stay safe and keep thinking good thoughts of us.

Your friend,
Rey

Another letter came several days later.

April 15, 1982

Dear Marisol

The weather here is terrible and I am stuck inside my tent so it is a good time to write to you. It has been cold, windy, and drizzling most days, but now it has turned bitterly cold and the winds have been gale force—very bad indeed. Our coats are not warm enough and the blankets we have are too thin to let us sleep well at night. The only good thing is that the officers don't want to be outside either so a lot of work parties have been cancelled, including mine. What a relief that is! Winter is clearly coming on and I hope we can get out of here before snow falls.

Thank you for your letters, they are very enjoyable. But please DON'T give my name to your class writing to soldiers on the Islas Malvinas. I am already getting so many letters from you and from my family that I don't have space to store them and I can't throw them away.

As more soldiers have arrived, it is getting harder to get food and to stay warm. Some days we have to eat out of our ration packs, mixing the dried food with water. It is pretty awful to eat this way. But the cold is what really gets to us. Many of us in the 25th come from Northern Argentina where the climate is practically tropical. Some soldiers have stolen fences from the islanders to make fires. A couple days ago when my unit was marching into town for work in the harbor, I saw two soldiers staked out for having misbehaved in some way. They were spread-eagled on the ground, tied to stakes and left exposed to the cold for hours. They even have a name for them: "the estaqueros"—the staked ones.

As I stood looking at them, an officer came by and said "Keep moving, xxxx-head, or you'll be joining them." I didn't argue and was glad when the officer went past.

I write about all the bad things that are happening here, but you should also know that there are many honorable and brave soldiers and officers here and if we are called on to fight, I know we will stand together. Despite the hardships of being on these islands, we are doing the right thing and we are ready to defend ourselves.

We are still very hopeful a settlement will come and the British will sail back home. But the rumors we hear are scary. It is said they are sending their strongest units: the SAS, the Parachute Regiment, the Royal Marine Commandos, the Scots Guards, and the Welsh Guards. But the worst are their mercenaries, the Gurkhas—ferocious Nepalese hillmen—who come in the night with their curved Kukri killing knives and cut off the heads of sleeping soldiers. It gives me chills just to think of them.

But those are just rumors and it is foolish to believe everything you hear. There are now thousands of us on these islands and more coming every day. We have canon and missiles and enough shells to blow the British away if they attempt to land. And every day our jets are flying overhead and our warships are in the harbor. These are our islands and they are going to stay our islands.

Thank you for writing,

Your friend,
Reynaldo

Lantana folded the letter and put it in his coat pocket to give to his daughter when he got home later that evening. The intelligence reports he had read earlier that morning indicated that most of those "rumors" were true. They were heading into war and the British were bringing the best they had with them.

Chapter Twelve

Ascension Island lies 500 miles south of the equator, almost exactly halfway between Great Britain and the Falkland Islands. This 34-square-mile slag heap is what's left of 40 extinct volcanoes. There is no indigenous population. It is British owned and leased to the United States who, during World War II, built an airport with a 10,000 foot runway on it. When the Falklands war came, the Americans turned the island over to the British and it became the forward staging area for the British Forces.

The hasty departure of the British task force—only four days after the invasion—was meant to intimidate the Argentines into an early withdrawal. Unfortunately, that meant most of the supplies loaded onto the departing ships were thrown aboard without much thought of how they would be used and how they would need to be unloaded when they reached the South Atlantic.

Consequently, an enormous resorting and redeployment process took place on Ascension Island. Dozens of helicopters moved tons of supplies between ships and onboard from the airfield. The work went on night and day. As plans for the retaking of the islands expanded, great quantities of supplies and personnel were flown down to Ascension from Britain on huge cargo transport planes.

Prior to the Falklands conflict, the airfield on Ascension had handled three landings a week. By Easter Sunday, April 11th, it had become the busiest airport in the world with over 400 air movements per day which surpassed even Chicago O'Hare which had held the record for many years.

On April 17th, the aircraft carrier *Hermes*, Admiral Woodward's flagship, lay anchored in the only port on the island. Onboard Ted Tomlinson and his office mates, Larry Burke and Tom Wingate, shared a tiny ready room one quarter the size of their office back in the Air Ministry in London. Even so, it was larger than their sleeping quarters, the size of a walk-in closet, which pushed two of them on upper and lower bunks against a bulkhead. Ted and Larry were together, Tom had to bunk with a fellow he'd never met before.

The three of them were sifting through requisition manifests and troop deployments trying to imagine what ships and troops would actually make the amphibious landing on the islands and what order their supplies should be taken ashore.

"I don't see how we're going to achieve air superiority with only twenty Harriers up against 200 Argentine planes" Larry said.

Ted looked at the topographical island map on the table before them. "It really depends on where we establish the beachhead. If we can find a sheltered area where the headlands give us a little protection, we can place our Rapier air-defense missiles along the ridgeline to take out incoming planes."

"The guidance system on those Rapiers is damned sensitive" Larry said, "and we don't even know if they will work in these conditions. Even if they do, knocking out a few planes will not establish air superiority."

"No" Ted said thoughtfully, "but we don't actually need full superiority. We just need to shoot down enough of their planes to discourage them from sending more. And the new Sidewinders we have, the AIM-9Ls, should give the Harriers a real advantage."

Tom asked: "Don't the Argies also have Sidewinders?"

"Some of their planes do" Ted replied, "but they're using the older Sidewinders and the new AIM-9Ls are much better. The onboard software is state of the art. With the early Sidewinders, you had to line your shot up straight from behind and the missile had to track in pretty much a straight line. But the AIM-9L is an all-aspect tracker and can follow planes moving across your line of flight. It can even be fired at planes coming directly at you. The Matras they're using will be no match for them."

A message came over the tannoy requesting all planning personnel to attend a briefing in the Assembly Hall. This was the message they had all been waiting for. The Admiral's staff and the ship's captains and upper level planners for the ground forces had been meeting all day onboard *Hermes* to set the parameters for retaking the islands. Now they would hear the overall plan for how this war would be fought.

Major Brockton conducted the briefing and he looked grimly happy to be doing it. About fifty of the mid-level planners were present and they all stood as he entered. He moved behind the podium. After everyone except Brockton had taken their seats and the room quieted down, he paused to look across the faces before him. His usual sense of self importance was fully on display.

"Right, then. As you all know, the launch of our task force, as *Hermes* and *Invincible* sailed out of Portsmouth, was done with maximum fanfare and Fleet Street publicity to let the Argentines know we mean business. We went to considerable lengths to impress them that we had a fully-staffed, fully-provisioned army ready to throw at them at a moment's notice.

"And you all know that was pretty much complete rubbish." There was brief tittering around the room. "This 'grand launch' stunt was done at the politician's behest with no regard for military necessities or contingency planning. We packed what we could and were pushed out to sea. The only positive thing about this launch was that it gave the Argentines the idea that we were fully prepared for them and an army in force was coming their way.

"The reality, of course, is quite different. We're desperately scrambling to get our supplies sorted out, our ships lined up, and our war strategy defined. In the last 24 hours, that strategy has begun to come into focus and we can now move forward.

"There are, in fact, two armadas heading south. Ours, the Assault Group, consists of the two carriers, *Hermes* and *Invincible*, and the attendant destroyers, frigates, and support ships. The second formation, carrying the troops that will actually land on the islands and recapture them, is the Amphibious Group. Due to assembly and provisioning delays, they will be joining us two to three weeks after we arrive within striking distance of the Falklands.

"The Argentines do not know this. We don't want them to know it. We must do everything we can to preserve their belief they will be attacked on land the moment the Assault Group arrives in Falkland waters. Our goal is to draw out their Air Force and Navy so we may engage them and establish dominance in the air and on the sea. Upon arrival, we will begin naval bombardment of beaches where they believe we might invade, launch airstrikes against the Port Stanley airfield, and commence air attacks against their defensive positions."

He moved to a large map projected on a screen and used a pointer to show the areas he was referring to. "The beaches we will be attacking lie here, around Berkeley Sound and along the north shore of East Falkland. They are anywhere from 30 to 50 kilometers from Stanley. They would be logical choices for an invasion beachhead and we believe the Argentines will have them heavily fortified. We'll also be bombing beaches south of Stanley around the Fitzroy area. We expect these areas will also be strongly fortified.

"We're counting on the Argentines to anticipate a head-on, Normandy style invasion where we fight our way ashore against heavily defended areas. That, of course, is the last thing we want to do. We're looking to establish our beachhead on an undefended beach or landing area somewhere on the western coast of East Falkland at least a hundred kilometers from Stanley. We want a protected inlet with high headlands where we can site our anti-aircraft weapons and give our landing forces as much shelter as possible."

Tom Wingate, sitting next to Ted, gave him a poke in the ribs and whispered "Well, you called that one right, didn't you?"

Brockton continued. "If we're able to surprise them and get ashore in a hurry, it is unlikely they will be able to organize and mount a counter offensive from the other side of the island. The price we pay is that it puts the range of low mountains in central East Falkland between us and Stanley. Port Stanley is, of course, the ultimate goal and the Argentines will defend it with everything they have.

"We must plan, then, for weeks of exposed fighting and a series of mountain assaults. We'll move our troops forward by helicopter and due to the open nature of the land, our attacks will be made at night. Unfortunately, we've learned that their night vision equipment is superior to ours, but we're hopeful the element of surprise will be in our favor.

"The period after the Assault Group arrives, but before the Amphibious Group goes ashore will be designated as the First Phase of the campaign and should be referred to as such in your planning reports. The First Phase will serve four distinct functions.

"First, it will allow us to draw out their Air Force and Navy and gage how committed they are and if they are able to effectively employ all the advanced technology we know they possess. This is an area where our NATO training and superior tactical experience should serve us well. We hope to establish clear air superiority during this First Phase and drive their navy back to the mainland.

"Second, the First Phase will begin the process of softening up their ground forces and breaking their spirit. The more Argentines we can kill prior to landing, the better. We will make multiple feints as if about to attack, and then shift our bombing to other areas. We believe this will cause the Argentines to move their troops around the island trying to anticipate where we will land. We'll continue to feed them false signals right up until the actual landing occurs.

"A third goal of the First Phase will be to land units of the SAS and SBS for reconnaissance purposes. We want to know troop deployments, cannon and missile sites, fuel depots, and ammunition storage areas. These recon groups will also be evaluating multiple sites for our main landing.

"Our fourth goal is to stage hit and run attacks on the airfield at Goose Green or on any fuel or ammunition dumps we can find.

Random and unpredictable attacks will raise their apprehension and confuse their planning. Again, the more damage we can do prior to the arrival of our main force, the easier it will be to complete our mission.

"Questions?" There followed a half hour of Q&A as the assembled planners tried to pin down particular areas of concern. Most of the information was familiar to Ted, but one area worried him. He raised his hand and Major Brockton pointed to him to ask his question.

"How will the Assault Group ships be dispersed during the First Phase?"

"A very pertinent question and one we should consider at length. But before we discuss ship deployment, we should consider the greatest threat our ships will face."

At the moment he said this, the map on the large screen behind him disappeared and was replaced by the picture of a long, white missile that looked like a huge, fat dart. Stretching horizontally, it was 10 feet long as projected on the screen. Ted watched the effect of this image on the audience and realized Brockton must have rehearsed this presentation with whoever was running the slide projector. It was a nice dramatic touch.

"This is the French-built *Exocet* anti-ship missile, the most dangerous weapon any navy has ever faced. In real life, it is twice the size you are looking at: a full 20-feet long with a warhead that weighs 363 pounds. It has an inertial guidance system, active radar homing, and GPS. Launched from the air by a Super Étendard, which we know the Argentines possess, it can be fired from 40 miles away. It will travel at 700 miles-per-hour, seven to twelve feet above the surface of the ocean and cannot be seen by radar until it rises to attack height only three to five seconds before it strikes.

"This missile is a ship killer. If a single one gets through our defenses and strikes either of our carriers, it is likely we have lost the war. We now believe the Argentines have five of them. Peru has attempted to buy more *Exocets* from France, but the French have refused them delivery until after this mess is settled. They believe, and we concur, that Peru will just sell them to Argentina.

"We have only two carriers and 20 Harriers to work with. We must have both carriers to achieve anything approaching air parity, much less dominance. Consequently, preservation of the carriers must take precedence. They will be surrounded with rings of protection in the hope that if we sustain losses, such losses will be ships we can replace, allowing us to carry on. To put the matter bluntly: those ships will be expendable."

A silence fell upon the room. Men looked at the floor, at the chair in front of them, or at the screen before them. They did not look into each other's eyes, as if to do so would make them complicit in the ships consigned to the deep. Major Brockton made no move to interrupt these dark meditations. Finally, he continued.

"We envision five rings of protection around the carriers. The outermost ring will be the Harrier patrols. Unfortunately, there is simply too much ocean for them to cover and they are unlikely to encounter, identify, and engage the Super Étendards before they acquire the range. We currently lack long range airborne early warning radar and the Americans, who could provide it for us, have drawn the line in their support at that point.

"So, first contact will probably fall to our Type 42 destroyers, *Sheffield, Glasgow,* and *Coventry,* which will protect us with their Sea Dart defense missiles. They will form the outer barrier, furthest out from the carriers.

"The next ring further in will be the Escort Screen consisting of four frigates. Behind them, just before the carriers will be three of our supply ships. Finally, maintaining station next to our carriers, will be *Brilliant* and *Broadsword,* both armed with the Sea Wolf point defense system."

Brockton paused a moment to look around the room. He was pleased to find that Ted was taking notes. "Now, I have heard the scuttlebutt going around that the fleet will be hanging back far east of the Falklands because Admiral Woodward is having a case of the wobblers. I can assure you, nothing of the sort is true. We have indeed designated lines of advance toward the islands that will keep us safely at sea. But the disparaging remarks I have heard that we will be hiding behind some Yellow Brick Road are ignorant and inappropriate. I trust you will discourage them among your staff or the ship's company."

At a nod from Brockton, the projector was turned off and everyone stood. "Dismissed. Colonel Tomlinson, please remain so we may have a word." The room quickly emptied leaving Ted facing the Major.

"I have an assignment for you. I'd like you to disembark and take station on *Sheffield*. We have serious concerns about the Sea Dart system and we need you to evaluate the software, hardware, and personnel during and after its first firing. I believe your group can take over your planning functions."

Here it was: the thing he feared most. He was being moved to the front line of defense in the war at sea, the first place the Argentines would attack. Ted saw there was no avoiding this job. Could he protest? What was the point? This was his to do. He saluted the Major.

"Very good, sir."

Chapter Thirteen

April 26, 1982
Portsmouth Harbor, England
Onboard MV Norland

Mike Ferrol stood at the rail of the ship, looking down at the carnival below him. The dock was covered with white, blue, and red bunting, a band was playing, and a huge throng of relatives and well-wishers were waving union flags and cheering. It wasn't quite the sendoff the crowds gave the two aircraft carriers, *Invincible* and *Hermes,* when they set sail three weeks earlier, but it was still an impressive demonstration. And the media were everywhere, filming every minute of it. The 2nd Parachute Regiment was going to war and Mike was sailing with them.

As he listened to the din of the crowd's cheering and the band playing "A Life on the Ocean Wave," Mike marveled again at his sheer luck in getting onboard this ship. The British government allowed only thirty journalists to travel with the troops to the Falklands and to be among them was like winning the lottery. As with so many of the good things that happened to Mike over the last two years, he owed this break to Reuben Blake.

When it was announced in the newsroom of the London Chronicle that one of the coveted journalist spots with the task force would be awarded to their newspaper, cheers rose up from the assembled reporters and editors. Before speculation could begin, the paper's publisher, Averill Hart-Dennison, announced that he had already selected who would receive this once-in-a-lifetime opportunity, and his choice was Reuben Blake. It made perfect sense. Not only did Reuben have seniority in the newsroom and the respect of the entire staff, he had been a seasoned reporter before becoming first an Assistant Editor and then the Metro News Editor. It was the logical choice.

More important than his reportorial and editing skills was his in-depth understanding of the political realities of London publishing. Reuben was a negotiator, not a crusader. He brought the news to the public in a form that facilitated future news gathering and never violated the government's trust. When there was scandal, he published scandal, but when there was reasonable doubt he gave the benefit of that doubt to the powers that be.

Like every other writer on the staff, Mike felt disappointed not to be going south with the armada. Even though it was unlikely there would be an actual war, traveling with the troops and writing about them would have been great fun and certainly broken up the routine of daily assignments. So it was surprising when four days before Reuben was scheduled to leave, he asked Mike to speak with him in the conference room.

"Mike, I need to speak with you about something I haven't shared with the staff yet" Reuben began. Mike noticed the closed door and wondered what was coming.

"Early yesterday morning, my wife suffered a stroke. It came quite suddenly and at this time she is paralyzed on her left side."

"Reuben" Mike said, "I'm so sorry."

"Yes, it's...well, it's tragic, really, but we don't know yet if this is permanent or if she will recover, only time will tell us." Reuben was quite upset and was clearly struggling to control his emotions. "For now, she's in hospital and I need to be with her as she goes through this, however long that takes. So I'll need someone to go with the task force since I cannot."

Mike's jaw literally dropped open. He couldn't believe what he was hearing.

"Reuben, are you suggesting I might go in your place?"

"More than suggesting, Mike, I'm offering you the opportunity."

Mike was dumbfounded. He hardly knew what to say.

"I don't understand, Reuben. There must be a dozen guys out there..." he pointed to the newsroom, "...who have more seniority and understand the British military better than me. Do you realize how many enemies you're going to make if you let me go instead of them?"

Reuben smiled ruefully. "Yes, I'm not going to be very popular for awhile here, but I've survived worse. And the simple truth is: you're the right man for the job."

Mike stared at him in silence for a moment. "Why? Why am I the right man? What have I done to..."

"Listen, Yank, we knew all about you before we hired you. We read your coverage of the 1967 race riots in Detroit. It was smart and honest and just a little poetic. You didn't pull punches. You got nominated for a Pulitzer for those stories."

"Yes and I got fired shortly after that. You remember that part of the history too don't you?"

"Yes, they canned you. As they should have for not checking your sources before printing allegations you couldn't support. You were very up front about that in the interview. Bollixed that one, didn't you? But that's not the point, Mike. The point is, what you wrote about the riots was true and honest and you told the story with compassion and insight. And you brought the story to your readers graphically with empathy for all sides. It was gifted writing and you could have easily won the Pulitzer for it."

Mike was stunned. "Reuben, I've never heard you talk about my writing like this."

"No, I suppose not." Reuben shook his head and looked away for a moment. "The truth is I've always known the crap I make you write is well below your talents. I've made you write down to my expectations. I've always felt a bit guilty about it. You're capable of doing better work and I'm sorry I haven't had the chance to let you do it.

"Mind you, sending you to the Falklands is not just my idea. Averill and the boys upstairs agree you're the right choice. So don't take this as some kind of favor I'm doing you. It's just an assignment and I'll have you back here writing obituaries before you know it. Anyway, if you want it, the assignment is yours."

"If I want it? Of course I want it! Reuben, I could kiss you."

"Oh, God, don't do that. I have grandchildren and I'm much too old for you."

They laughed together and four days later Mike walked up the gangplank to join the 2nd Parachute Regiment sailing south.

It was the culmination of a very busy month. Once the Argentine invasion broke, the newspaper swung into gear right alongside the military and the diplomats. There were countless stories to write and research and things changed so rapidly it seemed there was a new angle to be covered every hour. To add to the confusion, Mike's sister Eileen chose this time to visit London and camped out on his couch for a week and a half. Newly divorced and now "free as a bird," in her words, she took up all his spare hours and required counseling he was ill-prepared to provide.

Mike saw Madeline Tomlinson only once during April. They shared a brief lunch at an out of the way Italian restaurant where Mike often ate. It was a hurried affair as Mike was scheduled for a Defense Ministry briefing that afternoon. Maddie's husband Ted had sailed with *Hermes,* the flagship, and his sudden deployment had been a shock. Curiously, their daughter Edith had taken it poorly and was very apprehensive. Maddie talked about all she was doing to keep herself and Edith occupied. In this atmosphere, any thought of a sexual liaison seemed inappropriate and neither of them brought it up.

Mike had seen Ted two days before *Hermes* sailed, but it wasn't something he could talk about with Maddie. Ted had called Mike at the newsroom and asked to join him for a drink after work. Mike assumed there was some sort of military information Ted wished to pass along and Mike would provide his usual discreet back channel. But Ted's discussion of the current events didn't extend beyond anything both of them already knew.

"What I really wanted to talk to you about" Ted finally said, "is taking charge of my exit papers."

"Exit papers? You're not leaving the military, are you?"

Ted gave a pained smile and shook his head. "No, nothing

like that. Different type of exit." He handed Mike a sealed manilla envelop. "This is all the information Madge will need if I'm killed or seriously injured. There's insurance forms, instructions on how to file for military death benefits, house information, a list of contractors we've used to do work around the place, all that sort of thing. Enough so she can carry on in my absence. I'd give it to her myself, but she's in such a tizzy about this whole task force, I don't want to add to her worries."

"Well, of course I'm glad to do it, but don't you have some military buddy who might be...I don't know, more appropriate?"

"No, I think it would be better coming from a friend, someone she's known for a long time. Madge isn't good with these sorts of details, she may need some guidance."

"Okay" Mike said, "I'll hold onto these and give them back when you return."

They made an early evening of it. It seemed curious to Mike that this had even come up. Ted was sailing on *Hermes,* Admiral Woodward's flagship, certainly the safest ship in the entire fleet to be on. If *Hermes* went down, or even sustained serious harm, that would effectively end the war and the British would have to head home. So a screen of surface ships, aircraft, and submarines would be protecting it from the moment it left port. Ted was probably safer onboard that ship than he would be standing in Trafalgar Square.

Mike thought about this weeks later onboard the *Norland*, when he realized that the protection *Hermes* enjoyed did not extend to his ship. He was sailing on a civilian ship that had been converted to a troop carrier, a prime target for the Argentines. His ship had no anti-aircraft guns, no canon, no sonar to detect Argentine submarines, and no high speed capability to elude attack. All it had was 1,800 "Toms" from the 2nd Parachute Regiment whom the Argentines would dearly love to send to the bottom of the ocean. And Mike would go with them.

Well, it won't come to that, Mike thought. We'll cruise south for a few weeks until the diplomats work out some sort of arrangement. Few onboard believed the *Norland* or any of its passengers would ever see action. Still, even without actual combat, it would be fascinating to see how the military prepared for action and write about it. Mike was looking forward to the trip.

Before he realized it was happening, the ship had cast off and begun moving out to sea. The crowds on the dock slowly fell behind them and the sound of their cheering and the band playing faded until the ship cleared port and gently began to roll in the swell. Mike stood at the rail for half an hour watching the land recede, then picked up the duffel he'd been told to bring and made his way below.

The *Norland* looked like a small ocean liner. Five hundred feet long and eighty two feet across, it had eight decks and rose many stories above the waterline. It was previously a car ferry, hauling cars, trucks, campers and other assorted vehicles that were driven onto its huge open decks below. When it was converted to a troop carrier, a helicopter landing pad was welded onto the upper rear deck.

Now it was a warren of narrow passageways, hastily built cubicles, and tiny cabins with bunk beds and dressers, but nothing else. After carefully navigating his way down to Deck Three, Mike walked what felt like a quarter mile until he found his assigned cabin. There he met his roommate, Tyler Landry, a bookish-looking reporter with the Liverpool News Bulletin.

"I've taken the lower bunk," Tyler said, "but I'd be happy to move to the top bunk if you'd prefer to be down below."

"It's kind of you to offer, but at six foot two, I'm pretty sure my feet will stick out past the end of these bunks and it would be easier to do that on the top bunk."

"Right. Well, then I've taken the left dresser, you can have the other. You probably want to go to the Supply Office on Deck Four and get suited up."

For the first time, Mike realized Tyler was wearing army fatigues that bore no insignia, but had his name printed on a white band sewn above his left breast pocket. It read: "T. Landry – Correspondent."

"Thoughtful of them to give us uniforms."

"Yes, I'm pretty sure they did that to brand us so no one will talk with us."

"Really?"

"I've been onboard for 24 hours and no one other than the Information Officer has said anything of substance to me. I think they've been warned not to do interviews."

"Well, that will make it a bit sticky, won't it?"

"I expect things will loosen up after a week or two when they get to know us. Might be a good idea to head to the Forward Lounge and have a drink at the bar. Mind you, there's no hard liquor and we're only issued two cans of beer a night, just like the soldiers. They probably have a limited supply and are trying to keep the dust-ups to a minimum."

Mike went to the Supply Office and was surprised to find they had two uniforms prepared in his size with his name tag already sewn on. That explained some of the questions in the extensive questionnaire he'd had to fill out to get his boarding pass. The army now had a full file on him including his medical, educational, employment, and travel history. They knew where he lived and how long he'd lived there. They had his next of kin on file too.

After changing into his fatigues as he'd been instructed to do, he put his "civvies" into the lower drawer of his dresser and explored his deck to be sure he knew where the bathrooms, showers and exits were. Then Mike took an extended tour of the ship starting as high up as he was allowed to go. He quickly discovered that some areas of the ship were off limits to him and the officers and sentries were quick to tell him when he was trespassing in a restricted area. Everyone was polite to him, but no one extended themselves or offered to give him any kind of tour. Tyler was right, the word "Correspondent" on his shirt changed the way people responded to him.

There were troops everywhere and Mike passed classrooms and conference rooms that were already in use. Down a long hall at the end of one deck, he found an infirmary, a chapel, and a small, unmanned library where, apparently, soldiers could check out their own books. As Mike glanced into the library, he saw a lone soldier sitting at a corner desk reading a thick volume. Always open to an opportunity, Mike entered the small room and stood across from the man.

When the soldier looked up from the book he was reading, his gaze was hard and lean. He had a large frame, wavy blond hair, and the lightest blue eyes Mike had ever seen. There was no warmth or humor in those eyes. He appraised Mike as he might look at an animal he was about to slaughter.

"What are you looking at, Mr. Reporter? Hoping for a story? Fuck off and leave." He looked down and resumed reading.

Mike backed out of the room and left without a word. It was more than the rebuke or the hostile tone; there was something dangerous about this man, a pool of pent-up violence waiting to explode. Mike knew instinctively he could not be charmed or cajoled. Mike wondered what he was reading.

He followed the hallway to a door that led out onto the ship's fantail. There was a strong breeze and the sun shown brightly on the wavetops. Behind them, back a half mile or more, he could see the *Atlantic Conveyor,* a huge cargo ship with large containers and Chinook helicopters tied down on her upper deck. The *Conveyor* didn't roll with the swell the way the *Norland* did, she plowed straight ahead and seemed to be pushing the waves out of her way. She must be carrying quite a load, Mike thought, imagining her filled cargo bays below.

He was standing at the stern rail, looking out to sea, when a young paratrooper came up to stand next to him. The twenty-year-old was a full eight inches shorter than Mike, but his stature didn't bother the young man who looked confidently up at the older man.

"Hello, mate. Writin' some inspirin' words about this murderin' hoard comin' south to do for the Argies?"

Mike looked down into the round, smiling face next to him. "Well, I might if someone would talk to me."

"Boys are hangin' back from you, eh? Well, you can't blame'em. It's the imbuggerance factor. The Ruperts told'em to keep mum."

"The Ruperts?"

"Ruperts. Mini-brass. Officers. They're all lookin' to move up rank and they don't want any of us clods talkin' out of turn, spoilin' their chance. Silly bastards. Fresh out of Sandhurst and don't know jack shit about anything."

"You're a paratrooper, right?"

"Better than that, I'm a Scottish paratrooper. 2 Para is a Scottish Regiment, or at least a helluva lot of us are Scottish. I'm Tony Banks." He stuck out his hand and Mike gladly shook it.

"I'm Mike Ferrol with the London Chronicle. Never served a day in the army and don't know jack shit about anything either."

"Well, at least you're honest about it. You're a Yank, aren't you?"

"An American, yes. Try not to hold it against me. I'd be putting on airs if I told you I'm English."

"Don't make a difference. The Argies will be shootin' at you just like the rest of us."

"So you think it will come to war?"

"Nah. When they see this lot coming they'll be pissed off and knackered, but then they'll head home. At least, if they have any sense they will."

"How would you like to do an interview with me?"

"How would that play out, Governor?"

"I won't use your name or put in any identifying information. I just want to know your attitudes and perspective, and maybe a bit about your training. It won't give aid to the enemy. Anything I write will have to pass through the Information Office. What do you say?"

Tony Banks thought for a moment, then a smile came across his face. "Cost you two cans of beer."

"Done."

They met that evening in a small games room next to the off-duty lounge. It had a table and two chairs, big enough for a chess match, but not much more. Mike brought a pad and two pens. He'd supply the beer later in the Forward Lounge.

"So, tell me how you got into the Parachute Regiment."

"Well, before I joined the Paras, I was in the Territorial Army. Stationed in St. Andrews. *The Home of Gulf* they call it. I joined up just so's I could jump out of airplanes. What a thrill, I still love it. And St. Andrews was wild. We'd train all day and then they turned us loose in the evening.

"After training, we were free to roam the pubs of St. Andrews all night. And there was plenty of totty – much of it posh – in that student town. The girls always enjoyed spending some time with us army boys. I suppose we were a bit of rough for them. We'd go to the student's union and cause carnage, and we had the perfect chat-up line when last orders were being called at 11 pm: *"Do you fancy coming back to the barracks for another drink?"*

"Our place was open until 4:00 am. There were some big, big nights in there, with loads of drink and women all over the place. There was an unwritten rule that you could bring back as many girls as you liked, but you had to get them out of the building by morning. So there were some classic walks of shame when the sun came up."

Mike smiled, but he had stopped writing a while back. "Well, your night life is certainly colorful, but what I'm really interested in is you training."

"Got plenty of that in the TA. Fact is, I learned a lot more in the Territorial Army than I ever did in college. And you had to learn fast or you knew you would suffer. If you fucked up, you had to run up a hill or do press-ups on the icy ground. It was like training dogs: after a few smacks, a dog generally learns not to piss on the carpet. I liked the challenge, despite the pain.

"I can vividly remember my first jump. It was at Brize Norton. We'd arrived on a Sunday and the course started the following day. We spent time on the fan, jumping from thirty feet up with the fan resistance slowing our decent to the ground, so we could learn how to hit the ground in the correct fashion. Your first jump would normally be out of a balloon.

"All was going according to schedule, but the day I was up for my first jump, the weather kicked up too much for the balloon so

I was told I was going to jump from a plane. We were trucked to RAF Lyneham and then taken up in a C-130 Hercules. It was hot, sweaty and noisy, and we were in clean fatigues with no equipment, just our parachutes.

"On your first jump, despite all the training, you have no idea what is going on. Before you know it, you're out the door, there's turbulence, you're being thrown about, and then there's the tug of the parachute. At that moment, all your training goes out the plane with you: your head is up your arse. But when you touch down, you're buzzing. That's it. Hooked for life. Let's do it again!

"Strangely, though, the second jump is much more scary. You know what's coming and you start thinking about it. I got through it though and from then on, I just couldn't get enough of it. The buzz and the excitement never wore off. I clocked up over 100 jumps in the TA and the surge of adrenalin never diminished, even if it was the fourth or fifth jump of the day."

"What about weapons training?" Mike asked.

"Comin' from the city, I'd never had the chance to shoot a gun, so I was excited to get my hands on one. But you never got near to shooting a rifle or a machine gun until you could strip it down, clean it, and put it back together...and you had to do all that blindfolded. We would race each other, time each other, see who could do it fastest. And you could never be parted from your rifle. In the Parachute Regiment, you were expected to sleep with it. The same went for your Bergen rucksack. They taught you how to pack it right, so you know where every single thing was. That way, when you were in the dark or under stress, you could go straight to whatever you needed.

"But a lot of the training was about being part of the group. I saw how men dealt with things—how older men dealt with eighteen year old boys. The continuous banter and the dark, sick humor got people through tough situations. And we had to learn the history of the Regiment goin' all the way back to 1941. Which of our boys won the Victoria Cross and what they did to win it. We had to know all the battles the Paras fought in, how they went and which we received battle honors for."

Mike was writing furiously and by now had several pages of notes. "How did they train you to fight as a group?"

Tony scratched his chin for a moment. "Well, it's all about being part of the tribe, isn't it? See, tribalism is everything. We ate together, slept together, shat together, fought together. The buddy system means you're prepared to do everything for each other, including die. Guys charge into machine-gun nests and probably death, not for Queen and Country, but for their mates. You do everything with a buddy, you depend on each other. If one is asleep, the other is awake, if one has the front, the other covers the rear. You share the burden, the camaraderie and the teamwork."

Mike continued asking questions and taking notes for another hour before he finally said he had enough to work with. He promised to meet Tony at eight o'clock in the Forward Lounge to hand over his evening's beer allotment.

The scene in the Forward Lounge was even louder and more raucous than Mike had anticipated. It was packed with soldiers pressing up to the bar, demanding their two cans of beer and then returning to their tightly-packed groups surrounding tiny tables festooned with empty beer cans. There were ribald stories being told, or being made up and told, and various contests timing the speed of beer consumption.

When Mike finally found Tony, he was sitting on a stool at the end of the bar sipping a lemonade. "Really?" Mike said, "you're drinking lemonade?"

"Not my night" Tony replied, "my two cans are in the pool."

"There's a pool on this ship?"

"No, you dummy, not that kind of pool. It's a group of me mates, that's them over there holdin' up pictures."

"What are they doing?"

"Just havin' a bit a fun with the girlie photos we get. See, females all over England are sendin' us photos of themselves so's we know what the fuck we're fightin' for. And some o' them are lovely birds indeed, in quite revealin' outfits. Care to come over and have a look?"

"I'll pass, but how does this pool work?"

"There's ten of us, so we have twenty cans of beer a night. We give it all to a couple of blokes so they can get good and pissed. We rotate so everybody gets a go, but we have a drawing each night so you don't know if you're up tonight or not."

"Can you really drink ten cans of beer in a night?"

"Most of us can. But if you can't, you're allowed to pass out your remaining cans to your best mates."

"Very civil. Let me get the two cans I owe you." Mike passed his beverage card over to the bartender who stamped it and gave him two cans of beer.

Tony took the beer and pushed off his stool. "Right then, I'll just be headin' off to join my mates. You can come over too if you like."

"Thanks. I'm good right here for now." Mike didn't want to intrude or seem to be buying his way into Tony's group of friends. And he wanted to take in what was happening in the room before he became part of it. He sat on his stool and listened to the banter of the group nearest him.

"Ay, Charlie, enjoy your cannon fodder trainin' today?"

"I was chuffed to bits about it. Say, how'd they know all that shite about the Argies anyway? I swear, I think they know the color of Galtieri's underpants."

"Well, we know what color they're *gonna be!*"

A roar of laughter erupted and Mike smiled at the exuberance of youth. These healthy, confident young men were delighted in each other's company, pleased to be part of something bigger than themselves. But as he looked at them, he realized how old he was. Most of the soldiers were 18 or 20. At 38, he was old enough to be their father and he wondered how he would feel if one of them was his son, going into war, trained to kill and possibly be killed. It made him shudder.

Mike had been drinking a lemonade for twenty minutes when he saw the soldier he'd encountered in the ship's library. Even from far across the room, he could pick out the blond hair and laser blue eyes. He was sitting alone in a corner. Mike made his way over to Tony and inquired about the soldier.

"Who's that blond chap?"

Tony looked to where Mike had tilted his head.

"That's Leith Cullen. Bit of a hard case, that one. Lost a couple of his best mates in Belfast. Stays mostly to himself now. He's older than most of us, late twenties I reckon. Still a private and won't accept promotion. They tried to promote him several times, but he turned it down. Says he works best alone. I wouldn't go near him if I was you."

"No, I suppose I won't." If ever there was a man who was begging to be left alone, it was Leith Cullen. There was something dangerous about him, and something intensely private. Only a fool would intrude on his space and Mike was no fool.

Chapter Fourteen

The day after they sailed, April 27, word came that South Georgia had been retaken, a minor victory, but it carried symbolic value: it was the first place Argentina raised its flag on British territory; now it was lost to them. The soldiers Mike spoke with saw it as a harbinger of things to come. To a man, they thought the Argies would now retreat to the mainland.

But they didn't. They continued to fortify the Falklands and demanded the Islas Malvinas be recognized as Argentine. The British declared a Maritime Exclusion Zone extending 200 miles from the center of the islands and promised to sink Argentine ships within that zone.

In the weeks at sea, Mike wrote articles every day and submitted them to the Information Office for approval. Once approved, they were sent back to his office in London. He encountered only one instance of outright censorship: his description of the Milan Gun, a portable wire-controlled missile system, was a little too explicit for military approval. This surprised Mike since the missile had been in use for ten years and all the information he gave was already in the public domain. But he reluctantly discarded that article and moved on to other pieces.

Mostly, he wrote about the men, how they were training onboard and keeping fit, and the many competitions that were set up for both their entertainment and their training. His roommate Tyler was right that passengers and crew would open up and talk more freely as they got to know the journalists onboard. Through Tyler and Tony Banks, Mike found many sources for stories. As they moved south, the weather became progressively warmer.

When they got to the Equator, there was the usual high jinks of initiating those who had never crossed. King Neptune appeared in a long robe, carrying a tall trident. Next to him were Davey Jones, her highness Queen Amphitrite, and multiple members of the Court of the Deep. A beauty contest featuring sailors in outlandish drag costumes preceded the Initiation of the Pollywogs, those who had never crossed the line. These bathing-suited, hapless souls had their backsides greased up, were covered in shaving cream, and sent down a chute into a giant tub of foul smelling brine made with rotting vegetables.

When he was asked several times if he was a Shellback, one who had made the crossing, Mike wisely replied he had been over the line many times. The lie came easily to his lips. He justified it in his mind by asserting that his job was to report the event, not be a victim of it.

By the time they anchored in the bay at Ascension Island, the Assault Group was long gone, having headed south several weeks earlier. But the pace of activities at the airport and base was still frantic. 3 Para had already arrived onboard *Canberra* and the ship was being resupplied and reorganized as they came in sight of it.

When they approached the land, they could see helicopters darting across the bay with huge nets of supplies they were dropping into *Canberra* and other ships at anchor. It made Mike think of a bee hive and he would have loved to write about it, but the Information Office had asked journalists to refer to Ascension Island as little as possible. The Ministry of Defense did not want the Argentines to know how vital the island was to their campaign or the amount of support the United States was giving the British.

Despite the heat, they began training for landings using the volcanic cinder beaches to stand in for the Falklands. These were nothing like the beaches they would encounter down south, but the real point of the training was to learn how to board and exit from a helicopter with their full Bergen rucksacks, 120 pounds or more, and their weapons. Mike was able to ride with one group and land onshore to observe the whole training.

A welcome relief for the troops came when mail call was announced. It had been delayed almost two weeks during the cruise. There were cheers when the stuffed sacks were brought onboard, but it took a couple hours to get it sorted and distributed. Mike received two letters from his sister Eileen who was now in Paris tasting the continental life, and a large packet from Reuben at the paper which included clippings of several of his articles. He also had a stack of bills from his landlord and the utility companies, and various advertising packets he would have expected to be dumped before anyone bothered to forward them to him.

Down at the bottom of his stack of mail he found a small, pink envelop with the return address missing and in its place the name: *M. Tomlinson.* Madeline had written to him. How curious, he thought. He opened the letter in the silence of his room, Tyler had gone ashore.

April 12, 1982

Dear Michael,

It's been a week now since Ted left and I received a letter from him yesterday. He is very low in spirits and quite depressed about going into war. I have never known him to be this way. He has faced danger many times in his career and he is certainly safe enough onboard Hermes. But he talks about having played this hand once too often. It is rather unnerving and it has made me reflect deeply on the relationship I have with him.

Ted talked a great deal about our marriage and our lives together—the sacrifices we've made and the family we have created. He is far more sensitive and aware of the stress and anxiety Edie is going through than I had imagined. He spoke of the ways in which he has failed her, failed us both really. I was moved as I have never been by Ted's words. He was never one for poetry or romantic letters, and he is so closed off emotionally, I gave him little credit for self insight. But it appears I have been quite wrong.

Ted said that he has come to realize that he has failed us, failed his family, and failed himself. He says he realizes for the first time how dear we are to him and how irreplaceable. He

*says that if he lives through this, he wants us to make a new
start on our lives together. He promises to leave his work at the
office, to give Edie and me the attention we deserve, the love
we have been longing for.*

 *But, of course, the love I felt for him I have long since given
to you. The bond that we have formed, the ties that bind us, go
far beyond the physical thrashings of our bodies, the whispered
endearments, the stolen moments, the secret shared wonder of
our souls uniting.*

Mike put down the letter before reading further. God in Heaven,
he thought, how can she write this crap? Who does she imagine we
are? He thought of Scarlett O'Hara pleading with Ashley Wilkes in
the library. Is she really going to dump her husband for me? Or is
she just glamorizing our relationship so she can make the grand
gesture of ending it?

 Mike would have paid a lot for a bottle of bourbon at that
moment in his life. Reluctantly, he read on.

 *I have given myself to you, given the full measure of
my trust and the gift of my infidelity. But now I see that the
moral choice, the right choice, is to stand by the soldier I have
married, the father of my child, the man who holds my future
in his hand.*

 *And so, I must ask you never to see me or contact me
again. I trust that in the years to come, you will realize the
rightness of this decision and it will prove to be best for you as
well.*

 With all my heart, I thank you for your understanding.

 My love and best wishes,
 Madeline

 Fine, Mike thought bitterly, *stand by your man. Do the right
thing. Send me the worst Dear John letter ever written and go support*

our troops. Good for you. As his anger subsided, it occurred to him that Ted was quite safe whereas he was going ashore with the actual fighting troops and would probably get his ass shot off. For a moment, it struck him as funny. Then he realized that the most likely outcome would be that both he and Ted would make it through this and six months from now, he'd be sitting at Maddie's table again having dinner with her and Ted. What was the name of that tune the British sang after they surrendered to General Washington? Ah, yes, *The World Turned Upside Down*. That was it.

Chapter Fifteen

April 30, 1982
Stanley Airport Encampment
Islas Malvinas

After going through the outdoor mess line and eating his dinner, Renaldo made his way through long rows of tents to find Jury's. When he got to the right number, a soldier he had never seen was standing outside the tent.

"I'm looking for Jury Mitner."

The other soldier called into the tent. "Jury. You have company."

"Rey, come inside." It was a small tent and Rey had to duck his head down to enter. It was just large enough for two fold-up cots with bedrolls laid out on top of them. There were clothes, personal items, and boxes shoved under the cots. Jury was seated on one cot and he motioned for Rey to sit at the end of it.

"Wow" Rey commented, "You have cots. How did you get these? Everyone in my unit is sleeping on the ground."

"Turns out I have the right roommate. Army! Come in here."

The other soldier ducked his head as he entered and sat on the cot opposite Rey and Jury, facing them.

"This is Armando Gotarra, the smartest and best connected man in the army. And this is my friend, Reynaldo Poralez."

Rey extended his hand and they shook briefly. "You can call me Rey. Everyone does."

"Call me Army. It sounds funny at first, since we're in the army, but you'll get used to it." Army Gotarra was quite a bit taller than Jury and had a lanky, casual way of moving that radiated self confidence. Despite his height, he and Jury had the same bookish, studious look, and the same piercing, intelligent eyes. Rey thought it was interesting they had been assigned as tent mates.

"So, what makes you the best connected man in the army?" Rey asked.

Army paused and looked at Rey for a long moment, then he turned to look at Jury.

"He is my *mejor comarada,* the closest friend I have" Jury said. "You can trust him with anything. He won't betray us." Rey felt a burst of pride at being identified this way.

Army nodded. "All right, then. I'm the personal assistant to General Menéndez. I know everything that is going on, have a free pass to go anywhere, and I have deep connections into the supply command. I can get things that no one else can."

"Whoa, wait a minute" Jury said, "let's not get carried away, Army. You are one of four assistants to General Menéndez and you report to several officers in the command office and not directly to the general. You're basically a go-fer, doing whatever you're told to do."

Army laughed and looked a little embarrassed. "Okay, that's true. But I do have access to a lot of information."

"Yes," Jury said, "but that's only because your cousin lets you look at all the reports. If you were really important, you wouldn't be sleeping in this shit hole tent with me."

The three of them laughed together. Rey was beginning to like this guy.

"Hey, what's wrong with having relatives in the right places?" Army looked at the tent opening for a moment and then back at his roommate. "What do you say we break out a couple bottles?"

Jury smiled in surprise. "Okay with me."

Army began rummaging through the boxes below his cot and extracted three small, dark, two-ounce bottles. He handed a bottle to each of the others and unscrewed the top of his own. "Here's how" he said and drank from the bottle.

Jury and Rey followed his lead and in a moment Rey felt the burning sensation of strong alcohol coursing down his throat. It was so unexpected, he almost choked.

"What is that?"

"Rum. The officers get issued these bottles with their ration packs, but the supply post where I do inventory gets boxes of replacement bottles."

"And he steals them" Jury said.

"I don't steal them. I just change the manifest so it appears they were sent to Fox Bay. Then I *appropriate* them. I'm the only one keeping track of them so who's to know the difference?" He took another swig finishing his bottle and put it in a different box beneath his cot. "I have to be careful how I get rid of these bottles."

"Tell Rey about the ship yesterday."

Army smiled and took out another bottle from his hidden stash. "We've been unloading ships as fast as we can because the British are coming. Soon, everything we get will have to come in by air. So I was looking down the supply list for the *Río Carcarañá*, and what do you suppose they are bringing us?"

"Guns and ammunition, I hope" Rey said. "Maybe food."

"Television sets."

Rey's mouth dropped open. "What? Why is God's name would they send us television sets?"

"They're not for us. They're for the kelpers. They're going to lease them to the islanders so they will love us and become happy residents of Argentina." He laughed at the thought of it. "The generals are so stupid they think we can buy the islanders' cooperation and then the British fleet will turn around and go home. Fat chance of that."

"So you think the British will attack us?"

Army looked at Rey for a long moment. "Yes, my new friend, the British will attack us and when they do we're in for serious trouble. They won't stop until they have taken back these islands and all of us are dead, or at least enough of us so they can take over. I don't want to lose the Malvinas, but I have to tell you, I won't be sorry to leave this pile of rocks and sheep dung. I have only one goal in this war and that is to survive. It wasn't easy to get this job with General Menéndez and I'm sticking close to him. In war, the generals always stay safe, far behind the lines. It's the conscripts, you and me, who are expendable."

"But you don't think the British can win, do you? We have thousands of men, cannons, planes and helicopters. And we're dug in."

"You don't think the British can win?" Army said. "Let me tell you some numbers. My cousin shows me the supply manifests and I know all the numbers. Right now, we have 13,000 soldiers on this island, three quarters of them right here in Puerto Argentino. How many soldiers are the British bringing in their armada? We have no idea. We don't even know how many ships they have.

"But we know British history. In World War II, on D-day, the British put 73,000 men ashore ON THE FIRST DAY. And that was against the Germans, who had been preparing for them for years. The Germans had concrete pill boxes, siege cannons, mines in the water, and barbed wire on the beaches. They couldn't stop the British. They didn't even slow them down much." Army paused to take a long pull on his second bottle.

Rey was shocked to hear this jovial young man suddenly so negative about their situation. "But the Malvinas are our islands! We have to fight for them" Rey said.

"Oh, we'll fight all right. I'm just not sure we'll win. Look at the soldiers around you. Three quarters of them are conscripts, just like us, with one year of service behind them. Most of us have only fired a gun once or twice, and none of us have ever fought in a war. But the British have never stopped fighting. They fought in Korea, they fought in Ireland, they fought in the Middle East. They take part in every scrap around the globe. They're professional soldiers with lots of experience."

"But there could still be a diplomatic solution" Jury said.

"Maybe. We'll see." Army finished his bottle and offered second bottles to the other two. They both took one.

"I'll tell something else" Army said, "when the British get here, the first place they will bomb is right here. The Stanley Airfield will be their first target."

Chapter Sixteen

Rey stayed for another hour. Despite Army's dire warnings, Rey enjoyed the company of his new friend and his old one. After leaving their tent, he walked half a mile back to his own unit's area. As he got near his tent, he met his unit commander, Sergeant Moralvec.

"Poralez" he said, "you're going on night patrol. Report to me at 2:00 am."

"But Sergeant, I haven't slept."

"You can sleep now. 2:00 am at my tent. Don't make me come and find you."

"Yes, sir." The buzz he got from Army's little bottles of rum had worn off completely and Rey was ready to go to sleep, but he would have less than four hours before he would have to wake up. His tentmate, also drafted for the patrol, had the luxury of a wristwatch with an alarm function. He promised to wake them both up.

It had been warm during the day, but turned chilly in the evening and Rey went to bed still wearing his uniform. His blanket was not thick enough to keep him warm. When he awoke a few minutes before 2:00, he felt like he'd only slept for half an hour. The other soldiers who joined him in the patrol group looked equally exhausted. They were also new to these night patrols and no one was happy about them.

"We're going to do stationary patrol sites instead of trying to walk around in the dark" the Sergeant told the group. "We'll be on the periphery of the airfield and each of you will be spaced out about 300 yards from each other. I'll be coming around to check on you every 15 minutes or so. You won't be able to see much so you need to listen very carefully. We're on a peninsula here and the British could come from either side. They will sneak ashore and come very quietly. The British have a special forces unit, the

Special Boat Squadron, which does nothing but these kind of amphibious attacks."

Rey wondered how well the sergeant knew the strategy of the British forces. No doubt he had been briefed, just as he was briefing them.

"Now, one other thing. If you see the enemy, do not shoot at them. You may only fire your rifle if you are directly attacked. If you see them, fall back and report to me. You are much more likely to shoot an Argentine soldier than a British soldier. And by God, if one of you *accidentally* fires his weapon, I will personally take a strap to you."

Rey followed the group around the outer edge of the airfield as they were assigned positions. He was placed at the far end of the runway which was a little less than a mile long. This put him a quarter mile from the main tower and most of the buildings behind it, the hangars, parking area, terminal, and control tower. The runway and terminal were well lighted and a huge C-130 Hercules transport came in and landed as he was standing patrol. It passed right over Rey's head and touched down with a screech of tires and the roar of its four prop engines. Rey wondered how he was supposed to listen for the enemy creeping up on them with all this noise around him. After the plane landed, the runway lights were turned off and Rey was left in darkness.

The hours passed with agonizing slowness. Rey was sitting on the ground with his back to the terminal when Sergeant Moralvec appeared. His "every 15 minutes" visits actually took about an hour and a half. Rey hastily stood up when he heard the Sergeant.

"Stand easy, Poralez. Sitting is actually a better position. Makes you harder to see. Not that anyone is out there looking."

"You don't think the British will attack this way?"

"Listen. There are 4,000 Argentine soldiers camped around this airfield. If the Brits came by sea, we'd see their ships on radar. They can only put small groups ashore using submarines. So, if they put men ashore, it will just be for reconnaissance. We'd still like to kill them, of course, but they won't be attacking us."

"So why can't we shoot them?"

"Because you're more likely to shoot some Argentine soldier who has wandered off and is taking a piss."

Sergeant Moralvec lit a cigarette and offered one to Rey, but he declined. Rey had never smoked, believing it would ruin his lungs and make it harder to compete at soccer. His coach had once given him a stern lecture on this point.

The two men were standing next to each other, looking at the airfield terminal, when the blast came.

The bombs fell at 4:40 am. There was no warning, no sirens sounded, no anti-aircraft batteries opened fire; the bombs just fell from the sky. Twenty one bombs, each weighing a thousand pounds, cut a swath across the airfield damaging buildings, setting fires, and leaving a huge crater in the center of the runway.

The bombs came from a giant Vulcan bomber that performed the aerial feat of flying six thousand miles from, and back to, Ascension Island. It was the equivalent of a bomber flying from England to bomb Chicago O'Hare airport, and then flying back to England. Fourteen tanker planes, operating in relays, supplied fuel to the Vulcan. It was the longest bombing run in history and the most expensive.

When released, the bombs left the plane in just under five seconds. Dropped from 10,000 feet, two miles up, they acquired enough speed as they fell to bury themselves in the ground before exploding. The bombs did not hit at the same moment, some being delayed by several seconds, so the effect was of a mounting, prolonged explosion that went on and on; an earthquake, accompanied by a deafening blast and a wall of flame.

Rey was looking at the control tower when a red cloud rose up and raced toward it. In the second before the tower was engulfed, Rey saw the windows burst inward and the building seemed to bend as though struck by a giant fist. He later realized this was an illusion caused by the blast moving through the air before it hit him.

Both Rey and Sergeant Moralvec were lifted and knocked off their feet, flying backward like ragdolls, hitting the ground on their backs. The roar of the explosions left Rey momentarily deaf and his body aching along its entire length. The fall had knocked the wind out of him and his head had struck a rock when he landed, but he was saved by his helmet. Still, it was hard to breathe and it took several moments before he could move.

After his breathing returned to normal, Rey was able to painfully roll on his side to look at Moralvec. The sergeant was lying on his back, writhing from side to side, his mouth open. He may have been moaning or crying out, Rey had no way of knowing. His ears were filled with cotton and his brain was still hazy about what had happened. He rolled back and lay looking up at the sky, giving himself time to recover.

When he finally sat up, he was surprised to find the sergeant also sitting up. Neither could hear well enough to converse, but using hand signals they agreed to go to the terminal. It was hard for both of them to move, but as they crossed the airfield they fought through their pain to get to the site of the destruction.

It was a chaotic scene. Men were running everywhere, shouting, pointing, and trying to help the injured. There were bloodied soldiers standing while being examined, some were lying on the ground being assisted, others were being helped into trucks and Land Rovers that would take them to the hospital. Three bodies lay still on the ground, a blanket covering their faces.

Rey helped a group that was putting out fires and he saw the destruction of a Pucara airplane and the smashed offices next to the hangars. As his hearing returned, he became aware of a siren blaring and then heard the thump of the anti-aircraft guns, those surrounding the airfield and those from the town. But as he followed the trail of tracers firing skyward, he realized there were no planes above them.

———•◦•———

May 2, 1982

Dear Marisol,

I have survived my first bombing, the first bombing of this war, in fact. We had no warning, no time to prepare or even get out of the way. I was standing at the end of the runway when the blast knocked me off my feet. It sounds comical, but I am lucky to have survived. Three of my fellow soldiers did not. I knew one of them, at least enough to speak with him, and now he is gone forever. Many others were injured. I saw one man whose leg was badly shattered being carried away on a stretcher. He screamed in pain as they bounced along.

Raul, one of the men who was killed, was in school with Jury and Sonny and me, a year ahead of us. He was only 19. I can't help wondering how his family will feel when they learn of it. Why didn't we know this attack was coming? Don't we have radar protecting us?

May 1ˢᵗ was a very bad day for us. I stayed on the airfield helping to clean up and repair the damage. But then, just after dawn, the British launched Harrier jets against us, throwing more bombs onto the airport. Thank God we had warning this time, but only because another Harrier came over first to take pictures of the airfield after the first attack!

I dove into a slit trench and prayed the bombs would not come for me. It was the most terrifying moment of my life. When you burrow into the earth like that, like some animal, and reach beneath your helmet to cover your ears from the blasts, everything stops and you cannot breathe. When the all clear sounded and I got out of the trench, my hands and legs were shaking. We later heard that they shot down one of the Harriers, but no one believes that will stop them.

I know it sounds self-centered, but when I think about the others who were killed, I think about myself. What if I am killed? How will my family feel? My sister Amalia is only 14 years old and she believes the world turns around me.

Honestly, I think she believes I am some sort of film star. If I was killed, it would change the way she sees the world. It would make her bitter and sad forever. And I would lose the years ahead. It makes me feel desolate to think my life may be given up so we can rule these rocky islands and these English who don't want us here.

I am sorry to write you with all of these unhappy thoughts, but I don't want to give my family distress by telling them what is really happening here. I am very grateful I have you to tell about my experiences.

   Your friend,
   Reynaldo

At his desk in Buenos Aires, Vice-Comodoro Lantana lay down the letter from young Private Poralez. Should he give this letter to his daughter? He knew it would upset her, but maybe it would prepare her for worse news later. He regretted having given them permission to correspond, but Marie needed to grow up too and perhaps it was all for the best. He tucked the letter into his coat jacket and would take it home later that evening.

He valued what he learned from the young soldier. It was indeed tragic that the attack had come without warning. In typical fashion, the army had tried to lay blame for this on the air force radar posts for not sounding the alarm, but what could have been done? By the time the plane had shown up on radar, it was nearly upon them. Before turning loose the anti-aircraft gun teams, they had to ensure that it was not an Argentine plane and that took precious moments.

It was not a perfect bombing raid, but it achieved most of Britain's goals. It came without warning and shocked the troops. It did serious damage to the airfield. And the single plane that carried out the raid simply vanished, as if in a mist. Lantana's office could not determine how a bomber that large had come from an aircraft carrier. But it hardly mattered. May 1st had been so burdened with errors, oversights, and downright stupidities that it had not been simply a bad day, it had changed the course of the war.

The crater in the runway could not be fixed properly with the materials available on the islands. Even after two days of round-the-clock repair work, it was barely serviceable. The big Hercules transports could still land and take off, but none of Argentina's high performance jets, the Mirages, Skyhawks, or Daggers, could use it. So they would have to be sent from the mainland, 400 miles away, and could stay on station over the Malvinas for only a few minutes.

The British armada was now within striking distance and they immediately attacked. After the morning's Harrier bombing raids, they sent a destroyer and two frigates in to further bombard the airfield as well as sites for a possible amphibious landing along the northern coast. The British came within 16,000 yards of the shoreline and fired a stream of shells from their 4.5-inch guns. The thundering old style naval bombardment, with shells arching over the water to land on their targets, went on for hours. The ships remained just out of range of the Argentine field artillery.

Argentina sent twelve planes to bomb and destroy the three British warships. Four Skyhawk bombers, each carrying two 500-pound bombs, were accompanied by eight fighter jets, Daggers and Mirages. When the squadron reached the Malvinas they came under the direction of the local air force controllers. The inexperienced controllers identified two targets on radar northeast of the islands, but instead of ships, these turned out to be two Harrier jets on patrol from the British carriers.

The brief encounter that followed was indecisive. The Mirages fired their Matra missiles, but without hitting the Harriers. Running low on fuel, the Argentine planes headed back to Argentina. No bombs were dropped, they never saw a ship. In addition to the ships bombing the northern part of the islands, three other British ships were operating with impunity off the eastern coast, carrying out anti-submarine patrols and depth-charging.

The continuing bombardment caused a furious reaction in the high command in Buenos Aires. They decided to send the full force of Argentine airpower against the British. Vice-Comodoro Lantana did much of the planning for this air assault. Fifty-five planes were drawn from airfields all up and down the Argentine coastline: Skyhawks from San Julián, Mirages from Rio Galego, Daggers from Rio Grande, and six Canberra bombers, sold to the Argentines by the British, came down six hundred miles from Trevelo.

The planning was intense since all the planes needed to arrive at the Malvinas at the same time, but were traveling at different speeds, from multiple places. Fuel consumption had to be planned for and the role of each type of jet carefully laid out. The goal was nothing less than to completely overwhelm the British carrier-based air power and destroy the ships bombarding the islands.

The first planes to reach the islands were two Mirages and they immediately faced two Harrier jets. One of the Harriers fired a Sidewinder missile that scored a direct hit on a Mirage which disintegrated in a mass of flames and fell in two parts. Miraculously, the pilot, Lieutenant Carlos Perona, was able to eject the moment before his plane was struck and parachuted down, landing so close to the island he was able to walk ashore.

The other Mirage, flown by Captain Garcia Cuerva, was chased by a Sidewinder into a cloud. The evasive maneuvers were successful until the missile's proximity radar exploded the missile close enough to do serious damage to the Mirage. Knowing he could not make it back to Argentina, Captain Cuerva decided to land at the Stanley airfield. He made a slow and careful approach from the west, flying up Stanley harbor. Argentine anti-aircraft gunners, situated on the high ridge behind the town, lacked the training to identify their own planes and opened fire. The plane crashed and Captain Cuerva was killed. The initial jubilation at having downed a Harrier was soon replaced by the sad knowledge of what they had done. This was the plane Poralez had been told was a Harrier.

Ten minutes later, the main Argentine forces arrived: two formations of Daggers and one of Canberras. The Daggers found and bombed the three British warships, *Glamorgan, Alacrity,* and

Arrow. The bombs caused enormous geysers in the sea, but they did not hit the ships and did no damage. Two Harriers found the Daggers and a Sidewinder destroyed one of the Argentine planes. Lieutenant José Ardiles was killed; he was a cousin of the Argentine footballer who played regularly with Tottenham Hotspur.

The slower, lumbering Canberras made an even easier target. They had already made the fatal mistake of letting themselves be seen on the British ship's radar screens before ducking down out of range. Lieutenant Al Curtis of 801 Squadron shot down one of the Canberras forcing the others to head back to Argentina, but the Harriers were low on fuel and could not pursue them. As the Canberra slowly went down, it's two crewmen left the plane and parachuted into the sea, but neither was ever seen again.

Not a single British ship, plane, or officer was injured during this first day of combat. The three British ships had withdrawn after the attack and the Argentines reported one as sunk, but all three returned after sundown and continued bombing Argentine positions.

Vice-Comodoro Lantana dismally reviewed the reports on his desk and tried to draw out the lessons of this initial clash of forces. The Argentine pilots had acted courageously and had followed orders well. But they lacked the NATO-level combat readiness of the British pilots who were able to maneuver their slower planes more effectively and avoid losses. More critical was the deficiency in armament. The air-to-air Matra missiles the Argentine planes were using were no match for the newer, better Sidewinder AIM-9L missiles the Harriers carried. Clearly, the Sidewinder's improved software gave the missile much greater seek and destroy capability. And the proximity fusing made it capable of damaging planes without actually hitting them.

Lesson number one, Lantana thought to himself: in a direct confrontation with the Harriers, we will lose regardless of our greater numbers and speed. Consequently, we cannot use any further mass formations.

Lesson number two: we must avoid encounters with Harriers wherever possible. Dogfights will destroy our morale and our resources.

Lesson number three: immediate training must be given to the radar, anti-aircraft, and communications sections so they can identify the enemy and take appropriate action. There is no reason to pause when a plane is seen on radar to check if it is Argentine. We should already know what planes are in the air and where they are. And we absolutely must be able to visually tell which planes are Argentine and which are not.

Lesson number four: the faster speed of the Argentine jets will best be used in pinpoint operations against defined targets. Get in and get out. This is exactly the type of operation that will be required when the British attempt to land on the islands. Now that the British task force has arrived, that will be a matter of days, perhaps hours.

Chapter Seventeen

May 2, 1982
Onboard HMS Sheffield
100 miles southeast of the Falklands

Ted Tomlinson, sitting at a small desk in his cramped quarters, was also reviewing reports of the May 1st fighting, but his conclusions were quite different from those of Vice-Comodoro Lantana. He thought the British forces had been extremely lucky and he was quite sure that that luck would not continue. The Argentine pilots had fought bravely, with determination and skill; it was their misfortune to be outgunned. But they were outgunned by planes that were slower and fewer, the Harriers, and the British had not established air dominance. The shortened British carriers could only launch Harrier jets and there were only 32 Harrier airframes on the planet. There was no time to build more. This would be a war of attrition, as perhaps all wars were, and the count had only begun.

The air war, of course, was only one third of the equation. The other two thirds were the land war, yet to be fought, and the war at sea. While Argentina did not have the Royal Navy, they did have a formidable navy, including the aircraft carrier, *Venticinco de Mayo,* as well as destroyers, frigates, and submarines. And many of their ships were equipped with the naval version of the Exocet missile. The bulk of the Argentine navy had put to sea as the British arrived and were now hunting them.

Ted was considering all this when a messenger knocked on the bulkhead outside his curtained doorway. "Captain would like to see you, sir."

"Now?"

"Yes, sir. He's in his ready room."

Ted glanced at himself in the small mirror above his bunk. He'd remembered to shave that morning and his uniform was fresh so he headed directly to meet the captain. He saluted and stood at attention after entering the captain's ready room.

Captain Sam Salt was reclined in an easy chair, his feet propped up on a small coffee table leaving his desk empty. He was reading some reports and didn't bother returning Ted's salute. "Oh, hello, Ted. Here, have a seat." He indicated the chair opposite him.

Sam Salt was a short, quiet, precise man with a horseshoe of dark hair around his bald head. His crew loved him because he was decisive without taking himself too seriously. He had a mischievous sense of humor. At 42, he had the look of a man who would one day become an admiral.

"So, how goes the work evaluating the Sea Dart system? Are you getting the cooperation you need?"

"Well," Ted hesitated, "...they're giving me the information I need."

"But not very willingly, I'm guessing. They're all worried about those secret performance evaluations you're sending back to Admiral Woodward."

Ted was shocked. "Sir, I promise you I'm not sending any secret..." But the captain was already laughing and smiling.

"Of course you're not, Ted. I'm just having you on. I'm not sending evaluations of you either, at least nothing I wouldn't share with you. Look, what you're doing here is systems analysis, not personnel evaluations. I know that and if the crew were smarter, they'd know it too. Just do the work and reconcile yourself to not making any lifelong friends here. Of course, if you do observe any outrageous performance mistakes, I would appreciate a heads-up *before* you mention it to Sandy Woodward."

"Absolutely, sir. You may depend on me to follow protocol. I'm sure the Admiral would agree."

"Yes, I expect he would. So tell me, as a planner who has been looking at these issues for years, which should I fear most: Exocets from the sea or Exocets from the air?"

"Well, either could be deadly, of course, but I should say of the two, I would be more worried about the airborne version. They have a much great operational range, forty miles vs. twenty-six, and the Super Étendards that deliver them can be turned away immediately after launching, so they are far more likely to escape.

"For their ships to get within twenty-six miles of our fleet to fire their onboard Exocets, they'd have to get past the Harriers and the subs. Judging from their current fleet movements, they seem unlikely to take that chance. They are carefully skirting the Exclusion Zone. They appear hesitant to engage."

"Well, that doesn't fit with Northwood's playbook. They're looking for a confrontation and a decisive British victory that will force the Argies to withdraw their navy. I just hope they take the bait and come after us. It will look much better to world opinion if they attack us first."

"Haven't they already done that by invading the islands?"

"Yes, but the naval arena is a different sphere. We don't want to look like we're bullying them."

It was four hours later when Ted read a communique with the shocking news that a British submarine, *Conqueror*, had torpedoed and sunk the Argentine cruiser *General Belgrano*, the second largest ship in the Argentine fleet. He was still trying to sort out the implications of this act when he heard his name over the tannoy: "Colonel Tomlinson, please report to the captain's ready room immediately." He headed there on the double.

Captain Salt was in a carefully controlled rage. He held up a copy of the same communique Ted had received. "Did you know anything about this?"

"No, sir. I swear I did not."

"When did Northwood change the rules of engagement? Who authorized this attack?"

"Captain, I have no way of knowing that. I was not included in the planning."

"Well get on the phone and find out. Use a secure line and call whatever contacts you have on *Hermes* and find out why this was done and who is responsible for it."

"Yes, sir." Ted left the room and headed to the Communications Office.

He returned to the captain's ready room an hour later. The captain would not be happy with what he had to say, but he must be told.

"Captain Salt, I've spoken with two senior level planners and a communications officer. The attack on the *Belgrano* was authorized at the highest level."

"The highest level?" The captain sounded dubious.

"Yes, sir. Prime Minister Thatcher and the War Cabinet met just before noon at Chequers and changed the rules of engagement allowing our submarines to attack any Argentine warship."

"But why would they do that?"

"Captain, I gave you incorrect information when we spoke earlier. I told you the Argentine navy was hesitant to engage. I spoke out of turn. Apparently, they were just maneuvering into a better attack position. They split their forces to come at us from both the west and from the south. *General Belgrano* and her two escorts were just south of the Burdwood Bank and were being followed by *Conqueror*. If they had crossed the Bank, the water is too shallow for *Conqueror* to follow and we would have lost them. They could have steamed right up behind our line of defense."

"Couldn't the Harriers have held them off?"

"No, sir. The area is locked down in fog."

"So, based on that threat, we sank their second largest ship."

"Yes, sir. We did."

Captain Salt sat down heavily at his desk. "God help us. How fast did she go down?"

"She was hit with two torpedoes and went down in forty minutes. The Argentines have ships in the area now picking up survivors. They claim they have lost over three hundred lives."

"Well..." There was a long pause as Captain Salt sighed deeply.

"I think we can give up any hope of a negotiated settlement now. They'll be out for our blood after this."

Ted agreed, but felt it better not to speak.

"All right, Ted. Thank you for admitting your error, but of course it wasn't your fault. You could not have known what the current situation is. You're not on *Hermes* anymore. Now you're stuck out here on the picket line, with us. Get some sleep. You'll need it."

Two days later, *HMS Sheffield* was struck by an air-launched Exocet missile traveling at 700 miles per hour. The half-ton missile burst through the side, destroying the passageway, the galley, and penetrating deep within the ship. The warhead and remaining rocket fuel exploded in a ball of fire that soon ignited the ship's diesel fuel.

Ted Tomlinson's life ended in a millisecond. One moment he was standing at the galley counter, stirring his tea, then, in a flash of light, he was blown to bits. It was over before he could comprehend it. Eleven others died in the galley with him and the fire that raged at the center of the ship produced lethal black smoke that took nine more lives.

Despite heroic actions by Captain Sam Salt and the 261 surviving crew, *Sheffield* could not be saved. A last ditch effort involved towing the burned out hulk back to Ascension Island, but after several days in rough seas, the ship took on water and finally sank. The tow line was cut and Captain Salt, onboard the towing vessel, watched on sonar until his ship settled onto the floor of the sea two miles beneath the surface.

———◆◆◆———

Mike Ferrol learned of Ted's death while sailing south on board the *Norland*. One of the ship's officers found him in the Communication Office and took him aside to give him the news. Ted had designated Mike as one of the people who should be notified in the event of his death. At first, he found it hard to believe. "I thought Colonel Tomlinson was onboard *Hermes*."

"No, he was on temporary assignment on *Sheffield*," the officer replied.

"Are you certain you have the right man?"

The officer paused a long moment, looking directly into Mike's eyes. "I'm afraid his death has been confirmed. He was in the galley when the missile burst in and exploded. Colonel Tomlinson has definitely been killed."

Mike sat down and stared at the bulkhead. "Yes. All right, then. Thank you for letting me know." He felt dazed, lost, disoriented. How close had he been to the man? He had known him well, but had known his wife far better. A stab of guilt caught him as he thought of Madeline, now the widow Tomlinson. How curious to think of her that way, on her own, carrying on in the tradition of soldier's wives.

How would she live now? On the stipend the government would provide? To Mike's knowledge, Maddie had never worked a day in her life. How would she provide for herself and young Edith? There would be no more riding lessons, Mike guessed. Well, she was a beautiful woman and even with a child tagging along, there was always a market for beautiful women.

Mike felt like a cad and loathed himself for reducing her to her physical attributes. She would be devastated when she learned the news. All her plans for a rekindled marriage, a reconnected family, blown away. And what support could he offer her? None, really. He was a 38-year-old "journalist," a glorified reporter, with a failed marriage behind him and a history of drinking too much. As he thought this, it occurred to him that he had ceased drinking on this ship. The last couple nights, he hadn't even bothered to stop in to the Forward Lounge for his two cans of beer.

Mike returned to his room and dug beneath his civilian clothes to find the envelope Ted had entrusted him with, his "exit" papers. They were already addressed to Madeline. He only needed to take them to the Dispatch Office and see they got into the mail. Before he did so, he enclosed a brief note.

Madeline,

Prior to his passing, Ted gave me these papers which he felt would help you in the event of his death. I am deeply sorry to now have to send them to you. Ted died in an explosion. It was quick and painless. He was a fine man who will be missed in the service and by those of us outside the service who knew him.

I wish you and Edith all the best in the future. If there is any way I can help you, please don't hesitate to contact me.

Mike

The sinking of the *General Belgrano* changed the atmosphere on the *Norland*. All the boisterous carrying on of the troops onboard shifted to serious preparation for battle. These were young men on a ship who had learned of other young men on a ship who had died by the hundreds. They were not on a lark any more, they were headed into the fighting.

The loss of *Sheffield* steadied their nerves and hardened their resolve. The Argentines were clearly capable of striking back and had the will to do so. This would be no walkover and the training and practice took on new intensity. Gone were the sporting competitions. Now the focus was all on learning routines and following established procedures. Here is how you must pack your kit. Here is what you need and here is what you do not. For this type of field injury, this is the proper response.

Mike went through much of the training with the troops. He learned the nomenclature and the hierarchy of command. He wrote articles about the men and how they were coping with the stress of impending battle. He even began exercising with the troops and took up jogging around the deck with them. He was losing weight.

The weather turned colder as they continued south and the seas grew larger. Day after day, the ships pitched and ploughed through the huge waves, the bow throwing clouds of spray over the deck, the tearing winds, rain and mist cutting visibility to a few hundred yards. It was hard on the men. *A portent of things to come,* Mike thought.

One afternoon, Mike made his way to the library to check some facts, where he encountered Leith Cullen. The tall soldier's light blue eyes were piercing and intimidating. Mike turned to leave, but then heard Cullen's voice.

"Hold up there, Mr. Ferrol. I want to talk to you."

Mike turned and looked at the man seated in the corner. "All right," Mike said.

"Been reading what you've written about us and I don't think you get it."

Mike felt a chill up his spine. "Don't get what?"

"Come here. Sit down." They were alone in the library and Leith indicated the chair opposite him. "I don't think you get what we're doing here, how we operate, or what's about to happen. I don't think you get any of it. Your writing is all full of that Queen and country crap, the jolly band of brothers, one for all, and 'we fight to save our mates.' It's a pile of shite from where I'm sittin'."

Suddenly, Mike no longer felt intimidated by this man. His writing was the area in his life where he felt most secure. He paused and smiled. "Well, that's not a comment I hear very often. I suppose you have suggestions."

"Might be." Leith closed the book he was reading. "Let me ask you something. You ever been in the service, ever fought in a war?"

"No. I went to school and became a writer. It's all I've ever done."

Leith shook his head disparagingly. "Well, have you at least read about fighting? Ever read this book?" He held up the book he was reading. "*Goodbye Darkness* by William Manchester? Came out two years ago."

"No, I've read Manchester, but not that book."

"It's his account of the war in the Pacific. Now this guy understands killing. That's what it's all about, killing. That's what we do. But you won't get to that the way you're going. You need to stop talking to raw recruits who don't know their arse from a porthole and stop quoting the officer-johnnies with all their

Sandhurst, stiff-upper-lip crap. You need to talk with the older Toms who were already fighting when you got your first hard-on."

"The seasoned vets usually won't talk to me."

"No, I expect they won't, leastways not about how things really work." Leith rubbed his chin thoughtfully and looked down at his book. "We dress it all up in fancy words so we don't have to think too clearly about it. We talk about 'having a job to do' or 'going on a mission.' Well, we aren't missionaries and the job we have to do is sticking a bayonet in some poor joker's belly and twisting it until his guts come falling out. It isn't pretty and it isn't civilized and that's what you've got to understand.

"See, no civilized person would do what we do. We become savages so we can kill our own kind and the real training isn't to get us to do that, it's to get us to stop. In battle, the rules fall away and the killer comes out. All you think about is how to bring death to the enemy. Shoot'em, stab'em, blow'em up, whatever it takes to end their lives and keep your own going. But when they surrender, when they throw down their guns and put their hands up in the air, you're supposed to stop. Not all of us can. It's going back to civilized behavior that gets sticky. Legalized killing is addictive. It changes your psyche.

"I remember a night in Northern Ireland. We got word of a meeting that needed our attention. We went to the airport, loaded our kit, checked our ammo, and covered our faces in camo cream, war paint really. Then we loaded onto a helicopter and lifted off. As we passed over the lights of the city and headed into darkness, I looked down and thought: they're all down there, the ordinary people. Eating their dinners, watching TV, drinking, fucking, sleeping. Leading their ordinary lives.

"But I'm not one of them. I'm an outsider. Sometimes I'll mingle, but I'll never belong. This is what I do. I strike out into the night and make things right. And those poor sods ahead of me had better watch out. I'm coming for them."

Chapter Eighteen

The Town of Stanley
Falkland Islands

April, 1982, was a very bad month for the residents of the Falklands. The Argentines had promised to maintain "the continuity of the way of life of the people of the Islands," but this quickly proved impossible. They immediately restricted commerce, travel, communication, education, and health care, and inserted themselves into every aspect of the islanders' lives. By the end of April, there were seven Argentine soldiers for every British citizen. They filled the streets and parks, took over all municipal services, and appropriated land, buildings, and property for military use.

There was, during this month, a sincere effort by General Menéndez and the new town administrators to placate the citizenry by harshly punishing soldiers who stole from the residents or treated them roughly. Rather than simply taking over municipal services like the water department and the radio station, they tried to integrate their personnel with the existing infrastructure and create new services that would give them control, but would include the previous workers too.

This rarely worked. What happened instead was the creation of dual organizations that worked side-by-side. So the post office had a residents' section, manned by islanders, and a military section, manned by Argentine soldiers, that worked in the same building. The Falklanders were no longer allowed to issue or use Falkland stamps, a major source of income from philatelists around the world, but they could send mail out into the world.

The police department at first evolved into two policing organizations. The three island police split up, the police chief moving to Great Britain under fear of being arrested, while the female police constable went out to live in the camp. This left Officer Anton Livermore, now Sergeant Livermore, as the only civilian police officer in Stanley. Argentine military police moved into the building, dealing initially with only Argentine personnel, but under the leadership of the infamous Major Dowling they became focused on discovering saboteurs or any resistance movement. Sergeant Livermore was relieved of his duties.

St. Edwards Hospital had been run by Doctor Daniel Haines and his wife, also a doctor. But Dr. Haines was an outspoken opponent of the occupation and had tried to send military information to the task force using carefully phrased answers to medical questions on his daily radio program. When the Argentines discovered this, he and his wife, along with twelve other islanders suspected of being resistance leaders, were "deported" to an undisclosed location. This turned out to be Fox Bay where they sat out the rest of the war.

Hospital leadership then fell to Doctor Alison Bleaney, who had recently retired to care for her young family. Doctor Bleaney rose to the occasion and earned the respect and gratitude of every Falklander. The Argentines had wanted to simply take over the hospital, but she argued forcefully with Comodore Bloomer-Reeve that some of the residents must be allowed to remain in the hospital and be cared for there.

Alison Bleaney was not a shy woman and she discovered the most effective technique for arguing with Argentine military leaders was to take her five-month-old daughter Emma with her and breast-feed as she was talking to them. Armed sentries immediately dropped their weapons upon sight of her and their superiors became far more flexible. The male arrogance typical of Argentine officers seemed to dissolve in the face of maternal nurturing.

The Stanley School had been closed upon orders from the military, but after a time, the Argentines encouraged it to be reopened. The teachers would only agree to this if there were no military personnel present and no interference in their teaching.

The government could not accept this and the school remained closed. The teachers then began meeting clandestinely with groups of students in their homes to keep the lessons going.

As the weeks wore on, the dread of the British task force arriving grew among the Argentines and they became more jittery and demanding. But they were still trying to get the active cooperation of the islanders and on April 16, eight members of the British community in Buenos Aires were flown in to persuade the residents that life was good under the Argentine government. They met with a very cool reception by the islanders and were given no encouragement in their mission. The Falklanders were not insulting or confrontational, but they made it clear they had no interest in being ruled by Argentina. The group was flown back to the mainland the same day.

The program to placate the residents with television sets did a little better. Some of the islanders took the Argentine government up on the offer to purchase sets on the generous installment plan. The Argentines provided two hours of broadcasting a day, mostly in Spanish, but they did include some English programs.

But these minor goodwill gestures could not distract the citizens of Stanley from observing the furious preparations the Argentine military was making to defend against the British. Huge slit trenches were being dug everywhere, some with carefully built camouflage coverings. Sandbags were placed at the entrances to buildings. The military took over the empty school buildings and filled them with soldiers. Gun emplacements were put on the roofs.

Artillery and machine gun nests were set up around the airfield. The Airport Road isthmus that connected Stanley to the peninsula that held the airfield was heavily fortified. Barbed wire was strung along either side and mines were laid alongside the roadway. Signs along the way warned islanders and military personnel alike to stay strictly on the road or risk being blown up.

The Argentine artillery and anti-aircraft practice went on around the clock. It was as though they were trying to impress the islanders that resistance was pointless, even though it was not the islanders they would be fighting. On April 18, General Cristino Nicolaides, commander of the Argentine Army's 1st Corps, visited to inspect the troops. To honor his visit, the Argentines dropped napalm on Tussak Island setting it afire in a blaze that lasted many days. There were no civilians on the island, but everyone grieved for the wildlife inhabitants. The Argentines dismissed this as target practice, but the islanders feared there was a darker message: this was a warning of what the Argentines were capable of, they could destroy the entire settlement if they wanted to.

The personification of that darker message came in the presence of Major Patricio Dowling, whose actual name was Douglas Patrick Dowling. Of Irish descent, he passionately hated the British. During Argentina's Dirty War, Dowling had been a Captain in the Army Intelligence Battalion 101. He had been one of the "operators" of the El Vesubio detention center in La Tablada in the greater Buenos Aires area. The center functioned as a torture facility and many of the presumed political dissidents who were taken there then disappeared.

Dowling became the Chief of Police in Stanley and was ruthless in seeking out signs of resistance among the islanders. He instituted a program of arbitrary house searches, arrests, and questioning. He would frequently strike islanders he was questioning and was known for hitting one resident in the face with the butt of a rifle. After Comodoro Bloomer-Reeve received numerous complaints about Dowling's behavior, he recommended his removal to General Menéndez and Dowling was finally sent back to Argentina in disgrace. But he left a lasting impression on the islanders who were trying to figure out the many faces of the Argentine government.

Jenny Corbyn had made a decision. She wasn't sure her husband Grant would agree with it, but she felt strongly that it was the right choice. It was something she would have to discuss with him when they were alone together, a circumstance that seemed rare in these days of the occupation. That's how she thought of it: an occupation, not a change in government. This was temporary, this would pass. She knew this as strongly as she knew her own name.

But all that must wait. Now she had to get on with helping her mother and Darrell bake cookies. She found that simple domestic tasks calmed her, made it easier to accept that, despite the momentous events around her, normal life continued. Dishes still had to be washed, laundry done, bedtime stories read. Darrell seemed able to easily sleep through distant artillery fire and thundering jet fighters overhead. He adapted to wartime conditions far quicker than his parents.

Millie, Jenny's mother, had moved into their house and was now staying in the third floor storage room that Grant had fitted out with a light and a spare mattress. Jenny questioned whether this was the safest location for her, but Millie shrugged off her concerns. "Appropriate to my station in life. Nearer to God" she said, pointing up.

Now Millie was rolling out the cookie dough and helping Darrell use the cookie cutters shaped like sleighs and houses with smoke coming out of their chimneys. These were purchased at the None Such Shoppe, where Mrs. Featherstone gave Jenny a discount. They were too fancy for the West Store to carry, but two of the West Store employees had bought them.

"You know," Millie said, "thirty relatives of the West Store's staff have moved into the building."

"Yes, I heard that" Jenny replied. "It's all stone and concrete. Much safer."

"A lot of folks are moving out into the camp. Taking their children, of course."

"Mother, I know what you're getting at." Jenny couldn't hide the irritation in her response. "This is something Grant and I have to decide on our own. I'll speak with him tonight."

"I'm sorry" Millie said. "I don't mean to press my opinions on you. I'm sure you'll make the right decision for you and your family."

"Yes, mother, we will." It was, of course, Millie's family too and Jenny felt the distress any child felt at making a decision that might not agree with her parent's views. But this was too important, too critical, to simply make the convenient choice. She had weighed the factors and faced the possible outcomes. Now she must take the next step.

"Where is Grant anyway?" Millie asked.

"He's gone to St. Mary's Church. The Argies are taking over the annex, so they have to pack up the valuable things and lock up what's left so the cutlery and crockery won't get stolen."

"Has there been a lot of theft?"

"Not really" Jenny said. "They've gathered up all our guns and radio transmitters, but they've been very diligent about giving us receipts for those and promising us they'll be returned. Some people call them Nazis and it's curious because, like the Nazis, they keep very good records. But genuine theft has only taken place in the houses soldiers have broken into. Houses people have left to move out into the camp. You know, we're watching the Wilcox place next door. Grant goes over several times a day and turns on different lights. He bangs the doors when soldiers are walking by to give the impression the house is occupied."

"I heard the Runstable's house was vandalized. Food stolen, dishes broken. They used the living room for a toilet."

Jenny shook her head at her mother and nodded toward Darrell. There were some things he didn't need to hear. "Well, I'm sure many of their troops come from the rougher areas of the country and resent being stuck here in tents. They're desperate for food. I saw a couple soldiers going through the refuse bin behind the Upland Goose.

"I just wish they would go back home so Darrell can return to school and Grant and I can get back to work. When Mrs. Featherstone heard the edict that all stores had to accept pesos, she closed down the shop. Won't allow Argentines into the store. She told me: 'They'll sing a different tune when Maggie gets here!'"

Millie laughed. "I like Evangeline Featherstone. Evie's got a good head for business and she doesn't mince words. I hope they don't break into her place."

"She's got it boarded up pretty well. Grant helped her do it. We'll just have to hold out until all of this has passed."

Grant Corbyn was furious at what he saw. As he walked the streets of Stanley, his shock and dismay was turning to hatred. These bastards were destroying this island, tearing apart a gentle world that meant them no harm. They had no right to be here. They lost their claim to these islands a hundred and fifty years ago. And as he looked at what they were doing to their precious Malvinas, he hoped they would pay in blood.

They were already beginning to do so. Six days ago, they lost South Georgia, where the British flag flew once again. The Argentine commander had the good sense to surrender quickly so there were few casualties, but Grant doubted that would be true here on the Falklands. Here they would make their stand. And until they were gone, this island would pay the price for their trespass. Everywhere he looked, he saw the destruction and havoc they had wrought. Houses fired upon for no reason, buildings ransacked and taken over, parks and playing fields sullied and smashed by careless troops whose boots turned the grass to mud.

The smell of the city sickened him. The once pristine air, freshened by ocean breeze, was now fouled by the exhaust of their Amtraks, their Land Rovers, and their Panhard vehicles, and the stink of their cheap foreign cigarettes. Far worse was the smell they produced themselves, the foul stench of their latrines and the effluent the town's sewers could no longer contain. The sewers of Stanley were designed to support a population of 1,200 and now were collapsing under the strain of ten times that number.

He walked up Davis Street East where a lot of the houses had large bullet holes from 30 mm cannon. The Ionospheric Observatory Station had a rocket hole through the east end of the roof, a big black hole with jagged torn edges. On the other side of the road lay "White City," a row of white-painted prefab bungalows recently built for the government assistance personnel who had come to the islands with their families. They worked on contract from the UK, but the fighting left their "homes" pock-marked with bullet holes. What must they think of this place now?

As he got to the end of the street, Grant saw an old man struggling to ride his bike against the wind. It was Jud Muran and he brought his bike to a stop a few feet from Grant.

"Making deliveries?" Grant asked.

"Nay, there's no fishing boats come into these waters now with the Argies about. I'm just runnin' errands for me mum."

Grant smiled at the wonder of it. This ancient old reprobate had a mother who was still living! She must be close to a hundred and had spent most of her life drinking as hard as Jud did. He could well imagine what errands Jud had been sent out to do.

"Is Mrs. Wallborn still running her booth by the waterfront?"

"Did for awhile, now she's lit out for the camp. Won't be seeing her agin till these rodents have cleared out." Grant agreed completely with that characterization of the Argentines and just hearing someone else call them that felt cleansing.

"Take care, Jud," Grant called out as the old man rode away.

In the paddocks alongside the Ionospheric Station, there were rows of two-man tents with troops milling about. The tents were not well tethered and when the wind picked up they often collapsed or were blown over. Gale force winds also caught the waterproof capes the troops had been given causing them to billow up over their heads. Grant watched the comical struggle of one soldier desperately trying to get himself and his rifle free of his cape without blowing his head off.

Grant was walking up Philomel heading toward the docks to check on his boat when he met Monsignor Spraggon coming from the other direction. Though he was not Catholic, Grant had known the Monsignor for many years. He was a kind man, a noble man, someone who would always help others if he could.

"Good day to you, Grant" the Monsignor said.

Grant smiled and nodded his head. "I can't agree with you there, Monsignor. It's not a good day for this town."

Looking about him, the Monsignor replied "Yes, I suppose that is true. But we must keep faith and carry on. Did you know that President Galtieri was here? He only stayed a day and then flew back. I stood near him while he reviewed the troops. One young soldier gave him his rosary, but *El Presidente* gave it back and told him 'You'll need it more than I do.' Can you imagine the cheek of that man? Taunting his men about what they will be facing."

"I don't expect they took him up Darwin Road near Sapper Hill. I've heard there's between thirty and fifty Argentine dead up there, stacked like cord wood along the road."

"Yes, I've heard that too. It is most distressing. I hope they bury those men properly. I will speak to Commodore Bloomer-Reeve about it. Apparently, more died during the invasion than they are admitting. Or maybe they just can't adapt to the cold. Anyway, is there anything I can do for you or your family?"

"Well, you could persuade Bloomer-Reeve to send those padres packing, the ones staying at the Upland Goose. I believe there are eight of them now, spreading pamphlets all over town. Nobody wants their religion or their politics."

The Monsignor smiled ruefully. "Yes, they are irritating aren't they? They've found a captive audience in the citizenry, but they don't do much for their own troops. We get desperate soldiers at Saint Mary's all the time; cold, shivering teenagers who haven't had a decent meal in weeks. They're feeding them potato and onion soup, but a man can't sustain life on that diet."

"You'll forgive me, Monsignor, but sustaining their lives isn't a top priority for me."

There was an uncomfortable pause, then the Monsignor continued: "How are you doing at driving on the left hand side of the road?"

"I don't understand the purpose of it, but I'll do it if I need to."

"The Commodore explained it to me like this: would you rather have these 17-year-old Argentines driving their big military vehicles while trying to learn to drive on your side of the road, or would you prefer to just drive the way they're used to driving?"

"I suppose he has a point. They're certainly a hazard, hardly able to drive at all. I wish they could learn not to break the curbs and tear out fences."

"Well, let us pray their visit to the islands will be short."

"Amen to that."

The two men parted and Grant continued down to the docks. He was blocked from going near them by heavily armed guards, but even from a distance he could see his boat was not there. The guards spoke no English so he went to Jamison's Boat Yard to see if Tim Jamison knew where his boat was.

"It's in a cradle in the back yard. When the Argies took over the docks, they gave us just six hours to haul out every islander boat and put them in storage. I'm sorry I didn't get around to telling you."

"It's all right, Tim. I'm just grateful it didn't fall into the wrong hands." Grant went to the boat yard behind the building to see that the boat was properly covered, but Jamison had handled everything perfectly. There was a boom tent covering the cockpit and it was all securely tied down, ready for winter storage. He went back to the office to thank Tim.

"Quite all right" Tim said. "They won't let you sail anyway, so it was really time to put the boat up for the winter. I'll make another suggestion about storage. I think you should take that Land Rover of yours and park it in your garage. Put it up on blocks, take off the wheels, and remove the carburetor and bury it somewhere. You can tell them the car is 'undergoing repairs.' I'm guessing that when the task force arrives, the Argies will be appropriating every vehicle they can lay their hands on."

"Tim, you're a marvel! That's exactly what I will do." He shook hands with Jamison and headed for home.

Jenny and Grant had no chance to talk that night and the bombs fell the next morning. That initial bombing of the airfield, two miles from Stanley, took place at 4:15 am. The blast was so loud and so powerful, it shook the ground across the town and windows broke in some houses in east Stanley. Grant, Jenny, and Millicent were out of bed immediately, but Darrell slept right through it. There were more bombs on the airfield at dawn and the residents watched as dogfights erupted in the skies above them.

The next day, May 2, the *General Belgrano*, the second largest ship in the Argentine navy, was sunk by a British submarine. In the freezing waters south of the Falklands, 323 Argentine sailors died. The effect on the garrison in Stanley was immediate. Tension and urgent fear set in. There was no mistaking the British intention now: they aimed to come ashore and kill them. Everywhere preparations for the invasion escalated. Grant and Jenny watched as hundreds of troops moved out to the airport. Some sort of redeployment was taking place.

That night, after Darrell had been put to bed and Millie had retired for the night, Grant and Jenny sat on the front steps looking at the night sky. The rumble of planes at the airport was punctuated by shellfire from their anti-aircraft batteries. Rehearsing for the real show. They tried to ignore it.

"I had a visit from the Argentine press today" Jenny said.

"Really?"

"A reporter and his cameraman came to the door and asked what I thought about the current situation."

Grant looked amused. "And what, dear wife, did you tell them?"

"I looked straight into the camera and said 'I think the mothers of Argentina should know that their government is sending televisions for the islanders while their sons are rummaging through our dust bins searching for food.'"

Grant laughed out loud, a sound Jenny hadn't heard in several days. "I'm guessing that ended the interview."

"I'm afraid it did." They sat in contented silence for several minutes, listening to the sounds of Stanley at night. Finally, Jenny spoke.

"Do you think it will be long now?" she asked.

"No, not long."

"Is there anything else we should do?"

"There's still time to move the three of you out into the camp."

Jenny looked into the mug of tea she was holding. "No, I'd rather not do that." It sounded so simple when she put it like that. Just a minor preference of hers. But they both knew it was potentially a life or death decision.

"It would be safer for Darrell." It was the strongest argument Grant could make.

"Yes, I suppose it would" Jenny said, looking at her husband. "But if we're cautious, I believe we'll be safe here. The British won't bomb us and the Argentines won't harm us. And in the years to come, when Darrell is asked what his family did during the occupation, I don't want him to say 'we hid out in the camp.' I want him to say 'We held our ground. We stayed in Stanley and kept it safe.' This is our home. This is where we belong and they will have to kill us to make us leave."

Grant was not surprised by her answer. The responsible thing to do was to consider fleeing to the camp and now they had done that, but like Jenny, he believed they could survive whatever was to come. And he thought it important to do that.

Grant took Jenny's hands in his. "All right, then. We'll stay."

They made love that night; slowly, tenderly, in the shelter of their home, safe from the storm around them. Their bodies were old, familiar partners, yet the joining was always new and unexpected. When it was over, they lay still, holding each other longer than usual and Jenny cried softly on Grant's shoulder. She cried for the men and boys who were going to be killed, on the streets, in the hills, and as they came ashore from the ships at sea. She cried for the Argentines and the British alike. She cried for the beautiful town of Stanley that was breaking down around her and for the future she could not see.

Chapter Nineteen

May 7, 1982

My Dear Reynaldo,

I have done something quite wicked. I have violated my father's trust and broken his rules. But I cannot help it. His rules are not reasonable and he has no right to read all my letters to you. Our letters are for you and me, no one else.

Father sent me into his study at home to get his sweater and I saw your last letter to me on his desk. Next to it was a small stack of envelopes already addressed to you that he uses to send my letters back to you—after he has read them! Here is the bad thing I did: I stole one of the envelopes and copied all the mailing information so I can write to you directly.

I have also figured out a way you can write privately back to me. You must send your letters to my dearest and most trusted friend, Angelina Aspérez, at the address below. She has promised me she will not open them and we can trust her.

I am writing to you this way because—and this is what I cannot let my father read—I was so moved by your last letter that I cried. I am so sorry for what you are going through. This must be terrible for you and I think every day about how you are getting through it. I worry constantly that you may be hurt or worse and I pray for you every night.

What I really want you to know is this: I am with you. You are in my thoughts and in my heart and I will not lose faith that you will survive this. Even if we never see each other again and all we have together are the words on this paper, I am with you and will always remember your courage and your sacrifice.

I am only a schoolgirl, writing to a man who is at war,

defending our country. But I feel that we are linked and are going through this together. I hope you feel the same.

With great affection,
Your Marisol

P.S.: Please keep writing to me through my father's office. Especially about the military things you are experiencing and observing. Father reads your letters carefully and I have heard him discussing things you have written with people he is talking to on the phone. I think you may be doing good by telling him what is happening on the islands.

Rey sat on his sleeping bag inside his tent, reading the letter in the light from a lantern hung at the peak. When he had started writing to Marisol—when the idea first came to him—he had thought it would be fun, a way to keep in contact with a smart and pretty girl he might see later. Now it had become something else.

Perhaps the change was only within himself, but it felt like it was between them. He felt vulnerable and yet compelled to tell her all he was feeling. If she was truly with him, as she said, then he could share all that was happening, all he was experiencing. And he needed that sharing. It was about trust and she had given him hers, now he must do the same. Checking to see that his tentmate was still asleep, he took up his pen.

May 10, 1982

My Dear Marisol,
I can hardly tell you how grateful I am that you have found a way for us to write directly to each other. There is so much I wish to tell you, to share with you. And I agree, these thoughts are for you and me alone. Your father needs to know what is happening down here on the islands and I will keep writing to you through him, but I need to share with you what is happening to me.

Forgive me, Marisol, I am no hero. There is nothing noble or inspiring about what I am doing. You call me courageous, but I am just trying to survive. I hear the rumble of the cannon on the horizon and feel it coming toward me. I am as frightened as I have ever been. I do not know if I will survive this or if my life will be lost along with so many others.

I do not understand war. The closer I get to it, the more it eludes me. If these islands belong to us, why are they not just ours? Why must they be taken with blood and savagery and death? God gave us the ability to think and reason, but we seem powerless to do that and can only talk through the muzzles of our guns. I am losing faith that this is a right war, a just war. Please, tell me if you think I am wrong.

When I was a child and learned of the Islas Malvinas, I was taught they were Argentine, the people of the islands were Argentine. They had been taken over by the British and were ruled by them, like one of their colonies. Now we were coming to free them. We were the liberators come to their rescue. But when I landed on these islands, all I found were British sheep farmers. Many of their families have lived on these islands for over a hundred years. There are no Argentines.

My new friend Armando says this war is pointless and we cannot win. I don't understand all the politics he speaks about, but I think he is right that the British won't stop until they have retaken these islands. Which can only mean things will soon get very bad here. I hope that I am not a coward and will do my duty, but I feel no joy at the thought of killing English. I only wish to return home and see you again.

I hope you do not think me a coward or a fool. I am just trying to find my way.

Please take care of yourself and keep me in your thoughts.

Your devoted and affectionate friend,
Reynaldo

Rey had just finished sealing and addressing the envelop when he heard a harsh whisper outside his tent flap. "Rey, are you in there?" It was Armando. Rey pushed aside the flap and stepped outside to talk with him.

"Follow me" Army said. He led them to a corner of the field, away from all the other tents. Here they could speak privately as the wind covered their words. "There's going to be a major redeployment. Most of the troops will be posted out onto the mountains."

"Do you know where I'll be sent?"

"They are still making up the orders, but the 25th Regiment will remain here at the airfield. But you're all going to be broken into patrol groups and stationed around the periphery of the peninsula. You'll have to dig shelters as best you can to get through the bombing. It will only increase as the British attack."

"What about Jury and our friend Sonny? Will they be here too?"

"Yes, C Company was sent to Goose Green, but everyone else in the 25th is staying."

"I'd rather be in the mountains."

"No, trust me, you wouldn't. I've been to the mountains on supply runs and those troops are miserable. They are lucky to get one hot meal a day. It is cold and wet and the wind never quits. You may have to dodge bombs here, but if you jump quick into shelter when you hear the sirens, you'll be fine. Do you have shovels?

"I have one and Jury has his."

"Be sure to take them with you. And take all the clothes you have. I'll try to get you more blankets if I can find them. Is there anything you need before you move out tomorrow?"

"Just one thing. Could you mail a letter for me?"

The next morning, the 25th Regiment was assembled at one end of the airfield and they held a rollcall that seemed to take forever. Rey saw both Jury and Sonny standing in lines, but he was unable to break ranks and speak with them. The troops were divided into smaller and smaller units, and finally each soldier was assigned to a small patrol group. When Patrol Group 42 was announced, Rey heard his name called.

Then, incredibly, he heard the names of the other members of his Patrol: Juraich Mitner and Santana Dambolena. Could it be? Had he somehow been paired with his best friends, Jury and Sonny? What an amazing stroke of luck. He was still trying to digest this news when he heard the last part of the announcement:

"The leader for Patrol Group 42 will be Corporal Cabruja." A dark premonition stole over his heart. Could this be Sergeant Cabruja? No, it must be someone with the same name, a relative perhaps. Or some mistake. Anything, except...

Suddenly, there he stood, the former Sergeant Bartoli Cabruja, now wearing a single Corporal's stripe on his shirtsleeve. He gave Rey a sickening grin and pulled him over to where Jury and Sonny were standing.

"Did you think God had smiled down on you and put you three little love birds together? No. I picked you for this Patrol. They may have busted me down from Sergeant to Corporal, but I still have friends in the right places. And I chose each one of you because I know you and I know you won't give me any trouble, will you?"

"Certainly not, Corporal," Jury blurted out. "You are the designated leader of our Patrol Group and we look to you to lead us."

"Yes" the corporal said, looking closely at the other two who remained mute. "I am your leader. And let's be clear about one thing: I am still a sergeant. The sons of bitches who broke me down to corporal will pay for that mistake. But I am still a sergeant and I will soon have my stripes back. And when the four of us are together, you will call me sergeant. You may only call me corporal in front of officers or other troops. Is that clear?"

"Very clear, Sergeant Cabruja" Jury said. "We understand your feelings and will address you accordingly."

"All right then. I'm going over to the assignments officer to get our orders. You three remain here."

As soon as he was gone, Sonny turned on Jury. "Why are you

sucking up to that bastard? We may have to put up with him, but we don't have to like it."

Jury smiled at his friend. "You catch bears with honey, not with lemons. This particular bear is ill-natured and wounded. He needs proper handling. Flattery and subservience will serve us better than defiance."

Rey thought about this approach to "handling" the corporal. Cabruja was their legitimate leader and acknowledging that cost them nothing. It reassured him of control and that was his main concern. And Rey knew that Jury was highly skilled at giving people the illusion of control while persuading them to do what he wished.

Sonny looked dubious. "I don't think we should take any of his crap. We should stand up to him."

"No, I think Jury is right" Rey said. "He was always a lot more docile when Lobo wasn't around and they seem to have separated. I think his cruelty and the sadistic things he did were mostly to impress Lobo. Let's try to work with him and see where it takes us."

Corporal Cabruja soon returned. "Pack all your gear, but leave your tents. We will be issued tents when we get there. Meet back here in forty five minutes."

When Rey met the others later, all three of them were packing huge rucksacks on their backs with everything they owned in them and shovels tied on behind. Jury had wanted to bring his cot, but Army had advised against it. He told Jury all he knew about where they were being stationed and promised to look in on them when he could.

They were headed for the far west end of the airfield peninsula, to Engineers Point right on the water with a clear view across to Camber Peninsula. In theory, the British could land troops on Camber, which was unoccupied, cross over the quarter mile of sea at night using inflatable boats and attack the airfield from behind. This was exactly the type of attack typically done by the dreaded Small Boat Squadron. The assignment for Patrol Group 42 was to set up an observation point to warn of any approach by the British before they could land. They had no canon or machine gun; outside of their rifles, their only weapon was the radio-phone they could report with.

When the Corporal returned, he set down his rucksack and motioned to Sonny: "Dambolena, you come with me. You two girls stay here." Rey and Jury looked solemnly at the corporal until Cabruja was out of earshot, then broke into laughter. "He's very predictable" Jury said. "I like that about him."

Twenty minutes later, Sonny and the Corporal returned carrying two ten-foot timbers like a stretcher with a large tarpaulin resting on top of it. "You two will carry our sacks" Cabruja said as he and Sonny set off heading west. Rey and Jury could barely carry their own rucksacks, but somehow they managed to load each other up so they had one sack in front and one in back, then they followed the path to the end of the peninsula. It was hard going with moss and peat growing over the slippery rocks making for unsure footing.

After a mile and a half, Cabruja called a halt. "We will take a break" he announced, lighting a cigarette. They were all sweating profusely despite the chill in the wind. They sat on the ground resting for fifteen minutes, then the Corporal said "We will change loads." He began strapping on two of the rucksacks. Rey thought it was considerate of the Corporal to do this until he lifted one end of the timbers holding the tarpaulin. It was so heavy he could barely lift it and the round shape of the timbers, which were soaked in creosote, made it very difficult to grip them.

Jury could not lift his end at all. Try as he would, his hands were not large enough to grip the timbers and he was not strong enough to get both of them up off the ground at the same time. Cabruja swore darkly and came over to where Jury was struggling. He slapped him hard across the face sending him to the ground.

"What are you good for, you little dog turd? Dambolena! Get over here. Drop your packs and take this end. Mitner can carry the sacks."

"I'm sorry, Sergeant. I'm just not as strong as the rest of you."

"Shut your hole and pick up those sacks."

It was another two miles to the shoreline and each of them

fell at least once moving over the slippery rocks. The peat was thicker as they came toward the water and their boots sank down without warning, soaking their feet in the water below the surface. They were all exhausted when they finally made a halt. They were at the end of the peninsula and had a good view of the Camber peninsula across the bay.

"All right," Cabruja said, "dig a hole we can cover with the tarp."

"Sergeant Cabruja" Jury said, "I know it is your job to make the decisions and we will certainly follow them, but could I offer a suggestion for you to consider?"

The Corporal looked at Jury warily. "What is this suggestion you have?"

"Where we are right now, we are only four or five feet above sea level. But this is low tide and if we dig here, our hole will fill with water when the tide comes in."

"What are you saying?"

Jury pointed to the left. "On that rise, there are two large boulders about six feet apart. If we wedge our poles between them and cover that with the tarp, we can make a dry shelter that will keep us out of the wind and still give us a full view of Camber and the bay."

Cabruja stared at the two boulders for several seconds. He didn't seem to understand the concept. "Poralez, what do you think?"

Rey was also looking at the two boulders. He turned to Cabruja to face him squarely. "Sergeant Cabruja, Jury is the smartest person I've ever met. He will make a good shelter for us. If you don't like it, you can always take it down and do something else."

The Corporal shrugged. "Fine. Build whatever you like. I'm going on patrol."

Cabruja was gone for five hours. During that time, the three friends completed work on the shelter using rocks to anchor the beams and hold down the tarpaulin. The tarp was large enough that they could trail one edge down to the ground and make their shelter into a small cave. They cut out blocks of peat to seal the edges and keep out the wind and covered the top with tussock grass to provide camouflage from the air. Inside it was damp and thick with the scent of earth, but it was relatively dry.

When the Corporal returned, he smelled of alcohol. He brought them a small pail of grey soup. "Here is your dinner" he said. Looking around at the shelter, he grunted and lay down on his bed roll. He was soon snoring.

The next day dawned cold and wet, with a light mist coming down that made the horizon hazy and the water of the bay a deeper blue. Despite the weather, Cabruja decided to visit the other patrol outposts which were spaced a half mile apart up and down the coast. For this trip, he took Sonny with him. Rey and Jury were just as glad to stay inside the shelter. An hour after they had settled in, Army appeared at the entrance.

"This is quite a shelter you've built here" he said. "Dry, out of the wind, you've done a good job." Army came in and sat down. "I've brought you a few things: another tarp you can use for the floor, some ration packs, and a box of socks."

"Socks' Rey said, "you've brought us socks?"

Army looked at him seriously. "Yes and you must change them every day. This is important. Don't let your feet stay wet. Dry them off and change socks as often as you can. It's going to get very cold here soon and you risk trench foot or frost bite. Wash your clothes too."

"We have no wash basin" Jury said.

Army looked around at what little equipment they had. "All right, I'll try to find you something. But it may be several days before I can get back here."

"Thank you for all of this" Jury said. "You are a good friend to us."

Army shrugged. "Better than you deserve." The three friends laughed together.

"What do you know about when the British will be landing?" Rey asked.

"We no longer believe it will be soon. Apparently, their amphibious forces didn't come down with the aircraft carriers.

So it may be some time before they come. But we must watch for them. They won't attack here in force, we have too many troops around the airport. But they may send commandos in at night to raid the airfield. They won't come during the day, but you must keep a sharp lookout at night. They will think nothing of killing you while you sleep, so sleep during the day.

"They will keep bombing the airfield, but if you're careful you should be relatively safe. Still, I'd stay in this shelter whenever you can. The one thing we are sure of is that the attack will have to come before winter sets in. It will be a matter of weeks, not months."

At that moment, Corporal Cabruja and Sonny stepped into the shelter.

Cabruja nodded toward Army. "Who is this?"

Jury quickly spoke up. "This is our friend, Army"

"This shelter is too small for so many. Get out."

Army rose to his feet and stood in front of the corporal looking up into his face. He slowly removed his jacket revealing his shirt that bore the stripes of a sergeant. "Perhaps you don't remember me, Corporal. I am Sergeant Armando Gottara, an assistant to General Menéndez. We met in the requisitions office. And since I am a sergeant and you are a corporal, you will not be giving ME orders, I will be giving YOU orders. Are we clear about that?"

Rey was shocked by what he was witnessing. Army was a sergeant? It was news to Rey, good news to be sure, but Army had always been so friendly Rey never guessed he had a higher rank. Even more surprising was Army's tone of voice. He was clearly in command and was not the least bit intimidated by Cabruja's size.

Army let his words sink in for a few seconds, then continued. "Because if we're not clear about that, then we are looking at insubordination and that would have to be reported to Major Dowling. That would have...unfortunate consequences for your career. Wouldn't you agree?"

Cabruja's eyes were darting around the shelter as if looking for a way out. Finally, he muttered "Yes, sergeant."

"Good. Then we have an understanding. I have brought a few supplies for my friends here, a tarp for the floor, some ration packs and a box of socks. You will share them equally with your men. You will not take more than they get, nor less than they get. Is that clear?"

"Yes, sergeant."

"I will be heading back to Stanley to make my report to General Menéndez about the preparedness of our patrol groups, but I will be returning here on a regular basis to see how you are doing. In the meantime, someone has taken a shit and left it twenty feet from the entrance to this shelter. You will have your men dig a proper latrine and bury your droppings. It's unsanitary and we don't want the British to be able to smell your location."

Rey and Jury could not help smiling at this since they had already dug a latrine and everyone in the shelter knew who had not used it.

Army put on his jacket, nodded to his friends, and headed for the entrance. "I will see you soon."

Then he was gone.

Chapter Twenty

The weeks spent on that windswept point of land, looking out over the water, were bitterly cold and wet. Bombs fell without warning, usually far enough away that they could easily take shelter, but sometimes very close. The radar-controlled anti-aircraft guns in Stanley kept the British planes back from the land, but they were still able to make "toss bombing" raids from higher altitudes before sharply turning away to avoid Argentine fire. This technique was far less accurate than precision overhead bombing so it did little harm to the airfield, but it forced the Argentines to keep their heads down.

There was nothing to do but sleep and stand watches. Cabruja was overbearing and arrogant, but he stood his share of the watches and no longer physically abused them. Rey thought he was probably worried about Army discovering poor conduct and taking action. Jury's tentmate was turning out to be the best friend they ever had.

As the days wore on, Rey saw a curious shift within Patrol Group 42. Cabruja and Sonny had become friends. The corporal had little respect for Rey and Jury and always assigned them all the cleanup and maintenance tasks that needed doing. When he went on patrol, he always took Sonny with him. Sonny objected at first, but after a few days, he seemed to enjoy getting out of the shelter and away from the point. The "patrols" became longer and stretched to five or six hours. When they returned, both Sonny and the corporal now smelled of alcohol.

"I don't understand what has happened to Sonny" Rey said to Jury one day when they were alone in the shelter. "He's never acted like this before."

Jury was also worried. "I think he's found a warrior and he wants to be one too."

Rey was confused. "He used to hate Cabruja. Now they talk together like old friends. Cabruja calls him Sonny while you and I are still Poralez and Mitner. I don't understand what has changed in Sonny."

Jury was lost in thought for several moments before replying. "I'm not sure Sonny has changed. I think he's always been spoiling for a fight, but you and I kept the lid on. That's why he's being so diligent about the rifles."

Army had given Jury an expensive rifle cleaning kit he brought over from the mainland. It was far better than the basic rod and cleaning cloth the army supplied. The kit contained special solvents, oils, and cleaning brushes, pads to clean out the rifling in the barrels and the firing apparatus, polish for the stock, bluing for the barrels, and a tool to clean and align the sights. Jury freely shared the kit with the others, but Cabruja had no interest in it.

In the damp weather of the Falklands, the barrels and firing mechanisms of the rifles rusted quickly. Army forcefully told them they must keep their rifles clean and ready for action at all times. Jury set up a routine of cleaning his rifle every other day. Seeing the wisdom in this, Rey followed suit. But Sonny took this even further. He cleaned both his own rifle and the corporal's every day and he often checked to be sure the clips fit and the cartridges slid easily into place. It worried Rey that Sonny seemed to always be holding his rifle, cradling it in his arms or running his hand over the stock.

What worried Rey more was the crazy talk Cabruja had drawn Sonny into as they sat around in the shelter. The corporal had begun talking hatefully about the British as soon as they had set up the shelter. No one was surprised, the British were the enemy. But as the days and weeks wore on, his speech became progressively more violent. He didn't simply want to defeat the British, he wanted to kill every one of them and do it in ways that caused them the greatest pain.

Cabruja spoke of disemboweling them, or knifing through their windpipes and watching them drown in their own blood. He spoke of cutting off their genitals with his bayonet or shooting them in both kneecaps and then following them as they crawled away, carefully placing bullets at the base of their spines and slowly firing higher up their backs until they screamed their way into death. The images were so horrific, Rey and Jury could only stare at him in silence wondering what sickness brought these thoughts into his mind.

At first, Sonny treated this talk as a joke. He would try to join in and even top the corporal with more outlandish ideas. But Cabruja's sadism could not be outdone. He could work himself up into a fever pitch and then, without warning, suddenly sound normal and ask if they had any food left. These rapid mood shifts left Rey and Jury wondering where this fury came from, but Sonny seemed to take it all as normal behavior. Jury told Rey he thought it was anxiety over the battle to come and would disappear when the battle actually started. Rey doubted this was true.

Army was as good as his word and stopped in to see them every two or three days. He usually brought food, but still insisted that Corporal Cabruja let each of his men walk the three and a half miles back to the airfield for a hot meal once a day. On the frequent days when it rained, they sometimes skipped this. On those days, the rations that Army brought were much appreciated.

On Saturday, May 15th, Army showed up early in the morning and drew all four members of the patrol group into the shelter. "There has been a raid on Pebble Island. The British attacked our airfield there in the night."

"Where is Pebble Island?" Sonny asked.

"It's off the northern coast of West Falkland. That airfield was important to us and the British knew that, so they came in the night and blew up our planes."

"How many did they get?" Jury asked.

"They got every plane at the airfield, eleven all told. Then they blew up an ammunition dump and a fuel dump, and left a huge crater where the airstrips meet. They were able to sneak past the guards and plant explosives before anyone knew they were there. That airfield is now a total loss."

"How many of them did we kill?" Cabruja asked.

"None. We fired on them, but they were able to slip back into the night. We heard their helicopters taking them back to their ship. None of our troops were injured."

Jury looked thoughtful. "What does this mean for us, Sergeant?"

Army looked around the group, choosing his words carefully. "The British invasion is coming any day now and we expect them to land somewhere along the northern coast. The first place they will attack is right here. We believe the raid on Pebble Island was a rehearsal for attacking this airfield. The airbridge we have established in Puerto Argentino is the only way to bring supplies and more troops to come to our aid. They must destroy it to gain control of the islands.

"They won't come in force so don't look for big ships across the bay. Look for forty or fifty men. They'll either come in by submarine or by helicopter. After they land on Camber Peninsula, they'll cross over in rubber rafts. They won't use motors, they will paddle, so you won't be able to hear them. But I've brought you night-vision binoculars, the best in the world, better than the British have. From now on, post two men at all times during the night. That's when they'll come."

"What do we do if we see them?" the corporal asked.

"Phone in their position and the number of men you've seen and keep them in sight. But don't fire on them or send up a flare. Don't let them know you're here. If we can lure them in toward the airfield and then either kill or capture them as a group, it will discourage the British from conducting similar raids in the future. Don't be heroes. Stay invisible and keep reporting. That's your mission."

As he finished speaking, the bombs began falling around them. The earth shook, the wind blew smoke and cordite into the air, and the violent explosions pounded their ears. They moved to the corners of their shelter and took cover beneath the overhanging boulders.

A few days later, Rey opened a letter from Marisol that Army had brought and left with him. He had saved it until he was alone in the shelter. From the return address, he knew it was not sent through Vice-Comodoro Lantana's office. This was one of their "private" letters. He no sooner opened it than a picture fell out; it was a school picture of Marisol, her head and shoulders, looking very pretty with just the hint of a smile. Rey's breath stopped for a moment and he felt flushed with joy. This beautiful girl was writing to him among all the thousands of soldiers on this island. He quickly unfolded the pages.

May 15, 1982

My Dear Rey,

Here is my picture. I hope you will keep it with you. It's a school picture so it's not my best, but it is the only one I have to send you. It will give you a little bit of me to carry with you.

I was very upset that you wrote that you think you might be a coward. I KNOW you are not! You have great courage and strong beliefs. I don't know everything about you, but I do know this. On the first night we met, at the Marimba Palace, you spoke up to my father and got him to let us write to each other. That took courage. Most people are afraid of him. I've seen grown men he works with cower in his presence. You stood right up to him.

And when the bombs fell at the airfield, you did not run and hide. You went right to where others were bleeding and dying and did all you could to help them. You may be young, but you are kind and strong and have great courage. I believe in you. I will always believe in you. And I will always love you.

There, I've said it. I know I am too young to have these feelings, but I cannot help what I feel. I don't know if I will ever see you again. I pray I will. But wherever you are, whatever you're going through, I will be with you. Trust in my love and, please, keep yourself safe.

I know you have questions about the war. I don't know enough to answer them. I too thought you were being sent there to free the Argentine islanders. I don't know what is supposed to be done with the British who live there. These are government matters and we will have to leave it to them. What I do know is that you are an honorable, dedicated soldier of Argentina and will do whatever your country asks you to do. I pray for peace and for your return every day.

Please be careful and keep yourself and your friends safe.

From your dear friend who cares for you above all others,
Marisol

Rey felt dizzy after reading her words. How had he won the love of this girl he had only spoken with for one hour? How could he get back to her? It was agony not to be near her, to be freezing and wet and exhausted, mired in a war that would soon erupt around him. He could not lose her. Even if he had only another day to live, he must write to her. He took up paper and pen.

My Dearest Marisol,

God bless you for sending me your picture. You cannot imagine how I treasure this beautiful image of your smiling face. I swear it will save my life. When the bombs fall and the ground shakes, I will take out your picture and gaze at it knowing you are thinking of me. I dream of how our lives will be if I survive this war and we are able to be together. I imagine holding you in my arms and it takes away my fear.

Things are very bad here. We expect the British to attack at any moment, but no one knows where or when. Even though I am only in an observation post right now, a time will soon come when I must face their cannon and their rifles. Thank you for all the kind things you have written about my courage and my strength. I hope these will carry me through what is about to come. I only know that in the darkness of my fears, I often think of you.

And thank you for saying that you love me. I have done nothing to earn that love, but it is the dream of seeing you again that sustains me. I have never been in love before and we have only had an hour's time together, yet I feel your presence with me and your hand upon my heart. I will always love you, Marisol, whether I am here or at home or above you in heaven. I am far out to sea and you are the light on the shore calling me back. If there is any way possible, I will come back to you. I promise.

The worst of my fears come not from the British, but from the sad, evil forces that seem to have come into our patrol group. I've written to you about our leader, Corporal Cabruja. His bizarre behavior seems to get worse each day. His vivid daydreams about torturing the enemy have come to obsess him and sometimes he seems to lose touch with reality. The worst of this is that our good friend Sonny is drifting into his orbit.

This week the corporal told us about the "Ghost Warriors" who have infiltrated our ranks and are walking among our troops. These are supposed to be British soldiers who speak perfect Spanish and wear our uniforms and walk among us. He says they are gathering information and waiting for the right time to strike. A night will come, he says, when they will slit our throats as we sleep and then slip away into the darkness.

Corporal Cabruja believes the Ghost Warriors are everywhere among us and we must identify them to keep ourselves safe. He talks with Sonny about them and the two of them come up with questions they can ask other soldiers that only a true Argentine would know the answer to. Cabruja says we cannot trust anyone and he only trusts us because he knew us for a year before the war began.

I have written to your father about the corporal in one of the letters I sent to you through his office. I hope he will let the army leaders know about this man who is more dangerous to us than to the enemy. He should be in an asylum, not in the army.

My darling, that is all I can write at this time. Keep me in your heart as I keep you in mine. I pray our time together is yet to come.

With all my love,
Reynaldo

———————◆◆◆———————

At his desk in Buenos Aires, Vice-Comodoro Lantana lay down the other letter Private Poralez had written to his daughter and sent to his office. There was nothing, of course, that he could do about the crazy corporal who led Poralez's patrol group. The army was full of such people and the private would just have to take his chances. Interference from an Air Force officer would only muddy the waters.

Lantana noted that Marie seemed to have lost interest in this young man and was now only sending him one letter a week. Just as well, he thought, better she should forget him.

Chapter Twenty-One

May 21, 1982
Onboard MV Norland

Mike Ferrol stood shivering in a line of soldiers in the crowded passageway on the lower deck of the *Norland*. A cold wind blew in from the open cargo door toward the stern of the ship where men were dropping down into the much smaller landing craft that were rising and falling on the waves. It was a perilous jump for these combat soldiers, each straining under the weight of their fully loaded rucksacks, a hundred pounds or more, that bent them over like old men. But these were not old men; they were toughened twenty-year-olds, who routinely carried this weight on hikes of ten miles or more. Mike was the old man. The rucksack he carried weighed a mere forty-five pounds since he carried no weapons or ammunition, but Mike felt every ounce.

This was the invasion. The 2nd Parachute Regiment would be the first soldiers going ashore to establish a beachhead on the Falklands and Mike was going with them. In fact, he would be among the first wave. Though SAS reconnaissance patrols reported San Carlos was deserted, there was no guarantee that was true. It would only take a couple well-hidden machine gun nests to turn the shoreline into Omaha Beach. Mike listened to the cannon onboard *Antrim* already shelling the Argentine positions on Fanning Head that protected the entrance into San Carlos Waters. It was 3:00 am and Mike wished he'd been able to sleep more this afternoon. He wondered how much thought had been given to picking this particular beach.

The planning for the landing of assault forces against the Argentine-held Falklands began before any British ships sailed south. The When and the How of the equation were critical, but the most important question was Where? The myriad possibilities and the lack of clear information about the location of Argentine forces confounded the planners for weeks until a decision was finally made on May 12, less than two weeks before the landing parties would hit the beaches. In the end, it was again naval considerations that took precedence over the needs of the ground forces that would directly confront the Argentines.

For the commandos and paratroopers going ashore, a short approach to Stanley was best. It would shorten supply lines, ease reinforcement, and keep the troops fresh when they confronted the Argentines. But everyone understood that to retake the islands, the British must capture Stanley. To prevent that, the Argentines had concentrated the bulk of their forces, 9,000 men or more, around the town. They had fortified their positions, brought in field artillery, radar-controlled anti-aircraft batteries, and lay mine fields to thwart any British attempt to take the capital. A direct attack on Stanley would meet massive, immediate resistance.

For the Royal Navy, it was vital to have clear landing beaches that were unprotected by Argentine forces, with high headlands where Rapier batteries could be set up to protect the ships from air attacks. Sheltered beaches would eliminate the threat of an Exocet attack since the missile's guidance systems could not operate near land. The landing would have to be on East Falkland itself, but as far from any concentrations of Argentine forces as possible. To launch the recapture of the islands, a massive amount of men and materiel would have to be put ashore quickly.

The San Carlos inlet offered a crescent of sheltered beaches unoccupied by the Argentines and a protected bay that would make unloading and landing relatively safe, at least at night. The difficulty was its location on the far western coast of East Falkland, a full 100 kilometers, 62 miles, from Stanley. The plan, then, was to get men and equipment ashore rapidly, establish the beachhead, then move the troops across the island by helicopter. But, like any British beach assault, the plans were drawn in the shadow of Gallipoli, the 1915 amphibious assault that had turned into a naval and military disaster. It plagued its planner and chief advocate, Winston Churchill, for the rest of his life.

Mike Ferrol had few thoughts about the difficulty of amphibious assaults. At the moment, his full attention was focused on the seven-to-twelve foot drop he would have to make to get off the *Norland* and into the bobbing landing craft alongside. This drop, wearing his full pack, looked to Mike like a quick way to break both ankles.

"Now don't go getting all soft about this flying departure we're about to make" his friend Tony Banks said. Tony was the next man in line in front of Mike and they had been inching forward for the past 20 minutes. "I've swotted up the whole routine and there won't be nothing to it. There's two cabbageheads down in the boat who'll catch you under the arms before you even hit the deck. Just don't land on their feet."

"What if I can't bring myself to make the jump?" Mike said.

"Oh, they'll push you off if you don't jump, but don't bottle it in front of everyone. Just pick your time carefully and step well away from the ship. The LCU will be rising and falling three or four feet on every wave. Wait till it comes up to the top and then go."

"Couldn't I drop my rucksack down first and then jump?"

"Sorry, mate, by the time this lot hits the door, we'll be moving fast. Just bend your knees and jump. But get far away from the ship. You don't want to get caught between the hull and the launch. One of the lads missed his footing while they were cross-decking 3 Commando yesterday. Fell between the ship and the LCU. They caught him before he went under, but he broke his pelvis. Lucky bugger."

Mike stared at him in disbelief. "How was that lucky?"

"Bought him a ticket home. Won't be facing any Argie shellfire like you and me!"

In the event, it proved much easier than Mike imagined. The cold night air hit his face with a refreshing slap after the hot, moist dining hall where he'd spent hours waiting. He jumped without prompting and bent his knees. Two giant marines in the LCU caught him gently and pushed him away as other troops dropped down. He found a place to stand forward next to Tony. The wind and the darkness quickly enveloped them as their flat-nosed craft, carrying two hundred troops of 2 Para, moved away from the ship. In the bitter cold, the engine was roaring and the bow rose and fell with each new wave.

It was impossible to talk and Mike preferred to just rest his backpack against the side of the boat banging across the waves. He thought about all the D-day movies he'd seen, where frightened young men braced themselves for the moment the ramp would fall down and bullets would start flying. Mostly, he feared stepping off the end of the landing craft only to find they hadn't pulled close enough inshore and now he dropped into ten feet of water, his pack quickly taking him to the bottom. He'd practiced shedding his pack rapidly to meet this possibility. As the landing craft moved along, Mike felt a piercing chill from the spray coming in and the wind whipping into the boat.

When they reached the shoreline, the roar of the engine suddenly subsided to a quiet purr and they rode along searching the dark shore for any activity. Suddenly they came to a stop and a loud clanking and rattling of chains announced the dropping of the ramp. Then Mike was being pushed to the ramp and out of the boat. Incredibly, he sank only five inches in water before finding his footing. In only a few steps, he was fully ashore and eternally grateful to the "cabbagehead" who had driven that LCU all the way in.

The shore was first pebbly rocks, then spongy peat with lichen covered rocks that were slippery and hard to see in the dark. Mike heard a lot of cursing as men struggled to stay upright under their heavy loads getting ashore. What he didn't hear was any firing from the enemy. The beach was empty! His relief was palpable. He fell in with the line of troops moving south to the base of Sussex Mountain. They passed over a succession of streams and patches of marshes.

Tabbing they called it, this march under load, a curious term for the exhausting labor of carefully picking your way across peat and rocks and tussocks of grass. They said little as they made their way up the mountain, a steep climb. Mike heard the occasional cursing as men lost their footing and had to stop to recover.

The four mile climb to the crestline of the mountain, up 900 feet above the shoreline, was the hardest march Mike had ever made. The pack on his back pulled relentlessly on his shoulders and made it hard to keep his balance. His legs ached painfully and his frozen feet were sending shock waves up to his knees. Mike's lungs pulled in air roughly and he was soon gasping. He was close to giving up when they reached the crest. How the other troops managed, carrying loads two or three times his, he could only imagine.

It was dawn and the summit offered an amazing view looking south toward Darwin and back into San Carlos bay where the twelve amphibious landing ships were offloading. Men, tanks, mortars, and missiles were coming to the shore, a busy terminus with landing craft and helicopters in constant movement between the ships and the beach. They looked like water beetles darting across the surface. Local civilians from San Carlos Settlement, eager to help, brought their tractors and trailers and drove loads of ammunition, engineer equipment and general supplies up from the landing beaches.

The wind at the top of Sussex Mountain was brutal and constant. Digging shelters proved impossible; the ground was too hard. After a short rest, they began cutting into the peat with their shovels, making blocks of peat they could stack igloo-fashion into shelters against the elements and enemy gunfire. They offered scant protection, but it was enough. After an hour's labor, Mike lay out his bedroll on the ground, wrapped himself tightly in his balaclava, a close-fitting jacket with an attached hood that covered his head and neck, and fell asleep.

Two thousand four hundred British soldiers came ashore during the night of May 21. Another thousand would arrive during daylight. Tons of equipment, ammunition, tanks, fuel, and food came with them. The British launched multiple attacks on other sites along the north and east coast of East Falkland to keep the Argentines busy and confused as to where the real bridgehead was being established. But by early morning of the 21st, the ship activity in San Carlos Waters was unmistakable and reliable sightings were passed back to General Menéndez and to the war planners in Buenos Aires.

The first air sighting came soon after dawn. A Pucará attack plane piloted by Captain Jorge Benítez made a routine patrol from Goose Green, 17 miles away. Looking down on San Carlos bay, he saw an American-made Stinger missile flying toward him. In the brief seconds before his plane blew up, Benítez safely ejected and parachuted down. He walked ten miles back to the Argentine encampment at Goose Green.

Later, Lieutenant Guillermo Crippa was sent to investigate a report of the landings. He flew his Aermacchi combat plane until he saw the British frigate *Argonaut* guarding the entrance to the San Carlos inlet. He attacked it with cannons and missiles, wounding four sailors and doing damage to the ship's upperworks. Crippa then banked and flew over San Carlos Water where he was fired upon by missiles and guns, barely escaping. Realizing the importance of what he had seen, he turned around and made a second pass over the landing area, carefully counting the British ships amid the hail of fire from below. Again he escaped injury and returned to Stanley to report to General Menéndez in person. He was later awarded the Cross of Heroic Valor in Combat, the highest decoration given to any Argentine pilot in the war.

Mike Ferrol was standing on the crest of Sussex Mountain looking down Falkland Sound when he heard the first Argentine jets roaring toward him. War jets were nothing like the slower land-based attack planes. These were the engines of hell, ripping across the water of Falkland Sound at 1200 mph, flying only fifteen feet above the water to elude radar. At that speed and height, even the slightest disturbance would cause their destruction: a bird strike, a down draft, a shoreline tree limb. These brave Argentine pilots were flying through the eye of the needle and their courage and determination were remarkable, even to British eyes.

From the moment the jets were heard until they thundered over the headland and disappeared into the sky, the attacks took only six seconds. Starting at 10:30 am, they came in waves, Mirages, Skyhawks, and Daggers, screaming over in flights of two, four or six aircraft. As the planes approached, the shoreline and the ships below erupted in fire, throwing up a curtain of bullets and missiles that might snag the jets out of the air. Sometimes they did.

In addition to the Harrier jets flying combat patrols over the landings, Admiral Woodward had sent seven warships, six frigates and a destroyer, to guard the dozen landing ships now off the San Carlos beaches. The ships were posted up and down Falkland Sound, within San Carlos Waters, and at the entrance to the San Carlos inlet. Their armament ranged from the most modern weapons, like the Sea Wolf and Sea Slug missile systems, to the old Bofors guns from WW II. The soldiers fired Bren guns, rifles, and 66 mm anti-tank rockets. They even lashed machine guns to the upper railings of the ships and tried to throw bullets up ahead of the jets. Falkland Sound quickly became "Bomb Alley" and both sides paid a heavy price in their deadly encounters.

On the first day of the invasion, the Argentines sent 45 aircraft from the mainland, but due to weather and equipment failures, only 36 actually completed the 400-mile flight to the Falklands. Attacks on British ships were made by 26 Argentine jets, the other Argentine planes being turned back by the Harriers. Ten Argentine planes were shot down, over a quarter of their attacking force, all but one falling prey to the deadly Sidewinder Aim-9L missiles. During the course of the war, the British fired 27 Sidewinders and 24 of them hit their target, a phenomenally high percentage of success.

The pilots of Argentina did not hesitate, despite their losses. They flew straight at the British ships, hugging the water to elude the radar controlled anti-aircraft missiles. They only pulled up at the last second before dropping their bombs and sometimes hit the upper masts and antennas of the ships they were attacking.

But most of their bombs did not explode. The standard Mark 17 1,000-pound bomb they were using (made in Britain) required more time in the air to arm the bomb. Still, a thousand pound ball of steel, crashing through the side of a ship at hundreds of miles an hour did enormous damage. Many that lodged between decks would blow up later before being defused and dropped into deep water.

By the end of the day, the frigate *Ardent* was sinking, two other ships were out of action with unexploded bombs inside them, two more had been seriously damaged, and only two of the seven defending British warships were unscathed. Thirty-two British sailors were dead and another twenty-five were seriously injured. One man was blinded. Despite their losses, the task force ships had defended the landings and there had only been one ineffectual attempt to bomb the troops ashore.

Bombing the ships defending the invasion and ignoring the actual landing itself was a fatal error for Argentina. In that first 24-hour period, the British landed all of their fighting units, over 3,000 infantry, 24 field guns, eight light tanks, and a battery of Rapier missile launchers—a thousand tons of equipment plus the men needed to wield it. Despite the heroics of their pilots, the Argentines had effectively lost the battle of the invasion.

Mike watched the battles below in Falkland Sound and marveled at the speed of modern warfare. Within thirty seconds, each raid was completed and the guns would fall silent. Then hours would go by, or maybe just a few minutes, before the next raid. Men sat at their guns, refusing to be relieved, tensely waiting for the next raid. As he looked across from Falkland Sound to the sheltered bay of San Carlos Waters, Mike was amazed that no bombs fell on the landing craft, the troop ships, or the shoreline below.

The biggest target by far was the *Canberra*, an 820-foot long cruise liner pressed into service to carry troops to the islands. Nicknamed "The Great White Whale," plans to paint its white hull were given up so it could sail immediately after the aircraft carriers. *Canberra* was crammed with 2,400 troops from 3-Commando and carried them right into San Carlos Waters where it remained anchored for the whole day on May 21. The Argentines did not attack this giant target. They ignored the whole landing area, in fact, and remained focused on the warships out in Falkland Sound.

2 Para's mission was to patrol the Sussex Mountain area and prevent any counter-attack that might come from Goose Green or Darwin to the south. Due to highly effective diversionary attacks by the SAS, the Argentines never mounted any overland attack on the landing forces. So Mike and his friend Tony Banks were left with the rest of 2 Para, waiting for action for five cold, wet, miserable days. The troops were put on patrol shifts, four hours on and four hours off, but Mike was free to roam as he chose. Mostly, he just stayed bundled up in their makeshift shelter.

"Hello, mate" Tony said cheerfully after returning from patrol on their second afternoon. "Fancy a brew?"

"Sounds wonderful" Mike said, but without enthusiasm. Tony began fiddling with the hexi-burner, trying to find a place out of the wind where he could light it.

"I've got the tea," Tony said, "but we'll need water. You suppose you could head down the hill and fetch us a water bottle or two?"

"Don't know if I can" Mike said, "my feet are blocks of ice."

"That doesn't sound good. Get you boots off. Let's have a look."

Mike stared at him in disbelief. "You must be kidding."

Tony looked at him without smiling. "No, mate, we need to look at those feet. Let me tell you, we're losing more boys to frostbite and trench foot than we are to the Argies. Let me just have a look." He undid the laces on Mike's boots and pulled them off. The socks inside were wet and bitterly cold. Tony pulled the socks off and held one of Mike's feet up to get a closer look. It looked frighteningly white.

"Right, then. Bend your left knee and get hold of your left foot with both hands. I'll work on your other foot." Tony began vigorously massaging Mike's right foot. The pain was so great, Mike cried out. It felt like a thousand pins being jabbed into his foot. He gripped his left foot, but couldn't massage it. For the first couple minutes, he was just gripping it for dear life. He finally began to work the flesh and after several minutes, his feet started to feel better, still cold, but they had good circulation.

"Do you have any fresh socks?" Tony asked.

"They're in my Bergen. Lower right pocket in the back."

"Good man. At least you know where stuff is in your Bergen. Now let's see if we can dry out your boots a bit." Tony pulled a washcloth out of Mike's pack and began rubbing out the insides of his boots.

"Hey, that's my facecloth you're using there."

"Look, mate, you can't put dry socks into wet boots. Anyway, your face doesn't need washing, you're lovely just as you are." Tony laughed and after a moment so did Mike.

On their third night, they awoke to a tremendous explosion. Jumping up from their sleeping bags, they assumed they were under attack, but then saw black smoke pouring out of one of the ships anchored in San Carlos bay. The frigate, HMS *Antelope*, had been attacked by two Skyhawks earlier in the day and was left afloat out in Falkland Sound, but with two unexploded bombs inside the ship. It was brought into calmer waters in the bay so demolition experts could defuse the bombs. The crew were moved first to the fo'c'sle where they shivered for more than an hour in the icy northerly wind, then relocated to the shelter of the flight deck.

Staff Sergeant James Prescott and Warrant Officer John Phillips did the delicate work of disarming the bombs. A broadcast from the bridge announced they were trying a new method of defusing the bomb. They first detonated a small charge from a distance, then moved forward to see if it had worked. As they did so, the bomb went off blasting a metal door off its hinges hitting Prescott and killing him instantly. Phillips suffered a severely injured arm, but escaped to the upper decks with the help of two crewmen.

Fire teams immediately began work, but a raging blaze spread out from the center of the ship. Black deadly smoke poured over the decks and a column of sparks rose into the air. The fire would soon reach the missile magazines and the ship had now turned into a giant bomb waiting to explode. Despite the danger, every landing craft coxswain in the anchorage moved their craft to the crippled ship and began to rescue the crew.

Incredibly, they were able to get everyone away from the flaming wreck before it blew.

The captain, Commander Nick Tobin, escaped only five minutes before the blast shook the entire anchorage. Flames, smoke, and debris burst from the hull as the ship was blown apart. Thousands of troops ashore watched and photographers on nearby ships captured some of the most vivid photos of the entire war. Following the main blast, a series of smaller explosions continued over the next several hours.

In the morning, Mike and Tony looked down at the wreck that had been a mighty warship only the day before. Her back was broken and she settled slowly into the water, bow and stern gently slipping beneath the surface, leaving only a few life rafts and a handful of sailor caps bobbing on the water. It was a bitter loss and Mike felt it as much as any of the troops around him, but he was still surprised when he heard the savage rancor in Tony's voice.

"Don't you write about this, Yank. You wait until we get those Argies in our gunsights and then we'll give you something to write about. There's going to be some bloody payback and I aim to have my share of it." Mike was still in shock from all he'd seen. This was war: loud, savage, and unforgiving. He had expected heroics, and seen heroics in the rescue of those who could be saved, but now all he felt was vulnerable.

The next day, they learned that *Atlantic Conveyor* had been sunk by an Exocet missile. This enormous cargo ship, the same ship that followed *Norland* down 8,000 miles of the North and South Atlantic, was packed with vital supplies. Mike had watched it majestically plow through the waves and marveled at the size and power of it. After the missile strike, the ship was consumed by flames and had to be abandoned in 90 minutes. A dozen men were lost, including Captain Ian North, a much-loved 57-year-old veteran of the Second World War. He was the last man to leave the ship and swam to a life-raft, but finding it full, he made for another raft and disappeared before reaching it.

The *Atlantic Conveyor* had carried all the tents for the troops ashore, medical supplies, spare parts for helicopters and Harriers, many vehicles, and a storehouse of bombs. Most grievous of all, she took nine helicopters to the bottom, including three Chinooks capable of carrying 60 men each. These giant helicopters, costing three and half million pounds apiece, were the linchpin of the British drive across the islands. Without them, the troops would have to walk the hundred kilometers to Stanley. By sinking this one ship, the Argentines had changed the British strategy for winning the war, their tactics, and their timetable.

Chapter Twenty-Two

May 25, 1982
Sussex Mountain, East Falkland

Brigadier General Julian Thompson, commander of all five thousand British troops on East Falkland, had no intention of attacking the Argentine garrison at Goose Green. His plan was to bottle up those Argentine forces and pass right by them on the way to Stanley. The Argentines were positioned on a thin isthmus of land between East Falkland and Lafonia, the third largest island in the Falklands. The five hundred Argentine troops there were heavily dug in making them hard to attack, but easy to isolate.

Then politics reared its ugly head. In London, the war planners were terrified that diplomatic pressure from the United Nations and the major countries around the world would compel the British to halt their forces where they stood and conduct negotiations that could drag on for months. That would be intolerable. It would leave the British ground forces out in the open, without tents, as winter set in, while the Argentines would occupy the buildings of Stanley and the outlying settlements.

The newspapers and broadcast news agencies of Great Britain made matters worse by demanding action. It had been five days since troops had landed on the Falklands. Why hadn't they moved forward to attack? What was the holdup? Why weren't there any stories of British success in retaking the islands?

Meanwhile, logistics planners on the beach were frantically trying to reorganize the whole strategy of the war following the loss of *Atlantic Conveyor* and the nine helicopters that went down with her. Now the troops would have to walk the sixty miles to Stanley, at the start of winter, carrying their rifles and mortars and the shells they would fire.

The last thing Thompson wanted was a diversionary side battle that would take up a substantial portion of his fighting forces and waste resources he would need later for the assault on the main objective: Stanley. But the military leadership in London assessed both the political and the military situations and determined that a quick victory was required. They ordered that Goose Green, the second largest concentration of Argentine forces in the Falklands, be attacked and taken.

———————•••———————

Tony Banks wearily made his way up the path to the crest of Sussex Mountain where he found his friends Baz Grayling and Steve Dixon already seated outside their shelter drinking tea.

"Enjoy our evening's outing, did you?" Steve inquired.

Dixon was one of Tony's closest friends in the regiment. A young Essex boy, he was as kind and generous as anyone Tony had ever met. Steve had been with Tony all through training, one of the thirty members of their platoon, young men who slept together, ate together, played and fought together, and pledged to protect each other against all harm. Tony didn't mind the raillery from his friend, but it didn't mitigate his frustration.

They had made a futile march of five miles toward Goose Green, a grueling four-hour footslog in the dark, slipping on rocks and tussock grass, wading through streams and stumbling through the fog, while cursing softly but colorfully. Then the attack had been cancelled mid-march and they had turned around and trudged back to Sussex where they climbed the mountain again; all in the pitch black, freezing night.

"I'm pissed off and knackered" Tony said. "This is a royal cock-up if ever there was one. This is what you get for letting the brass make battle decisions from eight thousand miles away." He lay belts of ammunition down and checked their shelter to see that his Bergen and sleeping bag were still where he had left them.

"Oh, I don't think the crap-hats in London did the dirty to us on this one," Baz said.

"No," Steve agreed, "this bit of foul play came from Brigade on the beach. I was with Col. H when he got the news. He was royally pissed. You should have heard him: 'I've waited twenty years for this' he said 'and now some fucking marine's cancelled it!' He's a feisty dog, that one."

Lieutenant Colonel Herbert Jones, universally known as "H" because he loathed his first name, led the attack on Goose Green. H was 42 years old, a graduate of Eton who had served with the Devon and Dorset Regiment before joining 2 Para in 1980. Tall, handsome, and charming, H had a boyish passion about him, a quick temper, and a devastating smile. His codename was Sunray. He was intolerant in some ways—he wouldn't suffer fools. But when he made a decision, he was usually right.

The day before, they had been ordered to get their fighting kit together and attack Goose Green. The general belief was that the Argies' morale was low and they would probably crumble if attacked forcefully. In a land attack, a ratio of two or three British troops to each defender was considered optimal. This would be an even fight, at least in numbers, but against a well dug-in enemy. The planners felt confident of success if enough fire power could be brought to bear. They, of course, would not be going with the troops making the attack.

That evening, 2 Para assembled in "fighting order," which meant no Bergens, no sleeping bags, just 48 hours of arctic rations and what they would need to fight. Tony was the number two man on the "Gimpy," the general purpose machine gun, so he carried nothing but ammunition belts filling his pack, his pockets, and webbing. Once loaded, he and 450 other troops from 2 Para set off for Goose Green, eleven miles away. They moved down the mountain at 8:00 pm, concealed beneath the cover of darkness, in a long, single file.

After four hours, they were ordered back. It was infuriating!

Tony was still fuming at dawn as he sat on the ground next to Grayling and took a cup of tea Steve offered him. "Damned poor war-making if you ask me. Who the hell orders an attack and then cancels it four hours later?"

Baz nodded his head sagely. "Trust the gods; we mere mortals know so little."

"Oh, piss off, mate" Tony said.

They were still resting with their tea a few minutes later when Mike Ferrol came up the path from the beach. Mike was also frustrated, but for different reasons.

"Well, I finally got clearance to go with the troops on further missions" Mike said. "Last night, the deployment officer actually refused to let me join the raid on Goose Green. Said they already had two correspondents going and didn't need to be looking after another."

"Bully for him" Tony replied. "Saved you a night of pointless marching. Enjoy your beauty rest, did you?"

"Look, I'm a journalist. I need to see what is happening down here. I should not have missed last night's mission and I won't miss the next. I've seen to that."

"How'd you do that?" Steve asked.

"I went to H directly and pled my case. Told him I spoke fluent Spanish and it would be wise to take me along."

"Well, I do admire your spunk," Tony said. "Let's hope the Argies don't blow your bollocks off."

Getting clearance to go on future 2 Para missions had not been as easy as Mike made it sound. He'd had trouble getting past H's adjutant who wanted to know why he needed to see the colonel and what he was asking for. It surprised Mike because he had had no difficulty speaking with the colonel on board *Norland* during the trip down to the Falklands.

Mike had interviewed H twice for different articles he was writing and found him affable and down to earth. He didn't mince words or avoid hard topics. It was easy to understand why his men loved him. He was gung-ho without being arrogant; decisive, but open to input from others. He inspired trust and carried himself with the casual confidence and military bearing that let you know he loved what he was doing. Now, Mike felt lucky to be covering his first major battle, though he had no idea when that would be. He soon found out.

The next afternoon, the raid on Goose Green was back on.

That evening Mike loaded a small pack with his arctic rations, a pad, and two pens. He considered bringing a camera, but then thought better of it. This wouldn't be a holiday in Brighton. He had been offered a sidearm, but declined it. He hoped to stay just back of the action and preserve his objectivity. He wondered what he had gotten himself into.

When Col. Jones returned from an urgent "O" (orders) meeting at brigade, he assembled his officers to brief them. Mike was allowed to observe the planning session. It would be a surprise nighttime raid in darkness, since darkness was the only cover they would have. It would be short, sharp, vicious, and very noisy. The plan was to overwhelm the enemy before they could recover after realizing they were under attack.

The challenge they faced was that Goose Green was located on the southern end of an isthmus of land, only a mile wide and five miles long. It could only be attacked from the north and had been heavily fortified by the Argentines. There was no natural cover so the fighting would have to be done out in the open and there were 110 islanders living in the settlement. Goose Green had a small grass airfield, but the Pucara attack planes had been moved back to Stanley.

The troops would have to march to the battle carrying their own weapons and ammunition, but a British helicopter would be able to haul three 105 mm field guns to Camilla Creek House where they could shell the Argentine forces after 2 Para had secured it. *HMS Arrow* would be brought into range and would fire her 4.5 inch cannon against the garrison. Weather permitting, Harriers from *Hermes* would also bomb and strafe the Argentines. But even with this support, it was clear the bulk of the fighting would be left to the exposed ground forces.

Mike made the seven-hour march in the dark over broken ground and invisible clumps of moon grass. There were many fits and starts. The man in front of Mike fell twice and had to be helped up and have his load redistributed. At about 3 am, they saw a red torch ahead that signaled that Camilla Creek House had been secured. Four hundred and fifty weary men took shelter anywhere in the house or the surrounding sheds where they could get out of the wind and find a bit of warmth. Mike and Tony tucked in together in one of the sheds. They dozed and shivered without sleeping bags or blankets.

Dawn revealed that the house and sheds lay in a hollow invisible to the Argentine line 500 yards ahead. H, confident of their safety and security from view, planned to let his men rest during the day before launching an attack that night. This would give them the chance to dry out and prepare for battle. The cover of darkness and the swift surprise of their assault would then overwhelm the enemy.

But during the morning, men listening to the BBC's World Service news bulletin heard the astounding announcement that 2 Para was five miles from Darwin and was set to attack Goose Green. The battalion was first shocked, then enraged. No one was angrier than Col. H Jones, whose stream of profanity became legendary in the regiment. He swore he would sue the BBC and the Secretary of State for Defense if any of his men were killed.

The revelation of their position and intentions meant the house was no longer a safe haven, and H ordered the men to move out of the crowded shelter of the buildings and dig in across a widely dispersed defensive area. The element of surprise was now lost to them.

At noon, a British recon patrol south of Camilla House spotted a blue Land Rover advancing up the track toward them. They waited until the Argentines were close, then opened fire. Two of the three soldiers in the Land Rover were wounded when they surrendered, but they were taken before they could use their radio. One of the captives was the commanding officer of the enemy's reconnaissance platoon. He arrogantly revealed that the Goose Green garrison was substantially stronger than the weak deployment the British had expected. H was furious and demanded "What the hell have the SAS been doing down here?" The prisoners were given medical assistance and taken back to San Carlos.

At 4 pm, 2 Para's officers crouched in a half circle around Col. H as he gave them the battle plan. He described it as "a six-phase, night-day, silent-noisy battalion attack to capture Darwin and Goose Green." The aim was to dispose of the enemy's outer positions in darkness, then seize the settlements in daylight. The plan was to march forward in silence, then, when contact was made with the Argentines and fighting began, call in the mortars and 105 mm guns and "shell them hard, then move in fast." But British intelligence had completely underestimated both the strength and the resolve of the Argentine forces. The easy victory they anticipated turned into a bloody struggle that was much harder fought than either side had expected.

Tony Banks moved off the start line north of Burntside Pond and into the dark, cold night heading south toward the enemy. A cold rain began as D Company moved down the isthmus. The rain was probably a good thing, Tony thought, covering the sound of their approach. The Argie sentries might lay low in their trenches to keep dry, and not see them coming. Tony's pulse was up and he felt fear and excitement in equal measures. This was what he'd trained for, waited for, dreamt of.

When the fighting erupted, it was a sudden roar that tore into the quiet of the night. Mike had never seen anything like it. Machine guns and rifle fire were punctuated by rockets and mortar explosions. Mike ducked down as colored tracer bullets came cutting through the air. Shelling from the 105s began dropping on the Argentine lines, followed by shells from the 4.5-inch gun on the frigate *Arrow*. The Argentines returned fire with their 105s, mortars, machine guns, and rifles. Mike lost track of where Tony and the troops were advancing ahead.

D Company was quickly driven to ground and Tony realized the fire from the enemy's machine guns was very accurate and coming from multiple angles. It was hard to know where the guns were located. He felt terrified and disoriented, but then, as the adrenalin kicked in, so did the training that had been driven into his head. "Define your objectives. Open lines of fire. Keep your mates safe. Trust your training." Despite the shouts and screams he heard on all sides, the explosions and the general bedlam of warfare, Tony's senses were elevated and he felt as alive as he had ever been.

Then, amid the roar of battle, Tony heard an inhuman shrieking unlike any sound he had ever heard. "What the hell was that?" he shouted. He turned around and saw a terrible sight: silhouetted against a burning farm building, wild horses were running free in the smoke and flames, rearing up on their hind legs, pawing the air in torment. *Terrified by the madness of men,* Tony thought. A tragic tableau, but he could do nothing.

Mike Ferrol also saw the horses, desperate in their fright. They were running toward him and he realized these dumb creatures were the only ones doing anything sensible. Mike watched in awe as the battle erupted around him. Despite the ghost-like flashes of light and the explosions that pounded the air, it was actually quite beautiful. Tracers in green, red, and white crisscrossed the battle field and the rattling machine guns struck a cadence all their own. The Argentines began firing shamooli flares at the British. Designed to be launched like rockets to illuminate the battlefield, the flares were instead being fired directly at the forces advancing toward them. In the furor of the battle, it was impossible to see who was winning, whether the British were advancing or being torn to pieces where they lay.

Tony, in the heart of the battle, realized that his fear had disappeared and for the first time in a week, he did not feel cold.

He saw the battlefield before him with amazing clarity: it was kill or be killed and he need only keep moving forward, whatever it took, to survive. In the dark pure chaos of that night, men were screaming in terror and pain, but all that mattered was to keep up the momentum. Drive forward, take cover wherever it can be found, in any little dip in the ground or up a hollow, then hold until your mates can leapfrog past you. Keep moving until you get close enough to hurl a phosphorus grenade into their trenches, then listen for the screams and the death to follow.

Tony felt a twinge at the periphery of his conscience, a vague sense that something in this activity was not right, but he pushed this down deep and gave it no more thought. He was in the shit now and there was no chance but to go through to the end. He stayed focused on feeding the belts of bullets into the Gimpy while Wayne Rees poured a stream of destruction onto the enemy. They were taking hits, but the Argentines were taking more. All he'd been taught since joining the Territorial Army and then the Paratroop Regiment now focused his movements and actions. *Move forward,* he thought, *get the job done.*

When D Company got to Coronation Ridge, they were pinned down by a machine-gun nest. Lance Corporal Gary Bingley and his number two, Baz Grayling, moved forward to take position with their machine-gun. Bingley fired from the hip while running forward, killing two Argentine soldiers, but then took a bullet to the head and went down. Grayling was also wounded.

Watching them fall, Tony realized the gun that dropped on the ground between them was one of only three machine-guns the company had. It had to be recovered. He bolted upright and ran the 15 yards to where the men lay. It was pitch dark, but in the flashes of light he could see where they were. Tony lay on the ground and took Bingley's arm, but it was heavy and limp. Lifeless. Grayling lay moaning on the ground, but Tony discovered he had only been hit in his metal water bottle. Still, he was in pain and resisted moving.

"Come on you bastard!" Tony shouted, "we've got to go!" Pulling Grayling by one arm and holding the machine-gun with the other,

Tony dragged them back to their lines. Soon other troops moved forward and a well-placed phosphorus grenade gave a terrible death to the Argentines who had been firing at them. No sooner had the machine-gun nest been eliminated than sniper fire opened up. This kept the Paras held back until the anti-tank units moved forward and began firing Milan missiles at the snipers with devastating effect.

Breakfast time came and went, but there was no time for eating. The mission was far behind schedule and they were nowhere near the settlement buildings they were supposed to attack in daylight. After dropping 134 shells on the Argentine positions with their rapid-firing 4.5 inch gun, *Arrow* had to withdraw when the gun jammed. Mortars and shells for the 105s were nearly gone and bad weather precluded any attacks by Harriers. To make matters worse, the Argentines were fighting much harder than anyone had expected. Now it was up to the ground forces to fight on without the support of the bombardment they had counted on.

Around noon, word came that Sunray, Col. H, was down. The British had reached an impasse on their left flank when they were stopped by eleven mutually supporting trenches on Darwin Hill. To break through, Col. Jones had led a one-man assault up the hill, calling out "Follow me!" as he went forward past entrenched Argentine positions. He was brought down by small arms fire from behind him and fell to the ground. His men were able to retrieve him, but watched helpless as he slipped into death. His passing rippled through the British ground forces and men paused to mourn the loss of a friend as well as a leader. But the battle went on and everyone realized his death would not be the last.

On the right flank, D Company moved around the entrenched Argentine defense line along a beach below the Boca House ruins. They encountered a mine field and Tony's friend Taff told him he saw one man step on a mine and be blown up in the air and tossed to the ground like a rag doll. Then, incredibly, the man got back up, dusted himself off, picked up his rifle and moved forward. The Argentines, it seemed, had buried their mines too deep and most of the blast was absorbed by the peaty ground. Taff later said to

Tony, "The Argies must have thought we were fucking supermen!" But few British troops who touched off mines were so lucky.

Foot by foot, the attack proceeded. Milan missiles were fired into the Argentine trenches with devastating effect tearing bodies apart and killing others with the force of concussion. Tony followed the lead unit of D Company as they furtively moved around the far edge of the main Argentine defense line. Crouching and firing, he crossed the isthmus heading toward the schoolhouse. When he was out in the open, a Pucara attack plane came roaring down at them with its cannons blazing. The Paras pointed every gun they had and returned fire. Suddenly smoke trailed from the plane and it crashed to the ground. A cheer rose up from the troops and they continued forward.

The schoolhouse proved to be heavily fortified and the British were taking fire from trenches surrounding it as well. Tony heard a cry and saw Steve Dixon go down. *Jesus,* Tony thought, *I hope he hasn't bought it.* Desperate to save him, Tony ran to where Steve lay, but the color was already draining from his face and he was turning a bluish grey. His breathing was shallow and Tony realized he was about to die. In the horror of what Tony saw, the sounds of the battlefield faded away. A young boy's life was ending, a dear friend leaving him forever, and Tony was powerless to stop it.

Steve gave a sigh and uttered his last word: "Mum" and a single tear ran down his face. Then he was dead. Tony felt he could not breathe and this was harder to endure than anything he had ever experienced. It was more than the loss of life, it was the loss of innocence as well. Steve Dixon was dead and part of Tony died with him.

The fighting at the schoolhouse continued for another bloody hour. Finally, Platoon commander Jim Barry and two other soldiers approached the building under a white flag to try and negotiate a surrender. But as they returned to their lines, the Argentines opened fire and all three men were shot dead. A fury erupted among the British soldiers. "You dirty spic bastards! Filthy dagos! Greasy wop bastards!"

The British poured every ounce of firepower they had onto the schoolhouse. The Paras unleashed 66 mm rockets, Carl Gustav rounds and machine-gun fire into the building until it caught fire. When the British entered the schoolhouse later, they found only a dozen burnt and shot up corpses. There was no one left to surrender.

———————•••———————

At 11:45 am the next morning, Army Lieutenant-Colonel Italo Piaggi and Air Force Vice-Comodoro Wilson Pedroza formally surrendered the Argentine forces holding Goose Green. Mike Ferrol stood in the square as 500 unarmed men marched out to surrender. These, however, turned out to be only the Air Force personnel. They were followed by almost a thousand army officers and men, making a total of nearly 1500 Argentine troops attacked and overtaken by 450 British troops. As Mike watched these dirty, tired troops move past, he saw the shame and confusion they felt at being defeated by such a small force.

As part of the agreement to surrender, the Argentine leaders were allowed to hold a brief ceremony. Their troops were lined up, sang a verse of their national anthem, and were given a speech praising them for fighting well and assuring them that this defeat was not their fault. The officers were then taken to San Carlos and their men were moved into the sheep sheds and out buildings. Within days, the defeated Argentine soldiers were loaded onboard the *Norland,* the same ship Mike had taken to the islands, and returned to Argentina.

Mike was present when the 110 residents of Goose Green were released from the church and the village hall where they had been held captive for a month. There was enormous relief at being alive and safe, and many hugs and kisses were given to the troops who saved them. Mike spoke with the settlement manager, Eric Goss, and was given a tour of the bullet-torn houses of the residents. They had been vandalized and looted in the last hours of the Argentine defense.

Afterward, Mike walked around the battlefield and down into the abandoned Argentine trenches. He saw scenes of unspeakable horror, a landscape of nauseating carnage and destruction. The Argentine bodies had not been cleared and few had suffered clean, quick deaths. They had been blown apart, burned beyond recognition, bled to death as their entrails fell from their bodies. Heads and faces were missing and limbs were lying about like discarded rubbish. Most eerie of all were those struck dead with a single shot, staring ahead in shocked surprise, mouths gaping, eyes open, looking forward.

Sickened and unable to look at the dead any longer, Mike shifted his gaze to the trenches and defensive positions. Many were partially covered and had served as homes for the troops defending the outpost. They were stinking and filthy to a shocking degree. Helmets, rifles, packs, cartridge belts, canteens, shoes, ammo boxes, shell cases, all the detritus of war lay about, as well as personal items: toy cars, comic books, letters from home, photos, and discarded clothing. The weapons left behind were a curious testament to their Catholic faith. Pictures of the Lord and the Virgin Mary were taped to the butts of their guns. A rosary was casually draped over a machine-gun.

Most disgusting of all was the smell of the trenches. Aside from the stench of blood and guts trapped under the trench roofs, the Argentine troops didn't routinely use latrines. They defecated everywhere, leaving little piles of crap dotted with pink toilet paper. In some areas, it was hard to breathe and Mike wondered how they had lived together for weeks like this and why their officers would allow it.

Mike stepped out of one of the longer trenches and surveyed the battlefield again. There were blast holes and burning gorse everywhere, piles of spent shells and broken equipment amid embankments shored up to withstand assault. Two thousand soldiers had fought over this little village and now the 110 permanent residents of Goose Green would have to clean it up and turn it back into a safe farming community. Once the bodies were removed and buried, they would still have to fill in the trenches, restore their homes, and fence off the fields still strewn with mines. The cost of all that needed to be done would be enormous, and the work would not happen quickly with winter setting in.

This, Mike thought, *is what victory looks like; defeat as well. It is all the same.*

What he saw, he could not write about. Readers in Britain did not want to know how this place actually smelled and what it looked like. So he would tell the stories of gallantry and courage, how superior tactics and plain luck had won the day. 55 Argentines died here and 17 British. It was lopsided enough to make the sacrifice inspiring.

Chapter Twenty-Three

May 31, 1982
Engineers Point, East Falkland

Rey saw the section of tarp that served as a doorway to their shelter pulled back and Armando stepped out of the rain into the shelter.

"Where is your corporal and your friend Sonny?" Army asked Jury.

"Gone back to the airport to fetch water and supplies. But these trips usually take them hours. We don't know when they'll be back." Jury shrugged his shoulders.

Rey sat up on the bedroll where he had been resting and wrapped the blanket around his shoulders. It was cold in their shelter and they could hear the light rain striking the tarp that served as their roof. The tarp was holding up well and still kept them relatively dry. Army laid down the pack he had brought with him and found a place on the floor where he could lay out his wet rain poncho and sit down. Rey began coughing deeply.

"You don't sound so good" Army said.

After catching his breath, Rey replied "I have a lot of congestion in my chest. We've been stuck out here for three weeks, freezing our *cojones* off. Everything is damp. I feel rotten."

"Well, maybe this will cheer you up." Army opened his pack and brought out a tin with fancy European lettering on it. "Hot chocolate mix from Belgium. Jury, brew up some water and we'll restore our friend to the land of the living."

Jury quickly set to work with the burner. "What's the news?" Jury asked.

"None of it is good. We lost 1,500 men at Goose Green, dead or captured. The damn British are moving faster than anyone thought they could and we're just sitting and waiting for them to come. I don't think Menéndez knows how to use his men or his generals. He had Piaggi's 12th Regiment posted to Goose Green, a useless bunch of conscripts who couldn't defend a chicken coop. Then they sent in Pedroza from the Air Force, who outranked Piaggi, but he was only in charge of the Air Force staff so no one knew who was in over all command. Then two days before the place was attacked, Menéndez appointed General Parada to take command of the whole area and ordered him to move his headquarters to Goose Green.

"But Parada liked his house in Stanley and delayed moving. When the attack came, he tried to fight the battle by radio. He had no idea what the place looked like or how to defend it. At the last minute, they flew in a company by helicopter to reinforce the garrison, but it was too late and too little. The next morning they surrendered."

"Do you think they will be coming for us here?" Rey asked.

"Oh, they're coming all right."

The three men sat in silence, holding the cups of chocolate Jury had given them.

Jury rubbed the side of his cup thoughtfully. "What are the chances we will live through this?"

Army laughed. "Oh, things aren't that bad. Listen, 55 men were killed out of 1,500 at Goose Green. That's less than four percent. So even if the British beat us, just keep your head down and make sure you're among the 96% who go home. We're okay. We're all going to make it back, especially me. I've got plans."

"Yeah?" Jury said. "What are your plans?"

"My brother runs the docks at Bahia Blanca. He has two hundred men working for him and we're going into business together, shipping in goods from the Far East. We're going to make a lot of money. And the place is wonderful: white sand beaches, great nightclubs, and *very* sexy women! It's practically paradise."

"Well," Jury said, "one man's paradise is another man's perdition. I'm going to college. I already have a scholarship to the University of Montevideo. Then I'm going to teach."

Army gave Rey's shoulder a push. "What about you, Private Poralez? What's your future look like?"

Jury spoke up before Rey could reply. "Oh, his plans are all tied up with that picture he carries in his shirt pocket."

Army was immediately interested and reached over to Rey, signaling with his hand that he wanted Rey to give him the picture. "Let's see what your future holds."

Rey shook his head, but after both his friends stared at him, he finally relented and took out the picture of Marisol and handed it to Army.

"Well...I see what you're talking about. She is *very* pretty. But I'm sorry to have to say this...well, she is also *very* young. Are you sure she's interested in older men?"

Army and Jury laughed together. Rey tried to look exasperated, but couldn't help smiling himself. He was very proud of Marisol and it showed. Rey was about to speak when another coughing spell overtook him. When it subsided, he breathed deeply and wiped his mouth with toilet tissue. Then he took back his picture of Marisol and put it into the shirt pocket above his heart.

Over the next week, Rey's condition got worse. He was running a fever and had trouble standing his watch. He had already used up most of their meager supply of toilet paper to catch the phlegm he was coughing up. He was pale and had almost stopped eating. Jury forced him to keep drinking so he wouldn't become dehydrated.

"He needs to go to the hospital" Jury told Corporal Cabruja.

"It's just a cold" Cabruja said, "it will pass."

"It's more than a cold. He has been hacking all night. He needs medical attention."

Cabruja grunted. "He needs to stand his watch like the rest of us. Keep him moving. He'll get over it. And we will need him here for what's coming." He looked at Sonny and the two of them nodded to each other as though they shared some secret knowledge.

At one o'clock in the morning, Rey collapsed while standing watch with Jury. He was too weak to get up and Jury had to drag him into the shelter and put him into his sleeping bag. Then he covered him with both of their blankets. Jury went back outside and stood the rest of their watch alone.

The next morning, Army came into their shelter and said "Wake up! I have orders for all of you..." Then he saw Rey's condition and realized Rey could not get up.

"What has happened to Private Poralez?" Army went to him and felt his forehead. "This man is burning up! Why hasn't he been sent to the hospital?"

Cabruja looked at him sorrowfully. "It's just a cold. He'll get over it."

Army looked closely at his friend Rey. His skin was pale and damp, his breathing shallow, and he had dark rings under his eyes.

"This is no cold, you fool. Look at him. He needs to be seen by a doctor. Jury, help me get him up." They washed Rey's face with a damp cloth and got him to drink some water. Finally they were able to get him to stand, but Army had to steady him.

"I'm taking this man back to the hospital. Right now."

Cabruja shifted his position to face Army. "What are these orders you have for us?"

Army took a folded paper from his pocket and handed it to the corporal. "You are going to move out. Today. Pack all your gear and haul it to the airfield by 2:00 pm. Take everything except the poles under your roof. Leave those here. A truck will meet you at the west end of the airfield and take you to your next post. You're going to Wireless Ridge."

"Will there be a shelter there where Rey can recover?" Jury asked.

"No. You'll be out in the open and you'll have to dig or build your own shelter. Bring the tarps and all your shovels and equipment. Don't be late to the airfield."

Cabruja pointed to Rey. "If you're taking him, how are we supposed to carry all this to the airfield?" He swung his arm around indicating all they would have to take.

"Make multiple trips. After your first trip, leave a man with your supplies, then two of you can return for what's left. Just be damned sure you get to the truck by 2:00 pm or it will go badly for you."

Cabruja grunted.

The trip to the hospital was like a feverish dream to Rey. His chest was on fire and he desperately wanted to rest. Back in the shelter, he had heard the words they were speaking, but his mind could not process them. Now he just did what he was told to do. Army pulled him along holding him up by one arm. Rey only wanted it to be over, to lay down and close his eyes.

Rey fell once while they were walking and after that, Army let them stop to rest a couple times to keep him going. It took a full two hours to walk the three miles back to the airfield, but once there, Army was able to flag down a Land Rover that was willing to take Rey to the hospital in Stanley.

The next two days were a blur for Rey. He was taken into the army side of the hospital where he fell asleep in the waiting area before the doctor could see him. He was diagnosed with pneumonia and finally given a bed in a large room with rows of beds. Next to him lay another soldier who had been shot in the hip at Goose Green. He had been helicoptered out before the surrender, but now he was in great pain and frequently moaned in agony. In his own delirium, Rey was never sure if the sound came from the soldier or himself.

When he woke up in the afternoon of the second day, Rey felt a little better. The penicillin and aspirin he'd been given were taking effect. But his lungs still ached from coughing and he could only take a little food. He asked an attendant for writing materials so he could send a letter to Marisol. He had tucked an envelop into his shirt, meaning to write to her before he became ill. This was one of their private letters and he had memorized the address.

My Dearest Marisol,
I don't know if I can write to you today, but I will try. I

*am quite sick and my mind is foggy. I am in the hospital with
pneumonia. They try to feed me, but my stomach does not
want food in it and when I drink the water they give me, it
tastes bitter. It is very noisy here, day and night, and I'm never
sure if I am sleeping or awake. I think the war and the weather
and living outdoors for three weeks have beaten me down. My
spirits are very low.*

*As I lie in this bed, I've been dreaming about Teatro
Colón, the huge opera house in Buenos Aires. My father took
me there once when I was nine years old, but not to hear the
opera. We went in the afternoon when a flautist was giving a
performance in one of the side auditoriums. At the time, I was
taking flute lessons and my father hoped this would inspire me
to practice more. It had the opposite effect. Once I heard how
beautifully the instrument could be played, I realized I would
never rise to that level and I lost interest. I quit the lessons a
few weeks later.*

*It all swirls together in my mind: my childhood, today,
tomorrow. Even lying here in a warm bed, I still hear the
bombs falling on the airfield and feel the rain out on the point.
It's never a full rain, just a steady light mist, a grey apparition
of rain filling the air, seeping into clothes and blankets, pulling
the warmth out of my body. The wind, the rain, and the night
all conspire to rob my thoughts. My brain cannot function for
long periods and I cling to the rocks of our outpost like some
crustacean, waiting for something to happen. Forgive me, I'm
rambling now.*

*It is only thoughts of you that carry me forward. Whatever
life lies ahead for either of us, or both of us, I only pray to
see you one more time, to know you are real and I have not
imagined all of this.*

Hold me in your heart, I beg you.

*With all my love,
Reynaldo*

An hour later, a doctor appeared with two attendants. He took Rey's temperature, wrote some notes on a clipboard, and told him he was discharged. Rey protested, but the doctor turned and walked away.

"We have wounded coming in" one of the attendants said. "We need the bed."

They helped him out of bed, holding his arms until he got his footing. One of them even helped him get his uniform back on. Then he was given two envelops of pills and told he must report to the transportation center at the west end of town. He was being sent to someplace called Wireless Ridge. Rey had no idea where that was.

Out on the street, a cold wind was blowing and the sky was overcast. Rey saw the change in the town since he had last been here. The pavement in the streets was broken and there was mud everywhere. The green grass that had covered the playing fields and paddocks was now brown and lifeless, trampled by thousands of soldiers. Fences had been torn up and burned for campfires. A truck rolled past him and he saw an arm hanging beneath the canvas covering. The smell of death was unmistakable. They were headed to the cemetery and a moment later they were followed by a Land Rover loaded with wooden crosses.

Rey asked a couple soldiers where the post office was and they pointed him to the other end of town. He walked for several blocks before seeing it. Inside, a British woman behind the counter motioned to the army desk toward the back of the building. He thanked her and mailed his letter to Marisol.

He was more than a mile from the transportation center and he shuffled along, making the best time he could, but his legs were weary and he was still feverish. As block after block stretched out before him, he began to feel he might not be able to make this trip. He wondered if the pills they had given him were working. He took out the two envelops and read the directions written on them. One said that he should take two of the pills immediately upon leaving the hospital. He had not realized he was supposed to do that.

He opened the flap of the envelop and took out two of the white, oblong pills. Without water he could not swallow them. He looked around, but saw nowhere he could get a drink. There were soldiers walking by and riding past in trucks, but none of them had canteens and he was walking through a residential area without any public buildings. Finally, he saw a lone woman sweeping the walkway into her house.

It was against orders for soldiers to go into residential houses, but he felt faint and confused and desperate. He approached the woman. At first, she appeared a little frightened of him. But when he showed her the pills and mimicked taking them with a glass of water, she nodded and went into the house. Renaldo knew no English words and he realized this woman did not speak Spanish, but all he needed was the water. He wondered if she would report him to the authorities or bring out her family to force him back into the street.

The woman came out of her house holding a paper cup of water. She was older than Rey and quite pretty in an English sort of way, pale and soft-featured, but with strong hands that had worked hard. She held the cup out to him and he reached for it, but his hands were shaking and before he could drink, he spilled the water and dropped the pills. She spoke to him quietly now and guided him up the steps and onto the covered front porch of her house. It was a conservatory with three walls and the roof made of windows, all attached to the front of the house. After he went inside, she pulled a chair up to a table and motioned for him to sit down. It felt good to be sitting and out of the wind.

The woman went out into the yard and picked up the two pills Rey had dropped. She brushed them off and brought them back to the porch laying them on the table. Then she went inside and was gone for several minutes. Rey waited, unsure what else to do. He was too tired to move anyway. Finally, she returned with both a full glass of water and a bowl of soup.

The soup was made with white beans, leeks, and onions. It tasted better than anything Rey had eaten since landing on the islands. He felt enormously grateful and thanked her several times. It was the first time he had been able to truly hold down food in over a week.

Chapter Twenty-Four

June 7, 1982
Stanley, East Falkland

Jenny watched the soldier eat his soup. *He is very young,* she thought, *he cannot be more than a teenager.* The soup seemed to restore him and he began talking freely, even though they both knew she could not understand his words. But he was smiling now and was obviously thanking her. He wanted to share something with her and after a moment's hesitation, he took a photo out of his shirt and showed it to her.

The girl in the picture was very pretty and for a moment, Jenny thought perhaps it was his sister, but as he held it up for her, he touched his heart and it became clear: no, this was not his sister. She saw at once how proud he was of this crumpled little picture, how dear it was to him. Yet it struck her that here was a soldier, telling her about his love, whom he might never see again. It made her unspeakably sad, but he was smiling as he spoke so she smiled with him.

Before she realized they were coming, Grant and Comodoro Bloomer-Reeve stepped onto the porch. They stopped dead still and stared at Jenny and Rey sitting at the table.

"What's going on here?" Grant asked. Rey jumped to his feet and saluted the Comodoro.

"This soldier is sick" Jenny said, "I've given him some soup."

The Comodoro said a few words in Spanish to Rey who left the conservatory and waited outside on the walkway to the house.

"Carlos" Jenny said, "please don't punish him. I invited him to come up onto the porch. He nearly collapsed out on the lawn. He needed to take some medications and I gave him water. Then I gave him a bowl of soup. That's all that happened here."

Bloomer-Reeve looked dubious, but nodded his head. "He will not be disciplined, but he should not have been here. I will send him away."

"Wait. Before he goes, will you tell him something for me?"

"What?"

"Tell him..." Jenny struggled to find the right words, "tell him his girlfriend is very lovely and I hope they will soon see each other again."

Carlos shook his head, but he was smiling. "Yes, I will tell him."

After Reynaldo left, Jenny, Grant, and Carlos went inside the house where Jenny made them tea. They sat around the kitchen table and Jenny opened a tin of sugared biscuits.

"Where is your son?" Carlos asked.

"My mother has taken him down the street to play with Lonnie Forbes. We try to get him out of the house every day. Now that the curfew is from 4:30 to 8:30 the next morning, he gets very bored inside the house. But it worries me with the fighting getting closer."

"Yes, I understand." Carlos shook his head. "It's a bad business, for both sides."

"But it's worse for your side, isn't it?" Grant looked at Carlos intently.

"It would be...indiscreet for me to answer."

"We're worried about all the gun emplacements you've put around town" Grant said. "Are you really planning to keep fighting, street-by-street? We still have 800 residents living in town. Many are children and the elderly. If you don't surrender soon, a lot of civilians are going to get killed."

"It's not my decision. I don't decide military strategy. I'm only here to liaison with the residents."

"But Carlos..."

Jenny took Grant's hand before he could continue. "I know you're trying to help us," she said, "and we appreciate it. But the bombing keeps getting closer. We don't want to be in a war zone." As if to punctuate what she was saying, an enormous blast came from the airfield and the house shook, rattling the dishes and cutlery. It was followed by the roar of two Harrier jets passing overhead. Then anti-aircraft guns opened up, but they were just a little late.

"I assure you, we are doing everything we can to prevent injury to civilians. I'm sorry for the disruption to your lives."

"It's more than just disruption, Carlos, our lives have stopped. Neither my husband nor I can work, there is no school for our child, we sleep in a hole in the ground under the porch, we can't even go to the library."

"I thought the library was open?"

"Yes, it's open, but the town hall is being used as a casualty center and they've only strung up curtains to separate it from the library. The stench of the wounded and the unwashed is overpowering. There are men dying on the other side of that curtain and we can hear them moaning. How do you think I feel taking my six-year-old son into that building, holding his hand because he's frightened by the soldiers and their guns?"

Carlos put down his cup and shook his head. "I am so sorry for what you are going through. I wish I could tell you when this will end, but I cannot."

Grant picked up one of the biscuits and held it above his plate. "Do you know what happened yesterday when I went into Jimmy's Emporium to buy these biscuits and some groceries? Before I got to the store, I turned the corner and three soldiers stopped me and gave me a shopping list: three bottles of gin, some tonic water and a bottle of whiskey. They said to me: "Get this for us old chap," in perfect English."

"What did you say to them?"

"I said 'Sorry, old chap. You're not getting any liquor.' Then an MP came from the doorway of the store and those three disappeared."

Carlos nodded sadly. "Yes, I'm afraid that has happened many times. That's why we have posted MPs at the entrances of the stores. Mostly the soldiers want food or cigarettes, but they also want liquor. Please let me know immediately if they threaten you with a firearm."

"Thank you, we will. But it is not just the inconvenience, Carlos. It's the loss of our property. Your soldiers have emptied the town warehouse of our bales of wool. They're stacking them around General Menéndez's headquarters to protect it from bombs and bullets. Those bales of wool are worth 500 pounds each and can't be left outdoors. We can't replace them. You're destroying our livelihood."

"Again, my friend, I am deeply sorry. But we have given you vouchers for everything we had requisitioned. The government of Argentina will compensate you for your losses."

Grant seemed to relent and sat back in his chair. "I'm sorry, Carlos, I don't mean to attack you. I just want you to know what is happening to us so you can tell the general about it."

"Believe me, I understand your frustration. I will do as much as I can."

"Thank you. I know you mean us no harm. I hope we can still be friends when all this is over. Would you like to see our shelter?"

"Most definitely."

Grant led Carlos into the living room where a hatch opened in the floor. A steep stairway led down to a small windowless underground room beneath the porch. It was 18 feet long, six feet wide, and four feet high. Grant turned on a light and crouched down to sit on one of the eight bed rolls that were rolled up on the floor. He pointed to the walls.

"The foundation around the porch is concrete blocks and the roof of this root cellar is poured concrete. It was laid on sheets of corrugated tin with iron joists. If the porch is blown apart or the house hit, the roof of this cellar should keep us safe from any falling debris. It's a little damp down here, but I've built a wooden floor raised up above the earth and covered that with rugs and linoleum. We're quite warm down here during the nightly air raids."

Carlos looked at the unfinished walls and the shelves of supplies. "Why are there eight sleeping bags? I thought it was just the four of you."

"No, our friends the Carltons are staying here at night along with their two teenage sons. They go back to their own home during the day to clean it up. Soldiers broke into it two nights ago, stole their food, and did extensive damage."

"I'm most sorry to hear that" Carlos said. He was sitting on another bedroll across from Grant. "When all of this has passed, they should make a claim with the authorities."

"Oh, I doubt if our authorities would honor such a claim."

Carlos smiled and did not appear offended. He knew too well how the war was going and who was likely to win. Grant wondered what it must be like to be in his position, but it was not something he could ask Carlos.

"What supplies have you brought down here?"

"We have spare blankets and pillows, candles, biscuits, cards and games. And, of course, the radio. It makes it possible to spend hours down here during attacks. I've hung a blanket at the end there so Darrell has sort of a separate bedroom since he goes to sleep earlier than the rest of us. Of course, we have to go upstairs to use the loo, but we try to avoid that as much as possible. We usually leave the hatch open and I've rigged a fan to bring in fresh air, but we close it when the bombing starts."

"Well, this is an impressive shelter. You've done good work here."

Suddenly, there was a great commotion upstairs and the sound of stamping feet and several male voices. A soldier shouted down the hatch into the shelter.

"YOU IN THE CELLAR! GET UP HERE. GET YOUR HANDS ABOVE YOUR HEAD!"

Grant climbed up the stairway to be confronted by a soldier pointing a rifle at him. He held up his hands. There were other armed soldiers in the living room. When he looked into the kitchen, he saw Jenny backed into a corner being confronted by a large Argentine officer. She looked terrified, but he could only stay where he was. In a moment, Carlos came up the stairway, but he did not raise his hands. He stood for a moment letting his rank sink into the soldier pointing a gun at him. In a moment of shocked silence, the soldier dropped his rifle to his side and saluted the Comodoro.

Carlos moved into the kitchen. "What is going on here?"

Major Patricio Dowling turned angrily to him. "Who the hell is speaking..." he said before he realized whom he was addressing.

"I am speaking" Carlos said, "Comodoro Bloomer-Reeve. And now, Major Dowling, you will tell your men to stand down and leave this house."

"I have not completed my search of these premises."

"By what authority do you search this house?"

"I am the Chief of Police. I am my own authority."

"Do you have a warrant? Has an investigative report been filed? Why are you searching this house?"

Major Dowling was clearly angry at this intrusion, but he held himself in check and looked at Carlos steadily. "It is my job to seek out saboteurs and counter any resistance from these British. They are not to be trusted."

"Well, you can trust this family. I will vouch for them. So take your men and leave."

Without another word, Dowling and his men left the house and soon disappeared down the street.

"He is not the best representative for your government" Grant said.

"Yes, I know. We have had complaints. He will not be here much longer."

"Thank you, Carlos" Jenny said. "He's a frightening man. I'm just glad Darrel and my mother weren't here to see this."

There was a brief awkward silence for a moment, then Grant said "Well, I don't think he will be coming back to this house any time soon and for that, we thank you."

"Tell me if he or his men do return. It is late and I should be returning to my office. Thank you for the tea and the tour of your shelter. I hope you will not need it much longer." He shook hands with Grant and left.

After he'd gone down the walkway and into the street, Grant turned to Jenny. "What did Major Dowling say to you?"

"He told me they were going to search the house and if I gave them any trouble, I would be shot. When I protested, he told me to shut my mouth. If you had not come up from the cellar then, I believe he would have struck me."

"Jesus" Grant said. He took his wife in his arms and held her tightly.

Chapter Twenty-Five

June 8, 1982
Fitzroy, East Falkland

Mike Ferrol sat on top of his Bergen rucksack, warming his hands with a cup of hot tea that Tony Banks had brewed on his hexamine burner. It didn't taste like much, but anything hot was a deliverance from the unremitting cold and wind. They were at Fitzroy, on a bluff overlooking Port Pleasant, a misnomer if ever there was one, at least in Tony's eyes. Mike was tired and cold, but grateful they hadn't had to march the 38 miles from Goose Green.

They'd been given a five-day break after the battle, time to help the townspeople start rebuilding their settlement; then word came down: they had more work to do. The whole of 2 Para would be moving up the road to Stanley, the final objective, and the fighting would be fierce when they got there. They still had a long way ahead.

The trip to Fitzroy had been dangerous and harrowing. It was Mike's first ride in a helicopter. It felt more like being herded into a cattle car that had been turned into an elevator. Seventy men had been packed into the hold of a giant Chinook chopper and stood with their Bergens at their feet, rifles held at their sides, from lift off to touch down. There were only a few tiny windows, no sound beyond the roar of the giant engines, and only the unwelcome smell of unwashed men and their gear. One shot from an Argentine Blowpipe missile could easily have brought them crashing down, but the flight went as smoothly as a Mayfield bus ride.

After arrival, they settled into large sheep sheds, crowding into the vacant pens. Those that arrived later had to settle for trenches that frequently filled with water and offered little shelter from the wind. They made bivouacs to protect against the elements, but everywhere the snow and moisture seeped into their clothing, bedding, and boots. Mike's handwritten notes for articles mushed together and became illegible as the ink ran across his pages. He imagined hauling a typewriter with him, but that was a silly notion.

As the days went on, more troops arrived. There were 1,200 of them camped around Fitzroy now and the logistics of providing food and medical attention were a challenge. No one knew when the big push would come, but it had to be soon.

Mike and Tony sat looking down at the bay where two of the *Sirs, Sir Galahad* and *Sir Tristram,* lay at anchor. Each of these smaller logistics ships carried 500 troops as well as tons of artillery ammunition, vehicles, medical supplies, a large consignment of petrol for the Rapier generators, and two mexeflote pontoons to move it all ashore. There was a lot of activity between the ships and the shore.

"I'm going aboard *Sir Galahad*," Mike told Tony. "I have clearance to speak with the Welsh Guards before they disembark."

"I wouldn't advise it, mate. It's ten o'clock in the morning with clear skies. Those ships are sitting ducks anchored out in the bay like that."

"You think so? I think the Argies have given up on bombing shipping. We haven't had a serious attack in ten days. There was a half-hearted sortie two days ago with two Lear jets, but we shot them both down."

"We only got one of those Lears, the other one high-tailed it. But that's not the point. Look over there." Tony pointed north to one of several peaks. "See that? That's Mt. Harriet, only ten miles from here and with a clear view of this bay. Think they don't have telescopes? They know those ships are here and I bet Buenos Aires knows it too."

"Well, if they send jets from the mainland, the Rapiers will take them out."

"Those Rapiers just arrived. I don't even think they're set up yet. They take twenty-four hours to bed in."

Mike shook his head and drank the last of his tea. "I appreciate your concern, Tony, really I do, but I won't be on that ship for very long. Just a couple quick interviews and I'll head for shore."

"Well, then, let me give you one more piece of advice: don't go below. Your chances of surviving an air attack are a lot better topside."

Two hours later, Mike stood on the deck of *Sir Galahad* speaking with one of the Welsh Guard junior officers. As they were talking, Major Ewan Southby-Tailyour came aboard accompanied by Major Anthony Todd of the Transportation Corps. They moved rapidly across the deck and began talking with the commanding officer of the Welsh Guards. Though Mike could not hear the exact words that were said, it was a heated discussion and the sailors were giving the group a wide berth.

When it became clear the officer he was interviewing was also distracted, Mike asked: "Do you know what's going on over there?"

"Our commander is refusing to disembark the Welsh Guards here in Port Pleasant. He wants them to take us up the coast to Bluff Cove. That's where we're going and we were told we'd be taken there by ship. If we land here, we'll have to march to Bluff Cove and leave all our heavy equipment behind here on *Galahad*. If we meet the Argies without our equipment, there will be hell to pay."

As they were speaking, they heard the commander of the Welsh Guards shouting.

"NO! I WON'T DO IT! I'm not loading my men onto a landing craft that's already loaded with ammunition. It's a mixed load and there are regulations against it."

The conversation quieted down and Mike could see Southby-Tailyour pleading with the Welsh Guardsman. After ten minutes or so, a compromise was reached and the two majors left *Sir Galahad*. When Mike inquired about what had been resolved, he learned that the Welsh Guards had agreed to be transferred to one of the smaller landing craft along with their equipment and taken to Bluff Cove on that, rather than risking *Galahad* in broad daylight.

When the landing craft loaded with ammunition had gone ashore and been unloaded, it returned to pick up the Welsh Guards. But as it pulled along side, Colonel John Roberts, commander of 16 Field Ambulance and the senior ranking officer present, demanded it be used to take his elite medical unit ashore. It was loaded with twelve men and nine vehicles and headed to the shoreline. This took an hour.

On shore, another problem developed. The loading ramp on the landing craft became damaged and could not be lowered. The Guard's heavy weapons and equipment could not be loaded through *Galahad's* rear doors, but now must be lifted by crane and dropped into the landing craft. The 350 Welsh Guardsmen would remain onboard until this was completed.

It was a beautiful day, flat calm with sunshine glinting on the water. *Galahad* had now been at anchor for five daylight hours. Mike had been aboard for two. At 1:10 pm, five Argentine Skyhawks roared into the anchorage. When Mike saw the jets, they were only seconds away and he instinctively dropped to the deck. A thousand-pound bomb hit the ship and the blast that followed lifted the deck beneath Mike. A second bomb hit a moment later.

It was like a slow-motion car accident where time stretches out and all the senses become distorted. The explosions seemed to roll through the ship and make the air thick with noise. As he began to recover, time sped up again and Mike was left terrified, deafened and pushed against a bulkhead, his nose bleeding. As his hearing returned, he heard screams and shouts and more explosions. A door opened and soot-covered men came coughing and cursing out onto the deck as black smoke billowed out of the doorway. Mike had some vague sense that he should go through that door to help the men below, but when he approached the doorway, he was assaulted by hot, acrid, deadly smoke and realized the men below were probably beyond help.

The two bombs that hit *Sir Galahad* burst through the engine room and came down a hatch on the deck. They did not explode in the conventional sense. They "deflagrated" with the casings bursting open, spewing the explosives they carried which then burned fiercely. The inferno grew as the fire reached the Rapier fuel and then set off the tons of munitions the ship carried. At the stern of the ship, the explosions broke open the deck and a column of fire and black smoke shot up into the sky like a volcanic eruption. On the deck amidships, someone grabbed Mike by the arm and pulled him to the railing. As they crossed the deck, he saw men hurling cannisters over the side.

"JUMP YOU FOOL!" the man beside him shouted as he climbed over the rail and dropped below. Down on the surface, sixty feet below Mike, the cannisters were popping into bright orange life rafts and men were swimming through the freezing water toward them. Feeling light-headed and drunk, Mike climbed up on the railing and pitched his body into the air.

There was a peaceful moment of floating through space, then he hit the surface on his back, his body horizontal. It was like dropping onto concrete. It knocked the air out of his lungs and left him unconscious, sinking momentarily until hands grabbed him and pulled him onboard a life raft. Several minutes later, he came to his senses, still dazed and racked with pain. His spine felt like carpenters were hammering on it. He watched helpless as others tried to row the life raft away from the ship using only their hands. One of the life rafts near him burst into flames when a fiery chunk of debris blew off the ship and dropped into it.

A pool of burning oil was rapidly spreading out from the stern of the ship and formed a wall of flame. Despite their best efforts, the men paddling Mike's life raft were losing their battle with the wind and being driven toward the flames. Men were shouting and desperately stroking the water, but the life raft continued to be blown toward the inferno. Mike was too injured to do anything to help. As smoke came rolling over them, he saw one man leap off the end of the life raft and swim away. He lacked the strength to follow and was terrified as he realized he was going to burn to death.

Tony Banks was standing on the bluff overlooking the bay when the jets came in and the explosions began. *Jesus!* he thought, *that bloody yank has got himself killed now for sure.* He felt both angry and fearful. Tony joined everyone else as they ran down the hillside to the shoreline. By the time he got to the water, every man in Port Pleasant was responding to the disaster. Lifeboats were launched from *Sir Tristram* and landing craft came off the shore to begin taking survivors off *Sir Galahad.*

Three Sea King helicopters, a Wessex, and a Gazelle launched into dangerous rescue operations. They flew in low through thick smoke over the still exploding warship. The helicopters hovered while winchmen dropped into the sea to pick up men in the water. At the same time, ropes were lowered down the sides of the ship and men climbed down them to get into the landing craft below.

As the boats came ashore, hundreds of men, many badly burned, were being unloaded and given medical assistance. Guardsmen with blackened faces, blistering flesh, and terrible gashes were crying out in pain and anguish. Some had their hair and clothing burned off. Tony helped lift those so badly injured they could not get out of the boats. He tried desperately not to hurt them further. The air was filled with the smell of burnt flesh and fuel oil. It was a scene from Dante's *Inferno.*

As he worked to bring the wounded ashore, Tony looked out into the bay and saw the plight of three orange life rafts that were now being pushed by the wind into a wall of flame on the surface. The men on those life rafts were shouting and frantically waving their arms, but none of the landing craft could reach them in time.

Then, miraculously, two of the helicopters saw what was happening and moved to save the men below. They brought their helicopters between the flames and the life rafts and dropped down close to the surface to blow the life rafts to the shore. There was great commotion on shore and men waded into the water to bring the life rafts in.

Mike was starting to recover when his craft came ashore, but he was having difficulty getting out when an arm reached in and pulled him up. He was surprised to find himself looking into the laser-blue eyes of Leith Cullen.

"Are you injured? Do you need medical assistance?"

"No," Mike said, "I'm...just a little beat up. Perhaps you could help me."

As he came out of the life raft, his legs seemed to give out and he nearly fell. Leith put his arm beneath Mike's arm and around his back, lifting him up to help him walk.

"Well, Mr. Ferrol, I guess you have something to write about now, don't you?"

Chapter Twenty-Six

June 11, 1982
Wireless Ridge, East Falkland

Reynaldo huddled against the tall rockface at the top of Wireless Ridge. He was sick, exhausted, cold, and wet. It was his fourth day in Patrol Group 42's new "camp" and it made him long for the comfort of their well-made shelter back on Engineers Point.

"I'm freezing" Rey said to Jury. "I don't know how you can work in this cold."

"It helps to keep moving" Jury replied. He lifted the long barrel of the gun he was cleaning and looked inside it. "I think Army was right when he said we have more to fear from rust than from the British. If this gun jams when we're under attack, we're done for."

"Do you think Cabruja has actually fired one of these?"

"He says he's fired one and I believe it, but I'll bet he's never cleaned one. I doubt he understands how they work." The Belgian-designed machine gun Jury was working on required a tripod to steady the barrel and two men to operate it, one to sight the piece and one to feed in the belt as it was firing. Jury had laid the parts out on their small tarp and was carefully cleaning them and oiling them before reassembly.

"You'd better finish up pretty soon" Rey said, "you know it makes our lord and master nervous when that gun isn't loaded and pointing south." Jury smiled at the off-hand reference to Corporal Cabruja.

Sonny came into their shelter area through the "front door," an opening between the tall rocks on the south side of their little clearing. Farther back, they'd stretched a tarp between three rocks, but it didn't provide an enclosed space. At best, it only gave respite from the worst of the elements. Jury continued working beneath it.

"Are you finished with that?" Sonny asked. "The Sergeant will want that gun ready to fire when he gets back."

Jury looked at him for a long moment before responding. "You know, you don't have to call him Sergeant when there are just the three of us here. He is, actually, a Corporal." Jury and Rey were smiling, but Sonny did not look amused.

"He will get his stripes back" Sonny said, "and probably be promoted beyond that if we all do our duty."

Rey and Jury looked at each other without speaking. There was a long, quiet moment before anyone spoke. In the silence that followed, Rey thought about Sonny's father. Rey had been to Sonny's house many times and knew his father well. He was a drunken brute and had once been an army sergeant himself. Perhaps that explained why Sonny seemed so comfortable with Cabruja. He was a father figure for him.

After awhile, Sonny said: "He will lead us in the battle that's coming and we must be ready to stand with him. Many will fall in the days ahead, but not Sergeant Cabruja. He understands what's coming."

In the quiet that followed, Rey felt the tension within his group of friends. It was never the same after they came together in Patrol Group 42. He hoped somehow they could join back together the way they had been before all this happened. Jury finished the work he was doing and reassembled the gun. He took it to the tripod and locked it on with the machine gun facing south.

"Sonny," Rey said, "have you heard from your family? Any letters?" No mail was delivered in the hills, but when Sonny went into town for supplies, he would usually stop at the post office and bring back mail for all of them.

"Yesterday, I got a telegram from my father."

"A telegram? Not a letter?" This sounded ominous and Ray was concerned. "Is everything all right?"

Sonny looked steadily into Rey's eyes before answering. "Yes, everything's all right. I'll tell you what it said. The telegram said 'Victory or death. Your family will bless you.' That's all my father wrote."

Rey was dumbfounded. He didn't know how to respond.

Sonny looked away before continuing. "That is what my family said to me. They understand what must be done. I am not afraid to die."

Rey thought about the letters he had received from his own family, his mother's admonitions to keep warm and eat properly. He dared not tell her how badly they were fed. Since coming into the hills, the food was even worse than he'd had near the airport. He thought about Amalia's last letter. She told him he must get plenty of rest and stay out of the cold. He had hardly slept since leaving the hospital. He caught catnaps, but Cabruja often woke him to go stand guard. And the cold was unspeakable.

"It's all right to fear death" Rey said. "It's natural. I'm afraid to die. Jury, are you afraid to die?"

"Only if I die before you two. I want to be the last man standing."

This, finally, made Sonny smile.

Cabruja returned to their shelter on the top of Wireless Ridge a little after noon. He set a heavy pack down and inspected the machine gun. He grunted when he saw that all was in order.

"Here are your food packs" he said, handing one to each of them. These plastic wrapped ration packs were only distributed once a week and they did not last long. They contained two packets of sweets, four water biscuits, a tin of cold stew, a few fuel tablets and some matches. Rey ate his immediately. He'd had nothing that morning except *mate cocido:* hot tea with no milk and just a little sugar. He gave the fuel tablets and matches to Jury who was in charge of the burner and making tea.

Each evening, they were given a serving of thin soup made with dehydrated vegetables and a few very small pieces of meat. For this, they had to walk half a mile to the kitchen at the base camp. There was no bread or cheese and fruit was unheard of.

For water, they had to walk a full mile back to the Moody Brook barracks. There were storehouses of food back at the barracks, but this was not distributed directly to the troops and only doled out to the field kitchens in controlled shipments. But the guards at the storehouses had made a business of stealing the food and then selling it to the troops in the field. If you could not pay, you went hungry. The market for cigarettes was even greater.

Cabruja reached into his pack and extracted two packs of cigarettes, throwing one pack to Sonny. Rey and Jury did not smoke, but they would have welcomed cigarettes which were a valuable trading commodity. The corporal carefully opened his pack of cigarettes and lit one.

Sonny looked closely at the pack of cigarettes Cabruja had given him. "Look at this: these are stamped cigarettes!" He held up the unwrapped pack and pointed to the blue stamp on the top. The government provided "free" cigarettes to the troops, though these were rarely given out. Usually, the only way to get them was to pay unscrupulous supply officers and the price varied according to who you were dealing with.

The free cigarettes had no government control stamp and came in sealed containers from the mainland. The cigarettes that had the blue stamp were bought at home by relatives who mailed them to the troops along with other gifts. Cigarette packs with the stamp were stolen by the troops working in the post office who then sold them. The black market was very active on the Falklands.

"These cigarettes were stolen" Sonny said.

Cabruja shrugged and took a long drag on his cigarette. "Everything on this damned island is stolen. They stole the land, we steal their sheep. What does it matter? If you don't want the cigarettes, I'll take them back."

Sonny looked at the pack in his hand for a moment then put them in his pocket.

That evening, Army came to their shelter bringing a pack of supplies. Rey had not seen him since their trip to the hospital and Rey embraced him and thanked him repeatedly.

"It was nothing" Army said, "you would have done the same for me. But you don't look so good. Have you been eating? I thought they'd keep you in the hospital for a week."

"No, it was two days and then out on the street. They needed the bed for the wounded. But they gave me a week's supply of pills. I still have a few left."

"Well, what I've brought may help." Army unloaded his pack. It contained chocolate bars, a dozen water biscuits, packs of unstamped cigarettes for trading, a box of fuel tablets, fresh socks, and a round bag the size of a cantaloupe wrapped in plastic.

"What is that?" Cabruja asked, looking at the bag.

"Mutton. Enough to give you at least one good meal. You should eat it now, before it goes bad."

"How will we cook it?" Jury asked. "We aren't allowed to have campfires and there is no wood."

"You'll have to cut it into very thin strips and use your burner. It will take time, but from the look of you, you need protein. Now it is almost dark so I have to leave, but the enemy is getting close now and you must keep a good watch. Put a man at each end of your shelter. But don't fire unless you are absolutely sure you see the enemy. There are 500 of us manning this ridge now and you don't want to hit an Argentine. I'll return whenever I can."

After Army left, they immediately set up the burner and began carving the meat into thin strips. They held these over the flames at the ends of their bayonets and the sizzling smell made their mouths water. Rey had eaten better at the hospital, but for the others it was the best meal they had had in weeks.

As they finished eating, they heard a rumble coming from the western hills. It sounded like thunder and the flashes along the horizon looked like lightening, but the air was dry and the wind for once was still. It was artillery, booming from across the island, and each man knew what this meant.

The fighting to the west of them went on all night and only settled down when morning came. Rattling gunfire and occasional bombing could still be heard, but it was sporadic and punctuated by long periods of silence. There was great activity all along Wireless Ridge as troops mapped out approach routes and lined up defensive lines of fire. Jury drew a map showing the various trails and switchbacks leading up to their shelter. Their "back door" offered multiple possibilities for retreat, but it occurred to him that these also offered multiple possibilities for attack. At the front of their shelter, there was one path down, but after several hundred yards, it broke into a fractured landscape of boulders with no clear way down. This would be the hardest way to escape.

An hour before sunset, Army returned to their shelter. This time he brought nothing in his pack for them. He called them together to talk.

"Last night, the British attacked us across the outer mountain range. Mt. Longdon, Mt. Harriet, and Two Sisters have all fallen. They are closing the noose around us and we must be prepared for imminent attack. We can see them bringing their heavy cannon forward and their troops cannot be far behind. Wireless Ridge is the last elevated feature of our defensive ring before Stanley. There are only clear fields between us and the capital. This is where we must make our stand.

"Have your ammunition belts set to feed into the machine gun at a moment's notice. You may be attacked without warning. We don't know if the attack will come tonight, tomorrow, or even the night after. But we know it is coming and it will come at night. Don't go on any further patrols. Stay here and hold this position. Be sure to check the identity of anyone who approaches. The British will probably send scouts to identify our strength and mark our positions. Kill them if you can, but first be sure they are not Argentine.

"They will probably bomb here before attacking, but when the bombing lets up, that is when they will come up for the attack. I have five other patrols I must speak with tonight before I report back to headquarters, so I will not see you again before the battle. Take care, be strong, and I will meet you after this is over."

In an awkward gesture, Armando shook hands with each of the men beginning with Corporal Cabruja. Rey watched Army leave by the front of their shelter. Rey wondered if he would live long enough to see Army again.

Army made his way down the mountainside, looking for a path he had seen that would lead up to one of the other patrols. His footing was hesitant and the rocks slippery with the light snow that had fallen. It was bitterly cold. He was forced to take several turns that led through rock-strew gullies. He was grateful for the shelter offered by these towering rocks. Still, it was anything but a direct route and when he finally reached a steep ravine, he was unsure which way to proceed.

He tried to get his bearings, but the cold mist and the failing light confused him. *There are hundreds of us on this hillside,* he thought, *maybe I can find someone to point me in the right direction.*

That was when his footing failed him. He slipped on a rock outcropping and his knee slammed against the rockface. The pain was excruciating. He thought he must have broken his kneecap as he lay on his back, rolling from side to side. It was several minutes before his breathing returned to normal.

He was finally able to sit up, his legs straight out in front of him, but the pain from his shattered knee made him feel faint. He could not walk. He could not even stand up. His leg was now swollen and he could feel the flesh pressing against his pantleg. He sat upright for over an hour, staring ahead, confounded by his peril. It would soon be pitch dark and then he would be lost. He could not stay sitting here, he would die of exposure.

Keeping his bad leg straight, he painfully pushed himself up to a standing position using his rifle as a handhold. He pushed the butt of the rifle into the ground, then pulled with both arms to get himself standing. He tried to use the rifle as cane, but it did not offer enough support. He finally gave up and pushed the barrel into the ground tucking the stock end under his arm so it became a crutch.

He hobbled forward for a step, but had to stop when he nearly passed out from the searing pain. He rested for a minute, then moved ahead another step. It was agonizing progress, but it was progress. Maybe, if he could keep going, he could find someone who could help him. For the first time in many years, he prayed and vowed he would be a better person if he could just live through this night.

Finally, he heard the rustle of footsteps around a large boulder and knew his prayer had been answered. He was smiling when another soldier appeared. But as he looked into the other's eyes, he realized with a start that this was a British soldier and the smile fell from his face. For an endless second, an eternity of time, he wondered what to do.

———◆◆———

Leith Cullen did not wonder. He raised his rifle and fired point blank into Army's chest. The bullet shattered his sternum, shredded his heart and passed out of his back leaving a hole two inches across where his spine had been. Army dropped to the ground like a fallen bird and all he might have been fell with him: the friends he might have made, the family he might have raised, the work he might have done, the memories he might have cherished; all fell into the snow around this body that now lay staring up into the sky through sightless eyes.

Leith Cullen considered none of this. He checked to ensure the enemy soldier was dead, then instinctively began scanning the perimeter. How far had the sound of that shot carried? Would the echoes between the tall rocks conceal his position or reveal it? If this soldier was coming down, how many others were hidden above? Were they coming down too?

Leith carefully moved away, pausing often to scan and listen. He gave no thought to the body left behind. Someone else would deal with it later. He had no interest in the dead, only in the living he must make dead.

Chapter Twenty-Seven

June 13, 1982
Wireless Ridge, East Falkland

The four men of Patrol Group 42 were quiet during the day following Army's visit. There was no sleep after he left them, they expected to be attacked at any moment during the night and a tense 14-hour vigil left them all deeply exhausted. When daylight came, they could still see fighting on the western horizon and hear the distant rumble of artillery and the chatter of gunfire, but the firestorm remained in the distance. Now there was no more to do, no further preparations to be made, only the waiting remained. There was little talk among the four men, each shrouded in their own thoughts. Fitful sleep gave only brief respite.

Jury brewed tea and served it out to Sonny and Rey. Cabruja lay snoring softly wrapped in his blanket in a shadowed space along one wall.

"How long before they get here?" Rey wondered aloud.

"They'd be fools to attack in daylight" Sonny replied. "They'll come tonight. I just hope they don't send the Gurkhas in first."

"I think if the Gurkhas were anywhere near, Army would have told us" Jury said. They lapsed back into silence.

In the hours that followed each man took his turn standing behind the machine gun, looking out toward the battle field to the south, sighting the gun against an invisible enemy. *How will it start?* they thought, *how will it end? Will I survive? What if I'm wounded or maimed? What if this is the last day of my life?*

The desire to go on living is universal and undeniable. We think it odd if someone does not feel the impulse for self-preservation.

Yet there are causes we feel outweigh our lives, principals worth dying for. *But is this that time?* we ask. Or will this be some hollow sacrifice that passes into history without meaning or significance? What benefit accrued from those who lie in Flanders Fields?

The barrage began at 9:15 pm. The bombs rained down in unimaginable numbers. Hundreds, then thousands of explosions detonated up and down Wireless Ridge. The ground vibrated and the huge rock formations shook as pieces of rock were blown away. The British had two batteries of artillery firing continuously, plus guns from the Royal Artillery and giant shells from the 4.5 inch gun of the frigate *Ambuscade,* firing from just offshore. They were also using mortars, Milan anti-tank missiles, and cannon fire from four of their smaller tanks, the Scimitars and Scorpions. Before the night was done, 6,000 high explosive shells would be dropped all along the three-mile length of Wireless Ridge.

When the bomb blasts began, Rey and Jury dove beneath a deep outcropping within their shelter, laying against the rockwall as far under it as possible. A moment later, Cabruja jammed himself in front of them, the stench of his unwashed body nearly suffocating them. He washed much less than any of them, if he washed at all. As Rey lay pinned between Jury and Cabruja, he thought that at least the corporal was on the outside and his massive bulk offered some protection from shrapnel should they suffer a direct hit. He had no idea where Sonny was taking cover.

The barrage went on for hours. The sound was loud at some points and deafening at other times when shells fell closer to their position. They heard shards of rock ricocheting off the walls of their shelter and the air became thick with cordite and smoke. The blasts seemed endless. A piece of rock hit the corporal in the leg and he cursed the British, but his words were muffled and barely audible.

After what seemed like an eternity, the bombing began to fall off and move away from their shelter. Cabruja rolled out of his position and sat up looking around. Rey and Jury quickly got out from under the outcropping and found Sonny in a corner at the north end of the shelter. He was holding his face where a small piece of rock had cut into his cheek. The blood had now dried over the cut and he told them it was nothing.

"If the bombing has stopped" Jury said, "the attack must be starting. We need to man the gun."

They ran to the machine gun at the southern entrance to their shelter. It was dark below them and they could not see any indication of the enemy. There were no flashes of light, no signs of artillery, no tracer bullets streaming toward them. Suddenly a star shell burst high above them and the entire hillside and the fields below were lit up as if night had suddenly turned into day. They saw dozens, possibly hundreds of figures moving about. But they were not attacking up the hill, they were moving down the hill. These were Argentine soldiers in full retreat.

At the same moment, they heard the rattling of machine guns, grenades bursting, and mortars exploding at the other end of the shelter. The British had not attacked from the south. They had somehow brought their forces around Stanley and were attacking from the north and the west, where the Argentine defensive positions were weakest.

Cursing and grunting, Corporal Cabruja picked up the machine gun, still locked on its tripod, and dragged it to the rear entrance to the shelter. Before he got there, a spray of bullets came in through the opening, taking chips out of the rockface. He jumped back and the machine gun clattered to the ground.

"DAMN YOU!" he shouted at the unseen British forces, "YOU BASTARDS CANNOT DO THIS TO ME! I'll kill you and I'll keep killing you until I get my stripes back." He turned to the other three. "Get your rifles. We're going out there."

Sonny was already holding his rifle and stepped up to stand in front of Cabruja. Rey and Jury looked at each other, hesitating a moment, then picked up their rifles. Corporal Cabruja put both his hands on Sonny's shoulders and spoke to him.

"This is it. This is the hour. We're going to kill those fuckers and push them back. Go out shooting and pin them down and I will bring out the machine gun and set it up. I trust you to do this. Be a man for me. Be a man for your father."

Cabruja stepped aside to let Sonny pass. As he moved toward the entrance, Sonny turned for a brief moment to look into Rey's eyes. *How curious,* Rey thought, *he is smiling.* Sonny took three more steps to the entrance before a vertical stream of bullets ripped his body apart.

The machine gun bullets hit his head, his chest, and his stomach blasting through his body and throwing a splash of blood onto the wall of the shelter. The impact lifted him up and dropped him to the ground full length. A wide pool of blood quickly circled the body.

Sonny Dambolena was dead. The shock of it stopped time for Rey and paralyzed him, staring at the bloody heap of flesh that had been his lifelong friend. There was no right or wrong to it, only the immutable passing of a life, the stark absence of someone who was loved. Rey thought of how Sonny had grown from the boy of seven he had played with to the cocky young man who teased girls, triumphed at sports, and stood up to bullies. All his strength and courage and loyalty had now flown and Rey was left with only the memory.

Rey came out of his revelry to hear an incoherent stream of profanity from Corporal Cabruja. He seemed to take this death as some sort of personal insult, an attack against him alone. All his bitterness and fear welled up into a towering rage as though only he had suffered this loss. Now he was swearing revenge for what had been done to him.

"...I'm going to cut the hearts out of these goddamn bastards and make them suffer. I'll give them pain they have never dreamt of. They will be bathed in pain when I get my hands on them. But first, we finish Sonny's work."

Cabruja pointed at Jury. "You. You're next. Take your rifle and go out the entrance blazing. We will be right behind you."

Jury could not believe what he was hearing. "Are you insane? They have our range. They know we're in here. We cannot go out that entrance. They will mow us down."

Cabruja slapped Jury across the face. "GO YOU LITTLE BASTARD!" he shouted. "You are my soldier and you will do as I say!"

Rey, frozen in place, suddenly felt he understood this man. *This is how he was raised,* Rey thought, *'DO AS I SAY!' I'll bet he heard that a thousand times growing up.*

Jury abruptly sat down, holding his rifle across his lap. "No. We need to retreat. Regroup. It would be suicide to go out there now."

Cabruja turned on his heel and moved to his pack. He rummaged through it for a few seconds. When he turned back to face Jury, he was pointing a pistol at him.

"Get on your feet you cowardly little prick or I'll kill you myself."

Jury held onto his rifle, but remained sitting. "No. We need to retreat, it's our only chance."

Cabruja fired his pistol, hitting Jury in the upper thigh. A moment later, Jury fired his rifle, hitting the corporal in the stomach just below his navel. Corporal Cabruja doubled over and fell to the ground, his pistol dropping from his hand. Blood began spilling onto his pants.

"Jury! Mother of God, what have you done?" Rey could not believe what he was seeing.

"It was him or us." Jury opened his pack and took out a small medical kit and began dressing his wound. Rey knelt next to him, but could see no way to help. As they both looked at the wound, they heard a groan and, incredibly, saw Corporal Cabruja holding his stomach with one hand while crawling across the ground, reaching for the pistol. He almost had it in his grasp when Jury lifted his rifle with one arm and tossed it into Rey's hands.

"KILL HIM! SHOOT HIM! DO IT NOW!" Jury screamed.

Rey fired the rifle at Cabruja, hitting him in the neck, snapping his head backward. Then he fired a second shot into Cabruja's chest. The body began to shake violently, blood pouring from its wounds, then it went limp and did not move again. Explosions continued outside the north entry and bullets ricocheted off the walls taking chips of stone with them.

Rey sank to the floor and dropped the rifle. "Jesus! Look what we have done. We've killed our commanding officer. It's the firing squad for us now."

"Not if we get out of here" Jury said. "This is only a flesh wound. Thank God our corporal was a lousy shot. If you help me up, I think I can walk." Jury had torn open his pant leg and put a bandage over the wound, then wrapped gauze around his leg to hold it in place. Using his rifle for support, he was able to walk with Rey to the south entrance to their shelter. As they were leaving, Rey took a final look at Sonny's body, then a massive explosion outside the north entrance blew shards of rock into their shelter. They moved out and were only fifty feet down the hillside when a British grenade went off inside the shelter above them. It was one of the infamous phosphorus grenades the British used and it filled the space with flames.

They made it into the rocks that offered protection and moved down the hill. When they got to a flat area, Rey saw a path leading east. He turned to Jury.

"I think we can get back this way."

"No" Jury said, "I'm not going back."

"What?" Rey thought he hadn't heard Jury correctly. Then he saw what Jury was doing. Jury had torn off a strip of the white bandage cloth and was stuffing this into the barrel of his rifle, leaving a foot of it hanging down.

"I'm going to surrender to the British. Come with me. We can get out of this alive."

"No. We can't. The British will kill you even if they see that pitiful white flag. Come with me back to our lines. You're wounded. You won't have to fight."

"I'm sorry, Rey. I can't do that."

They stood together for a moment looking at each other while the war raged on above them. They heard the machine gun fire, the thump of mortars, and the screams and shouts of those still fighting. But for that little bit of time, they were out of the conflict. Two friends silently saying goodbye.

"We'll meet back at your house in Buenos Aires" Jury said. "I promise." He turned away and found his own path between the rocks, heading west.

Something in Rey would not let him surrender. Even if he had thought it safe, as Jury did, he could not abandon his country. This war was not of his making, but it was his war none the less. He gripped his rifle and moved east.

Flashes of light from the battle cast long shadows among the rocks as Rey desperately struggled to find a pathway through. It was a treacherous passage, the rocks underfoot were slippery from light snow and everywhere he had to check his position to be sure he was heading correctly. With a start, he realized the darkness was beginning to fade and dawn was coming up. It gave an urgency to his steps.

He paused at the sight of a soldier lying on the ground. A rifle lay a few feet from him and Rey realized with revulsion this was a dead, lone soldier. As Rey approached the body, a star shell went off above him giving the scene a ghostly artificial light. In that light, Rey saw that it was Army. Armando Gottara, one of the kindest people Rey had ever met, laying on his back with a bullet hole where his heart had been. The sadness of it struck Rey so fully, he stopped where he stood to look at his friend.

A shot rang out and Rey's right arm went limp, his rifle dropping to the ground. Another shot was fired, barely missing Rey's head. He stumbled forward to get out of the line of fire, finding shelter where he could behind a large boulder. The numbness in his arm disappeared and he felt a river of pain up and down his arm. With his left hand, he gripped his right arm just above the elbow and realized the bone was broken clear through and the dangling appendage at his side had no life of its own. His rifle was behind him, somewhere on the ground, but it did not matter. He could not have fired it anyway.

He stumbled ahead holding his arm, dodging the bullets that rang out of the night and flew past him taking chips out of the rocks. After a quarter mile, the shooting ceased. Perhaps the shooter had lost interest or maybe he was coming after him on foot. Rey had no way of knowing. He drove himself forward, but felt weak and exhausted. He was bleeding beneath his jacket, he could feel it. He finally came to a small rock with a flat surface and tried to sit down to rest, but the rock was slippery and he slid off landing on his backside with a sharp pain up his spine.

This was the end. He could move no more. He lay among these timeless boulders as the sun came up and the sky filled with light, but he was powerless to get up and continue his flight. He wondered what death would feel like and why the cold did not lessen the pain in his arm. He dozed off and when he awoke, he saw a British soldier standing in front of him, pointing his rifle at his chest.

He would die, just as Army died, with a bullet through his heart.

Chapter Twenty-Eight

Leith Cullen looked at the Argentine soldier in front of him. He was young, wounded, and defenseless. He didn't appear to have any weapon at all. Judging from the odd angle of his arm, and the blood that had soaked through his jacket, the bullet must have shattered the bone.

He could kill him now. Perfectly reasonable. He was the enemy and this was a war. But something held Cullen back. He had killed four men earlier in the night and he hesitated to end another life without reason. This one could not harm anyone. He was out of the war.

Leith nodded his head and motioned with his rifle for the Argentine to stand up. But Rey was too weak to stand. He could not raise himself from the ground. Leith finally reached out his arm and grasped Rey's good arm, pulling him to his feet. He motioned for Rey to walk in front of him and pointed the way back to a British staging area.

Mike Ferrol was the first one to see the pair approaching. He was standing with a group of seven Paras who were reloading their weapons and checking their webbing. Several yards away, a dead Argentine soldier was lying on the ground, all but his feet covered by a tarp. As they came near, Mike realized this was the first Argentine prisoner he had seen taken during the attack on Wireless Ridge. He watched as Leith and Rey approached the group.

"Here now, what's this?" a tall soldier said. "Didn't you get the message, Cullen? We ain't takin' no prisoners."

"We're taking this one. He's mine and I'm taking him back."

The tall soldier and another soldier stepped into the path blocking Leith and Rey's way.

"Put him under the tarp and we'll do for him. Won't be no trouble at all."

"No. He goes with me. I'm doing you a favor. You don't want to be seen killing prisoners in front of the press."

The tall soldier glanced at Mike, shook his head, and looked at his mate. Then the two of them reluctantly stepped aside. "Don't see what's special about this one. What's he to you?"

Leith spoke over his shoulder as he walked past. "Read the last sentence of *Moby Dick*."

The tall soldier turned back to the group. "Who the fuck knows what the last sentence of *Moby Dick* was?"

"I do" Mike said, "the last sentence is '*And I only am escaped alone to tell thee.*'"

Back at the British base camp, Leith turned Rey over to a triage medic and left without a word. The medic started an IV to restore Rey's fluid levels and carefully cut away Rey's jacket and shirt exposing the arm with jagged splinters of bone poking out through the flesh. Somehow the bullet missed the major arteries and nerves, but the sharp edges of bone were dangerously close. A doctor dressed the wound and marked Rey for transport to the aid station at Ajax Bay. A cease-fire had been declared and Rey was taken by helicopter to Ajax Bay, then airlifted to the hospital ship *Uganda,* the only ship with full operating rooms.

Before hostilities began, Argentina and Great Britain established a "Red Cross Box" out in the ocean, 20 miles north of the Falklands. Within the two-square-mile area, the British hospital ship *Uganda* and six ambulance ships, three Argentine and three British, could operate freely, safe from any attack. The ships were closely inspected by the International Red Cross and were not allowed to carry any armament or surveillance equipment. These seven ships worked within the guidelines set out in the Geneva Convention.

Most of the Argentine casualties were treated onboard one of the three Argentine ambulance ships, the *Almirante Irízar, Bahía Paraíso* and *Puerto Deseado*. Once treated, the soldiers were then taken back to Argentina. But the most serious cases were transferred to the *Uganda,* which had better facilities, more doctors, and surgeons. Both British and Argentine soldiers were given intensive care and the British treated 150 of the Argentine wounded who were then transferred back to one of the Argentine ambulance ships to be taken home.

Reynaldo Poralez was one of the Argentine soldiers operated on by the British. They did extensive restorative work on his arm and put him in a cast from his shoulder to his wrist. He stayed on *Uganda* for three days before being put on one of the ambulance ships and taken back to Argentina.

The war was over, not only for Private Poralez, but for Argentina as well.

June 18, 1982
From onboard Bahía Paraíso

My Dearest Marisol,
I am coming home at last! I have been wounded, but there is a good chance I will recover fully. I was shot in the arm and had to have an operation to put the bones back in place. I have a cast covering my whole right arm. The English did this on board their hospital ship, Uganda. It feels very strange to have to thank them for saving my arm. They did this freely and actually saved many Argentine lives. I feel grateful to them.

I dream of you daily and hope you can forgive a soldier who lost the war. We fought as hard as we could, but the British were simply too strong for us. In the weeks before the end, I caught pneumonia from living outdoors and had to be put in the hospital. I wrote to you from the hospital, but I was so delirious, I can't remember what I said. I was released before I recovered fully and sent into the hills. We were camped in a place called Wireless Ridge when the end came. I cannot describe the savagery of the last attacks on our position. Such things are better left unsaid.

I have lost my dearest friends in this war. This morning I saw the list of casualties and there on the list were my two closest friends, Santana Dambolena and Juraich Mitner. I actually saw Sonny die and I will never forget the horror of it. We have been together since we were seven years old and no one can ever replace him. Jury was my best friend and I loved and trusted him just like my family. We became separated, so I did not see what happened to him. The British must have killed him before the surrender.

I also lost my newest friend, Army Gottara. I only knew Army for two months, but he was one of the kindest and best friends I have ever had. When I was feverish with pneumonia, I might have died, but Army dragged me two miles through the snow and got me to the hospital. He saved my life and when I found his body on a hillside, I felt crushed and hopeless. That is when I was shot and I only survived through the unexpected kindness of some British soldier. I never learned his name.

So I am coming home, but I am fearful. Have your feelings for me changed? I know I am older than you and perhaps your father will not allow us to see each other, but I have dreamt of you so long and held you in my heart so tightly, I can only hope you feel the same. I am not the person I was before this war. I am no hero, just a soldier, defeated in battle, returning home. Can you care for such a person? Can you love me as I love you? I pray that you can.

You are just as important to me as any member of my family, or anyone else I have left in this world. You are the only light out of all the darkness I have seen in the past two months. It is only thoughts of you that have sustained me and given me faith.

I will love you and be grateful for you whatever your feelings may be. I bless the providence that brought us together and hope we find each other again.

Your loving and constant friend,
Reynaldo

Marisol never received this letter. She was already gone when it arrived. Her father, fearing he would be put on trial, as many Argentine officers were, moved his family out of the country. He forbid contact with anyone back home, fearing reprisal. Rey was unable to discover where they had gone.

Chapter Twenty-Nine

June 14, 1982
Stanley, East Falkland

The war ended in capitulation. There was no final battle for Stanley, the Argentines realized their situation was hopeless and General Menéndez surrendered his forces. He hesitated at first, fearing he was surrendering all the mainland forces of Argentina as well, but the British persuaded him they were only seeking a resumption of local sovereignty.

In the late afternoon of the first day of the ceasefire, when the streets and hills around Stanley were eerily quiet, Mike Ferrol walked the three miles into town, alone and without authorization. The British troops had been ordered to cease fire, but hold their positions at the racecourse, outside of town. Mike went into Stanley knowing there was the off chance he would be shot by some Argentine patriot, but he wanted to be the first correspondent into the capital. He wanted to beat Max Hastings of the London *Evening Standard*, who always appeared wherever the action was. With luck, he would not be too late.

Mike was exhausted and bone weary. He had not slept for two days and had never been this tired in his entire life. He felt drugged. He had given up shaving two weeks ago and hadn't bathed in many days. Mike did his best not to look like a combatant. He carried no rifle or weapon of any kind, no helmet, not even a backpack. All he had were a few sheets of paper carefully folded in his pocket and a pen. There were many Argentine soldiers standing in groups along the street, but they made no move to stop him.

He walked a couple streets into Stanley without seeing any civilians. He wondered if they were ordered off the streets during the surrender negotiations. Finally, he found an elderly woman in front of her little house, patching holes in the walls. He was relieved to see her smile when he approached.

"Hello. I'm Mike Ferrol. I'm a correspondent with the *London Chronicle*. I wonder if you could direct me to Stanley House?"

Millicent Varnay sized up the young man in front of her. He was obviously an American, regardless whether he worked for a London paper, he looked so tired he might fall over, and he didn't impress her as being terribly bright. Walking into this town at this moment was not smart. Maybe he was just so exhausted his judgment was impaired.

"Mr. Ferrol, you look a bit washed out. I think you had better come inside and let me give you a cup of tea before you get yourself shot out here in the street."

Mike paused to consider and then smiled. "Well, yes, that would be nice. Thank you." He followed her inside her small bungalow. It consisted of a living room with an open kitchen area, a small bedroom and bath at the back, and a utility room off the kitchen area. There were a surprising number of bullet holes in the walls, but these had been plugged up using mismatched bits of cloth. She asked him to take off his boots at the door and then looked disparagingly at his muddy clothes.

"We'll need to put a sheet down before you sit on the couch." She brought a sheet from the bedroom, spread it on the couch, and indicated he should sit down. "Now, I'll just make the tea. I suppose you've been with the British forces?"

Mike collapsed on the couch and felt his head spinning. "Yes, I've been with the 2nd Parachute Regiment since the landing: San Carlos, Goose Green, Fitzroy, Wireless Ridge, and now Stanley. I'm hoping I can witness the surrender."

"You won't get there the way you're dressed. The Argies are mostly young boys and they fire off their rifles for any reason at all. It's dangerous to walk around in a uniform they don't recognize. You are likely to get yourself shot. Of course, you're about the same size my husband was. If you don't mind wearing a dead man's clothes, I can suit you up in his togs. How's that sound?"

Mike was too tired to care, but he was aware this woman was being very kind to him and he didn't want to seem unappreciative. "That would be fine." Millicent went into her utility room and began rummaging through storage boxes. When she came back fifteen minutes later, she found Mike fallen on his side and fast asleep, his head resting on a pillow which thankfully was covered by the sheet. She sighed and lifted his legs, tucking them into the end of the couch. Then she covered him with a blanket.

Millie paused a long minute to look at the man lying asleep on her couch. She remembered another boy lying on a different couch thirty years earlier: her son, Martin. Born prematurely, he had never been strong and fell prey to every illness that came along. He was five years old when they lost him and would now be about as old as this fellow. It was the central tragedy of Millie's life, far harder to endure than the later loss of her husband. They had waited several years before trying for a family again, but then were rewarded with Jenny, a robust, self-directed child who always knew what she wanted. *Worth the wait,* she thought.

Things past. Millie went back outside.

When Mike awoke, it was bright daylight and he could smell fried eggs and buttered toast. It was the best smell he had ever woken to. He sat up on the couch and stretched his legs out. His back was aching from the cramped position he'd slept in, but even so, he felt wonderfully restored.

"How long did I sleep?" he asked Millicent who was standing at her stove.

"Fourteen hours. It's Tuesday morning."

"Oh, no! I've got to get to Stanley House for the surrender."

"I'm afraid you've missed that. They signed the papers at 9:30 last night. They didn't let reporters in anyway, nor civilians either. Didn't want to embarrass the Argentines. I would have, if I'd had a say. Tell you what, why don't you let me feed you breakfast and wash up your uniform. You can get a bath and a shave and then

I'll take you down to the Upland Goose and you can meet some of the real Falklanders."

"That sounds too good to be true. Are you sure you don't mind doing all this for me? I have no way of paying you."

"I don't mind. But when we're down at the Goose, I wouldn't press too hard about the three women who were killed."

"I'm sorry...did you say women were killed?"

Millie looked at him for a long moment before replying. "Yes, three days ago. A British bomb struck a house here in Stanley killing three women. Friends of mine, actually." Millie spoke the words, but her voice was beginning to falter. She didn't want to cry in front of this stranger.

"Oh, I'm so sorry. I didn't know. I've been up on Wireless Ridge with the fighting. I never heard."

She pulled herself together. "Well, it's a tragedy of course. We nearly got through this war without civilian loss, but then this happened. I suppose it could have been worse. Anyway, we're holding a memorial service at the Cathedral tomorrow and you should probably come."

"I wouldn't want to intrude on the women's families."

"You needn't worry about that. Everyone in Stanley will turn out. There will be hundreds of us. I'm sure other members of the press will also be there. After we've chatted up my friends at the Goose, we can go over to the Cathedral and help with the cleanup. The Argies left the place in a shambles."

Millie was as good as her word. She seemed to know everyone at the Upland Goose and they were all happy to talk with Mike about their experiences during the war. He gathered enough material for several articles. Then they went to the Cathedral and joined the team of islanders who were cleaning it out after the Argentine occupation. They had left it filthy, strewn with debris and rubbish, and left behind a surprising number of weapons and ammunition.

Later Millie took Mike home and cooked him dinner. She asked where he would be staying that night. Mike told her he had no idea and she offered to let him stay with her. They made a bed for him on the living room floor using cushions and an old comforter. It let him stretch his legs out and was more comfortable than sleeping curled into a ball on Millie's short couch.

The next day, they arrived an hour early for the memorial service and still had trouble finding seats among the pews. As Millie had predicted, everyone in Stanley seemed to turn up and there was only standing room when the priest finally took the pulpit. Prayers were said and hymns sung and Mike realized it was the first time he had attended a religious service in almost thirty years. It took him back to his childhood, back to a long forgotten faith. Friends of the deceased gave eulogies, stories were told and poems recited. Finally, the priest stood before them for a final benediction.

"As we say our farewells to Susan Whitley, Doreen Bonner, and Mary Goodwin, let us remember all they gave us during their lifetimes. They were beloved family members, cherished neighbors, and dear friends. Let us hold them in our hearts and be thankful for the time we had with them, but let us never deny or disparage our sorrow. We cannot help but feel the depth of loss and the heaviness of grief. When the funeral bell tolls, it is not for the deceased alone. Every person's suffering belongs to us all. Let us pray.

> *Dearest Father and Almighty Creator,*
> *We know that by your gift, we have life, but must endure death as well. We are joined and then we are parted. Help us to accept the turning of the wheel of life and the wisdom of its completion. Give us strength and frailty in equal measure, that we might know your majesty and accept our weakness before it. Our lives are but a flash of light in the infinity of your time, but we are grateful to have them. We give you our thanks.*

"And now, dear friends,

May the Lord bless you and keep you;
May the Lord make his face to shine upon you
And be gracious unto you;
May the Lord lift up his countenance upon you
And give you peace."

Chapter Thirty

Standing outside the Cathedral, Mike was introduced to Millie's daughter, Jenny Corbyn, and her husband Grant and Millie's six-year-old grandson Darrell. When Jenny heard that Mike was staying with Millie, she immediately protested.

"Oh, Mum, you can't make him sleep on that cold floor in that drafty little house of yours. He'll catch pneumonia."

"Well, given the difference in our ages, I can't see the alternative" Millie said.

Jenny shook her head. "You're impossible. I think you just want to stir up your neighbors. All right, why don't the two of you come to dinner tonight and we'll figure this out. We eat at 5:30 sharp."

That left several hours open and Mike took the time to find the newly established Information Office and submit several stories to be sent back to London. Though the war had ended, the military was still censoring news coverage. Since his stories dealt with the islander's experiences, he doubted they would cause any alarm.

"Do you need billeting?" a sergeant at the Information Office asked.

"No. Thank you, I'm staying with a local family."

"Just give us that information, then, in case we need to contact you." Mike wrote down Millie's name and the street name. He did not know her exact address.

For dinner that night, Jenny cooked lamb chops, a salad, and cooked carrots Millie had canned before the war came. As she passed the carrots to Darrell, Millie said "These are my best carrots, grown with these hands." She held up her hands to show Darrell.

The boy looked closely at his grandmother. "Grammy, do you grow carrots out of your hands?"

"That's right" Millie told him. "And I grow onions between my toes!"

"EEEOUUU" Darrell said, holding his nose. "I don't want any onions!"

The conversation turned to the "liberation" of Argentine supplies.

"Down at the Defense Hall, it's a warehouse of foodstuffs," Grant said. "There's anything you could want down there: cheese, rice, flour, vinegar, oil. And the soldiers have told us to take as much as we can store and use. The rest they're going to haul out to sea and dump. We've been making trips to rescue as much of it as we can."

"Where are you storing it?" Mike asked.

"We've filled the kitchen and the pantry. Now we're putting it down in the root cellar that served as our shelter during the bombing."

"Do you need help with loading? I'm writing about how the island is recovering from the war. It would help if I took part in the work."

Grant looked at Jenny who gave him a brief nod. "Certainly, we'd love to have your help. The fact is, Jenny and I have talked it over and we think you should move in here with us."

"What?" Millie said, "You're stealing my house guest?"

"Oh, mother" Jenny said, "that little bungalow of yours is hardly big enough for one person, let alone two. We'll put him upstairs in your room on the third floor. You can come and visit him every evening if you like."

Mike turned to Millicent. "I do appreciate your hospitality, Millie, but she's right. That house is really too small for two people. And that makeshift bed we laid out on the floor last night is not really the accommodation of my dreams."

"Oh, all right. But I plan to keep tabs on you, young man."

"Well, I shouldn't be here too much longer. Whenever 2 Para is sent home, I'll sail with them. But I'll come and visit, Millie, and I'll help you fix those bullet holes in your house. I'm pretty good with paint and plaster."

Millie smiled. "I would appreciate that very much."

Grant told them about the Argentine container units that were left all over Stanley. These huge metal boxes were filled with supplies of all kinds. "The ones marked *Explosives* are loaded with bombs and shells and they parked several of them right downtown. If one of those had been hit by our artillery, it would have blown up an entire block. Out at the edge of the Common, there are rows of those containers.

"We thought the ones marked *MUN* were munitions, but they don't have any munitions in them. They're mostly food and clothing. It's amazing how much they never unpacked and got out to their troops in the mountains. We found one container filled with cigarettes, enough to keep their whole army smoking for a year, and another had nothing but Wellington boots. One unit was filled with clothing for women and children. We believe they were hoping Argentine settlers would come to the islands."

"I've heard they left booby traps everywhere" Mike said.

"Yes, the troops keep finding them. A soldier showed me one house where the Argentines had been staying. Before they left, they carefully set the table for tea, but the four teacups were turned upside down. One of the teacups had a grenade under it with the pin already ajar. All you had to do was lift the cup and it would have gone off."

"I spoke with Valerie Bennett yesterday, the matron at the hospital" Jenny said. "She told me that before they left the hospital, they put a grenade between the mattresses stored in a closet. Can you imagine wanting to blow up people in the hospital? She said that after the tragedy on Ross Road , two reporters from Argentina wanted to take pictures of the three British women killed. She refused, of course; locked up the mortuary and took the key home with her."

"If you really want to see what damage has been done" Grant said to Mike, "you might want to talk with Val's husband, Neville, he's the Acting Superintendent of the Stanley Fire Service. The Argentines have set fire to many buildings. They burned the Globe Store down to the ground."

"Yes, I'd like to speak with him. Perhaps tomorrow you could show me where to find him."

The ships that brought the troops down from England were used to take the eleven thousand Argentine troops left on the islands back to Argentina. The speed of the return of the Argentine soldiers was almost unprecedented. Within a few days, most of them were gone, leaving on *Canberra* and on *Norland.* The bulk of the British forces remained on the islands for two more months until replacements could be brought down from England.

Mike stayed in the Falklands for another six weeks. He learned that during the surrender negotiations, the British military leaders back in London had taken part in the talks in real time using an advanced communications link up. They left almost all the decisions to Major General Jeremy Moore and his staff in the Falklands, but they did overrule one request the Argentines made: they would not allow any Argentine troops to be transported back to Argentina on Argentine ships. They could only return home on British ships. It was, perhaps, a way of demonstrating to the Argentines who had won the war.

The junta would not allow the British ships filled with their returning soldiers to land at Buenos Aires. Instead, they were sent to nearby La Plata and docked at the Rio Santiago shipyard, a deliberately isolated location. The government was slow to acknowledge they had lost *las Islas Malvinas.* Many of the Malvinas veterans were home before the junta finally admitted their defeat. General Galtieri was forced to resign on June 17.

With the fighting over, Mike turned his attention to the cleanup of the islands and the restoration of public services. He wrote about the Commons where so many spent Argentine shells were embedded in the mud, they had to be dug up with shovels. He wrote about the busted water mains and the struggle to get the sanitation systems working properly again. The thousands of Argentine soldiers who had overpopulated Stanley were replaced by thousands of British soldiers who created the same problems. He wrote about mine fields that were poorly documented and unable to be cleared. But as he corresponded with his editors back in London, Mike became aware that fewer of his stories were actually being printed.

Finally, three weeks after the surrender, Mike received a telex communique from Rubin Blake, his editor at the Chronicle, telling him they were "wrapping up" their Falklands coverage and he should proceed back to London at his first convenience.

Rubin asked Mike to write a final summation piece, something that would "capture the significance of the victory and convey the gratitude of the islanders for their liberation." Mike thought about this for two days, but felt unsure what he might appropriately write. The truth was the islanders were very muted in their appreciation of the successful campaign and there were no open celebrations, no victory parades, no speeches with soaring superlatives about being liberated from the invaders. There was, in fact, a sense of loss among the populace, a dull awareness that life in Stanley would never be the same; that now the islands had changed forever.

Ruben's request also left Mike thinking about his own experience of the war. There were images of horror burned into his memory, scenes of carnage and waste that left him sick in the pit of his stomach. While he understood the need for this war, the rationale behind preventing any nation from taking over territory based on a hundred-fifty-year-old claim, the brutality of it still staggered him. It was senseless, irreparable destruction. He could think of nothing inspiring about it.

After hours spent pondering how he could write the article Rubin wanted, Mike finally gave up and just wrote what he was thinking. He doubted Rubin would run it, but the piece said what he felt, so he sent it anyway.

The Lives We've Lost

They came from Chaco and from Portsmouth, from the streets of Córdoba and the slums of Liverpool. Young men we armed and told to go kill each other. Nearly a thousand of them are gone now, from two countries that didn't hate each other, but only claimed sovereignty over the same obscure islands buried in the South Atlantic. Now the status quo has been restored and we can go back to our lives, except for those thousand boys and men who lie beneath the ground on East Falkland.

Somewhere on a street in Corrientes and down a back alley in Birmingham, two mothers wonder what it was for. Their daughters were not drawn into this clash of arms, this was men's business and they will only be expected to raise the next generation of men to carry it on. Men who will fight the good fight, raise the flag, and pin pieces of metal to each other's chests.

This thousand men who will not return from the Falklands or the Islas Malvinas, whatever name you give them, will never suffer the rigors of old age, never reflect on the decades they've missed, never write memoirs of the battles that left them behind, lying on the ground. Their stories died with them. And this minor skirmish, miniscule in the history of warfare down the centuries, will soon be forgotten.

It's been said this was a better war than most, a cleaner war, free of the atrocities that sully so many conflicts. It was confined to the military, a mere three civilians were killed, quite a record in these days. But the question lingers, was it a necessary war? Did it accomplish anything beyond the desecration of these once pristine islands? Did it settle the issue of sovereignty or give either country a sense of resolution?

No war is better than any other. They are all an abomination. At the height of our civilization, when we glory in the beauty of the Bolshoi ballet and celebrate Shakespeare's sonnets, we seem powerless to keep from killing our own kind.

There is a better world somewhere before us. A world where we lay down our arms, not in triumph, but in submission to a greater good. And someday, perhaps the loss of a thousand lives will be seen for the tragedy it was.

Chapter Thirty-One

Mike stayed in the islands another three weeks after the funeral. He wrote more articles and sent them back to Rubin, but he doubted they would get published. He spent the bulk of his time working with the crews that were cleaning up Stanley, hauling out debris and rebuilding the town. He worked on Millie's house, sealing up the walls and repainting. As winter set in, much of the work moved indoors and often had to be put off while the town accommodated the British soldiers who remained. The residents who had moved out into the camp returned and began cleaning and rebuilding. Mike helped wherever he could.

He stayed with Jenny and Grant and Darrell the whole time he remained in the Falklands. They were gracious and brought him into their family life with a generosity he had not expected. He found he could talk to them about things he had only thought to himself.

One evening after Darrell had been put to bed, he told Jenny and Grant about the terrible fighting on Wireless Ridge, the bombs exploding and the bodies he found torn apart on the ground. He told them about picking up his rucksack after the battle and realizing there was blood on it. As he told them about the horrors he had seen, he cried, openly and without shame, an outpouring he had not expected, but came unbidden.

They were warmly supportive and unembarrassed, but only within the confines of their English reserve. They did not hug him. They held his arm, spoke kind words, and served him tea and biscuits. It was enough for him to know they genuinely cared and were struggling with their own feelings as well.

The next morning, after Grant had left to take Darrell to the newly opened school, Mike sat with Jenny drinking tea at a small table in their kitchen.

"I don't really understand how you've processed all of this," Mike said, "the sudden changes in your lives, the upheaval, the loss of so much of your world."

"Well, I'm not sure I can tell you" Jenny said. "It seems much like this pregnancy." She patted her rounded tummy as she spoke. "I get up each morning, throw up for a few minutes, then carry on. That's all there is to do. But I know what you mean about the upheaval. And I will miss and probably long for our islands as they were before the war. But in some ways, the changes have been good as well."

"How have they been good?"

"We've been forced to take more of a stand for what we believe in. We didn't physically resist the invasion, but we didn't give in either and I'm proud of that. We stood our ground. The Argentines encouraged us to go back to England and would have happily given every one of us passage. But almost no one left the Falklands. We stayed to claim our islands and the war has defined us more as Falklanders.

"It's brought my family closer and taught us to rely on each other in deeper ways. The weeks living with my mother, which I thought would be a burden, proved a blessing instead. I've been able to give my mother shelter, something that has never happened in our relationship and it's brought us closer.

"And it's brought our community closer. Having the Carlson's and their sons stay with us was more than just the right thing to do. They became, for a period of several weeks, part of our family. They met our friends and we theirs, and this happened all over Stanley: a community forged in the crisis developed networks that never existed before. The 1,800 residents of the Falklands have always been close and supportive, but never as much as we are now. It's made us all proud to be Falklanders, proud to have carried on through the storm and survived."

"Well" Mike said, "you certainly have my admiration."

"It's changed you too, I can tell."

"Yes, it certainly has."

"No, I don't just mean the bloodshed and the destruction you've seen. I think you've changed as a person. When you talk about your life back in London, about being a journalist in one of the world's capitals, there's something of regret in the way you speak of it. And I've seen the way you play with Darrell. It's very imaginative and engaging. I know you're divorced, but I'm wondering if you want something different now."

Jenny's observations struck Mike to his core. He wasn't sure whether to be offended or grateful. But nothing Jenny said carried any malice and she was clearly sincere. He realized, with a shock, how comfortable he had become living with this family; being, even for a brief period, part of this family.

Later that evening, Mike sat at the small desk Grant had found for his room at the top of the house, a place where he could write his articles. It gave him privacy and he was grateful for it. Now he used it to write a letter to Madeline Tomlinson.

My Dear Madeline,

In your last letter you asked me not to write to you or contact you, but so much has changed over these past three months, I hope you will be willing to hear from me again. At the least, please just read these words so I can share what I am thinking and feeling.

I am not proud of our relationship before the war. I treated you dismissively and took advantage of your vulnerability. I am sorry, genuinely sorry, for using you so badly. I also feel sorry for how I treated Ted who was a friend as well as a source of information.

I know you well enough to know that you are not proud of our affair either. I am sure you feel guilty for the hours stolen from your family and the infidelity to your husband. I think both of us chose convenience over dealing directly with our problems. For myself, I was still coming to terms with issues from my divorce and the failure of that marriage. I feared serious, long-term commitment and instead found release in a shabby affair that went on too long.

Though I regret the circumstances of our coming together, I have no regrets whatever about being involved with you. You are an exceptional woman, beautiful, gracious, kind and giving, and a wonderful and dedicated mother. I'm sure you have made a successful life without the attentions of Ted or myself. I wish only the best for you and Edith.

I want you to know that I have changed. That may be a premature judgment after only a few months, but I feel the change as deeply as I have ever felt anything. It is partially because of the war and the destruction I have seen. Mortality has never been as clear in my mind and I now realize how precious every day is. The horror of young men dying in front of me has made me question what I am doing with the years I have left. Journalism has been a good profession for me, but I'm feeling the pull of an older dream, from back in my early twenties, when I thought I might write a novel or two. These tentative plans are still hazy in my mind, but they become clearer each day.

Something else has changed: I have been living with a family here on the islands and it has changed a lot of my thinking. For the past six weeks, I have been staying with Jenny and Grant Corbyn and their six-year-old son, Darrell. They are islanders, kind and gentle folk who have a profound understanding of how to be together as a family. It is hard to put into words what I've learned from them, but it has to do with acceptance and unwavering commitment. What they have gone through in this war has been hellacious, but going through it together has brought them closer and made their history richer.

I think what has passed between us could be seen that way as well. I think we could reframe our past together and see it, not as a tawdry passing affair, but as a tentative reaching out, a first connection, misguided perhaps, but sincere and rooted in affection and acceptance. It could be a bridge to our future.

I'm not asking you to marry me or even consider marrying me. I'm only hoping you will let us meet again, as different people, and see what happens.

I fear this may all be too late and sound like fantasy to you, like some passing phase—but I believe we have a future together and I will work for that future and fight for that future as hard as I can.

Please don't respond to any of this right now. Consider it and let your mind dwell on the possibilities ahead. I will call you when I return. I will be here for at least the next week before I can book passage to England and whatever ship I take back will need at least two weeks more to get back. That should give us both time to think about what we want in the years ahead. I only hope you will give us a chance.

Believe me when I tell you that I loved you before and I can love you again.

All my best wishes for you and Edith.
Mike

On the morning of the day Mike left the Falklands, he walked the streets of Stanley and paused outside the Cathedral. He could hear the townspeople singing the hymn *Jerusalem* inside and he caught the last two stanzas.

Bring me my bow of burning gold:
Bring me my arrows of desire:
Bring me my spear: O clouds unfold!
Bring me my chariot of fire.

I will not cease from mental fight,
Nor shall my sword sleep in my hand
Till we have built Jerusalem
In England's green and pleasant land

Epilogue

Chapter Thirty-Two

February, 2022
Médanos, Entre Rios, Argentina

Reynaldo Poralez and his nephew Marco worked for many hours on Marco's essay about the Malvinas war. Marco not only interviewed his uncle, he did research in the library and carefully took notes. He was able to shape these into a full story of the war. When he had finished the writing, he gave the paper to Rey who read it over and gave it his blessing.

What Rey told Marco about the war was true, mostly. In the end, Rey gave himself permission to simply lie about the death of Corporal Cabruja. In his telling of it, Cabruja became a British soldier who stormed into their shelter and was shot dead by Rey after the deaths of Sonny and the corporal. Rey was uncertain if his feelings about the death of Cabruja would have been much different if he had been a British soldier.

The project brought Rey and Marco closer and they often spent time together doing chores on the farm and Rey sometimes came to Marco's school to watch him play soccer. Any time Rey went into town, he took Marco with him. Though Marco liked spending time with his uncle and helping purchase supplies for the farm and loading them into their truck, he also used these occasions as opportunities to meet up with his friends from school. This left Rey with an hour or two to fill during each trip.

To pass the time, he went to Joley's Café to sit and drink coffee, and here he met the owner of the café, Jolianne Callera. She was ten years younger than Rey, about fifty he guessed, but she retained much of the beauty of her youth and a figure that caught men's eyes. She was a widow and this was not lost on the men of Médanos who often made ribald propositions she easily fended off. After one such exchange, Rey told her she brushed off men as easily as a horse whose tail swept flies from its backside.

"A very accurate description" she said, laughing as she said it. "I've had all the attention from men that I need. Now, it is just me and my café and my son. And, sadly, my son is very far away."

Thus began a series of conversations during which they told each other their life stories. Their relationship developed into, not a romance, but a deep friendship. Rey felt like a floodgate had opened inside him and all his thoughts about his life came pouring out. Joley was so open and unguarded, she seemed unafraid to tell him anything. He had not felt such intimacy since his wife had died.

The café was a small, simple building. There was a long serving counter with stools for the customers and facing that, six booths that could each accommodate four people. At the far end of the counter, on the opposite end from the door, there was a seventh booth set around the corner, behind the counter. Joley had made this into an office space, but it retained the booth table and she sometimes welcomed her employees or even customers to join her there. It was in this private booth, over a period of weeks, that she told Rey about her life.

Joley grew up on a hill farm in the nearby town of Mazaruca. She had three older brothers and grew up wild, fighting constantly for her place in the family. She smoked cigarettes and cursed like her brothers and caused many problems. Before she finished school, she met a soldier, fell in love, and found herself pregnant at 16. When her father learned of it, he took a strap to her and drove her from the house. Her brothers were forbidden to speak with her, but they helped her in secret when they could. The soldier disappeared.

She stayed with friends for a time, but this led to problems with their families and she had to keep moving. When she went to the church, the priest was not sympathetic. He told her she had been used by the devil and was now unclean. He told her to go to a nunnery, but Joley hated the nuns she had encountered at school and refused to go.

Toward the end of her pregnancy, when her belly was round and full, a strange thing happened. A farmer she had known for many years offered to marry her. He was old and fat and lived alone on a small farm outside of town where he kept chickens and a few cows. He said that she would have to work around the farm, do the cooking and the cleaning, but she could stay until the baby was born and he would pay for the hospital and see that she was cared for. But he told her that after the baby came, she would have to become fully his wife and give herself to him physically.

"He was certainly no beauty" Joley said, "and I dreaded the thought of sharing his bed, but I was desperate by then and had nowhere to go. I decided that I would stay with him until my baby was born and then move out and take the baby with me."

They were married quietly by the town clerk with an office worker as the witness. They kissed very briefly. She moved into his house and he gave her a small bedroom to stay in. He told her it would become the nursery after the birth and she would move into his bedroom. She said she was grateful and began doing all the cooking and cleaning.

As the last six weeks of her pregnancy wore on, Joley came to appreciate the farmer in ways she had not expected. He was kind, he was clean, and he never spoke harshly to her. The farmer worked hard every day and was very frugal, but he gave her money to spend when they went into town and paid for the doctor when she had visits. She felt grateful and was happy to cook and clean for him. She began to decorate the little house they shared and was happy when he bought her furniture for the nursery. On her birthday, he brought her a cake he had purchased in town and gave her a few small gifts. She was so moved by it, she kissed him on the cheek.

The birth was surprisingly easy. It was painful, but pain has no memory and when she held her son in her arms and nursed him, she felt only grateful. She was surprised by the farmer's reaction, he seemed as pleased and as excited as if the baby were his own. When she returned home two days later, he had stored her bed away and now there was only a bassinet and a dresser in the nursery. She would sleep in his bed now.

For two weeks, he made no demands, but she knew he was waiting and she was also waiting. She considered leaving, as she had planned, but she had nowhere to go and no way to support herself. And the farm had become her life as well as his. It would be a good place to raise a boy. Finally, she rolled to his side of the bed and gave herself to him.

The years that followed passed easily. The old farmer was as good a father to her son as she could have hoped for. He played with the boy as a child and gave him chores to do as he grew older. They became very close. His demands on Joley lessened as he grew older until his last year when she became his caregiver. She came to realize she loved this fat old farmer and would miss him terribly.

After he passed, she learned that he had left her everything he owned: the farm, the land, and all the animals. Within a few weeks, she sold all of it and moved with her son to Médanos, where she bought a run-down restaurant and renamed it Joley's Café. She opened it for twelve hours a day, from 7:00 am to 7:00 pm, and kept it open six days a week. It became her life.

Rey shook his head and smiled when she finished her story. "I hardly know what to say. You've told me so much about yourself. When I asked about your life, I didn't mean to pry."

Joley laughed and reached across the table and squeezed his hand. "I'm not one for having secrets. Everyone in Mazaruca knows my story anyway. Tell me about your life."

"I grew up in a large house in Buenos Aires. My father was a successful doctor and we were strictly raised, but given a lot of freedom as long as we did well in school. We never lacked for anything. Then the war came and I was sent to the Islas Malvinas."

He told her about his service in the army of Argentina, about the weeks living outdoors, being wounded and the care he received from the British, and how he had lost his dear friends Sonny and Jury. And for the first time in his life, he spoke about the death of Corporal Cabruja and his part in it. He told it just as he remembered it. He told her that even though he felt they had done the only thing they could, he still regretted it and the act haunted him.

After he finished speaking, Joley took Rey's hand and held it.

"In this life," she said, "we do what we must, and then we go on."

He felt a great weight lift from him and for a moment, Rey thought he might cry. It would have been safe to do so, but the moment passed and he felt only deep relief after sharing this dark secret. Still, he regretted that he had not shared it with his wife.

Rey told Joley about Marisol, how they had met, how they had written to each other, how he had carried her picture with him, and how the hope of being with her had sustained him through the worst time of his life. And he told her about returning home to find that Marisol, the girl he loved, was gone.

"Did you see her again?"

"Not for two years. After my arm healed, I went to engineering school, but I did not do well and it became unbearable. I could never master the math and all I really wanted to do was work with my hands. So I went to a trade school and studied tool and die making. I also learned welding and industrial fabrication. If you give me the engineering plans, I can build anything short of a nuclear submarine."

"But what about Marisol? What happened when you saw her again?"

Rey smiled, not wishing to rush the ending of his story. "We were different people then. She was older and I was still recovering from the war and the wound I had suffered. But our feelings had not changed and we dated for a year before I proposed. We were married for 27 years. It was the best time of my life. She was beautiful and kind and we spent the golden years of our adult lives together. But then I lost her."

"What happened?"

"We wanted children, but Marisol was not strong. She had two miscarriages. The doctor finally told us that she would not survive another pregnancy. So I had a vasectomy and we accepted that having each other would be enough. She was healthy during her twenties, but became frail in her thirties and in her forties had a series of fevers. She died at age 46. That was ten years ago." He smiled again. "Now I have my memories and my brother's children to play with."

They were quiet for a few moments, then Joley said: "Thank you for sharing all of that with me. The last ten years cannot have been easy for you."

"Well," he said thoughtfully, "easier than working myself to death at Joley's Café."

They laughed together. "I'm not working myself to death" Joley said. "I have employees I trust and I often take afternoons off before the evening trade comes in. But you're right, most of my time is spent right here in this café. It was better when my son was here, helping me. But he went away to college and then moved south. I see him once or twice a year now."

"Do you ever go to the movies?"

"Well..." she hesitated. "I've been a few times. Not recently."

"Why don't you let me take you to the movies this Saturday night?"

They went to a theater the following Saturday and watched a poorly written comedy, but it was enough to entertain them. They did not buy popcorn, but ate snacks Joley made at the café and snuck into the theater in her handbag. A posting said they could not bring outside food into the theater and they waited for the lights to go down to consume their forbidden snacks. They whispered together like children.

Rey walked Joley back to her house and before he left, bent forward and kissed her lightly on the cheek. She smiled and said goodnight, then went inside.

A few days later, Rey and Joley were sitting in the back booth at her café having coffee together. It had become their special meeting place. Rey timed his trips to town so that he got to the café when the lunch rush was over. Now she had time to sit and talk with him.

"Is your nephew with you today?" Joley asked.

"Yes, he's around town somewhere, probably meeting some girl. He'll be at the truck at three so we can go home."

Joley started to talk about the café, but stopped when she realized Rey wasn't listening. His gaze was fixed on someone who had entered the café, an older man, slim, short and a little stooped, with salt and pepper hair. Rey looked shocked to see him, as though he had appeared from the dead, as indeed he had.

Rey rose from the booth and went to meet him. They stared at each other in wonder for a moment before embracing. Then Rey was crying. Joley had never seen Rey cry before.

"Jury, how is it possible you are alive? I've thought of you so often, but...here, come sit down." Rey was smiling now, wiping his eyes. They sat together in one of the empty booths. There was only one other patron in the café, sitting at the far end of the counter.

"Oh, I'm not as easy to kill as you might think" Jury said. "Did you really think I was dead?"

"You were listed as dead. It was in the papers. And I never heard from you again. How did you survive?"

"After what happened, when you went down the mountain, I decided it might be safer if I was thought to be killed as well. I found the body of Leandro Pacheco. Do you remember him from the Third Division? He'd been blown apart, most of his face was missing. I took his name tag and gave him my own, then I surrendered to the British. I promised to give them all the information they needed about the defenses in Stanley if they would just let me live. Of course, I didn't really know all that much, but I made things up. We surrendered the next morning so it never mattered anyway."

Joley came to the booth and gave each of them a fresh cup of coffee. Rey introduced her to Jury. She was pleased to meet him, but she saw they had much to discuss and excused herself to go back into the kitchen.

"Why didn't you contact me after I got back?" Rey asked.

"I feared retribution after what we did on Wireless Ridge. I knew it would not go well for anyone involved in that war and I never felt safe. I fled the country and moved to Ecuador. I've been living there for forty years. I have a family, a wife and two daughters, and three grandchildren. I teach at the university. After I moved to Ecuador, I wrote to Pacheco's family and told them what I had done. I didn't want them to be left wondering what happened to their son."

Rey sat back and looked at his old friend, at the lines in his face and the grey in his hair. He wondered what he must look like to Jury. He'd put on weight in ways Jury had not, but they were still the same people, the same young friends beneath their years.

"What about you, Reynaldo?" Jury was smiling. "Did you ever see that girl whose picture you carried around?"

Rey smiled and felt a burst of pride. "Well, I didn't see her for two years. Her father was a Vice-Comodoro in the Air Force and feared being put on trial. It happened to many in the military. So he moved the family out of the country, to Bolivia. When they returned, she was eighteen years old. She found me and we started dating. A year later, I married her. We were married for twenty seven years. She died ten years ago."

"Oh, I'm sorry to hear that. Did you have children?"

"No, but we loved each other and had a good life together. I became a machinist and she ran a kennel where she boarded and trained dogs. Those dogs became our children. It was a good life we shared."

"What was it like in Argentina after the war?"

"It was hard. I was shot in the arm after we parted on the mountain. It shattered my upper right arm. The British operated on my arm on their hospital ship *Uganda*. They did a good job. I recovered almost complete use of the arm. But the government wouldn't allow us to be shipped back to Buenos Aires. The British had to take us to La Plata and there we were told not to talk about the war when we got back home.

"There were no parades or homecoming celebrations. It was just the reverse. People treated us like pariahs. They blamed us for losing the war. It was hard to find work and we quickly learned to lie about being Malvinas veterans. Many of the survivors who fought there became beggars. It was a very bad time for us. I was fortunate to have a supportive family."

They were silent for a moment, then Rey asked "Why did you come back to Argentina after forty years?"

"My father died and I wanted to talk with my brother and sister to make sure my mother will be taken care of. And I wanted to see you. It wasn't easy to find you. I finally got an address for your brother and visited there this morning. They told me where to find you in town. Go to Joley's Café, they told me, he'll be having coffee with her."

"Yes, she's a good friend."

"Do you think it will it ever become more than that?"

"I don't know. We're just finding our way."

"Say," Jury asked, "did you ever talk to Army after the war? Do you know what he's doing now?"

The smile fell from Rey's face. "I'm sorry. I thought you knew. Army didn't make it off the islands. He was killed there. I saw his body as I came down the mountain."

Jury pushed back into the booth and looked down at the table miserably. He breathed heavily and when he spoke his voice was raspy. "Oh, God. That's awful. He was such a good man."

"Yes, we left a lot of good men back there. Sonny and Army and so many others, they are still back there on the islands."

They were silent for several moments before Rey spoke again.

"Was it betrayal, what we did?"

Jury whispered fiercely: "He was a ravening dog, out of his mind, we had to kill him."

"No, I don't mean Cabruja. Did we betray Argentina? Should we have stayed and fought to the end? Given our lives even, if that's what it took to beat the British?"

Jury smiled sadly. "You're still a believer, aren't you Rey? Thrusting your lance for the noble cause. But we had no chance to recover those islands. We could not have won. We were fighting for the land, they were fighting for their people."

"But I grew up believing in the Malvinas."

"So did I, Rey, but it was a dream. It was never anything more than a dream."

"But what did our friends die for? What about Sonny and Army and all the others we left back there? Didn't it mean anything?"

"It meant the end of Galtieri, the end of the junta. That's what we fought for. We were pawns, but we were pawns for the right cause. It was the same struggle your brother Christobol gave his life for. We gave the government back to the people and the hundreds who died on those worthless islands, the hundreds who are still buried there, they ended the Dirty War and gave us back democracy. We may never get those islands back, but we saved Argentina."

Rey's mind was reeling now, processing Jury's words. Could it be true? Could they have been part of a larger scheme that actually saved their country? He wanted to believe it was so, he wished it was so. Perhaps it was.

They spoke for another half hour and then it was time for Jury to go. Rey walked him outside. They hugged each other briefly and then said goodbye, warmly as old friends will, but knowing they would probably never see each other again.

When Rey came back inside the café, Joley was waiting in their booth. He sat across from her, but said nothing. He felt drained.

"So that was Jury from your time in the army" Joley said.

"Yes, from very long ago. Some day I'll tell you more about him, but not today."

"Come to my house tonight. I'll make you supper."

He felt old and weary, but managed a smile.

"Yes, I'd like that."

THE END

Historical Notes

A Better War Than Most is a novel set within historical events. I have included historical figures sparingly and tried to use quotes or put words into their mouths that were appropriate to their circumstances. The main characters are, of course, fictional. The notes below elaborate and comment on the historical setting. Chapters with no notes are completely my invention.

CHAPTER 1
The infamous *Dirty War* conducted by the Argentine military junta against its perceived domestic enemies is well documented and a low point in the troubled history of that country. My description of it is based on many accounts.

CHAPTER 2
Nightmares from combat experience are very common among veterans. Warfare is a known source of PTSD and we are only beginning to give our veterans the psychological counseling and support they need. The incident of soldiers being "staked out" for disciplinary reasons is based on numerous reports.

CHAPTER 5
The rivalry between different branches of the service is very common in every military establishment. Indeed, there is often bitter rivalry between different units. There was also great rivalry within the British military.

CHAPTER 6
The incident with Constantino Davidoff and his scrappers is factually recounted here. It did start the war, but it threw the junta's timing off. They had planned to take over the Malvinas later in the year so that winter would set in and close down any chance the British

could retake the islands. But once the British got confrontational, Argentine pride took over and they launched the repossession of the Malvinas immediately. It was a fatal mistake.

CHAPTER 7

Ted Tomlinson and his office mates are all fictitious, but every military has similar planners. Major Brocton is fictitious, but Admiral of the Fleet Sir Henry Leach was a well known and highly respected figure. The speech I have given him here is my invention.

CHAPTER 9

While my description of Stanley and the Falkland Islands is factual, I have perhaps made it a bit more colorful than it was in real life. The None Such Shoppe, Fish and Flowers, and Jamison's Boat Yard are all my imaginings.

CHAPTER 10

This account of the Argentine invasion from the islander's point of view is based on three books written after the war by islanders and several other books that include interviews with the islanders. I've tried to render the night prior to the invasion exactly as it transpired down to the timing and the actual radio commentators who broadcast what was happening. Governor Hunt's messages are verbatim, according to sources, and the Argentine Four Communiques are summarized here and were considerably longer.

CHAPTER 11

The initial paragraphs in this chapter factually recount Argentina's actions, the British response, and the United Nations actions. Vice-Comodoro Lantana (a fictional character) speculates about Argentina's position, but I've given him foresight no one in the Argentine command structure possessed. The incident with the large Argentine flag blowing over and breaking the flagpole, described in Rey's letter, did take place.

CHAPTER 12

The description of Ascension Island is factual and it was, for a brief period, the busiest airport in the world. Countless tons of supplies, equipment, and thousands of personnel passed through this island and it is hard to imagine how the task force could have proceeded without it. The dominance of both the Sidewinder AIM-9L missile and the Exocet missile shaped strategic and tactical decisions throughout the war. The five rings of defense around the British carriers were constantly shifting as resources and missions off the Falklands coast dictated.

CHAPTER 13

The 2nd Battalion of the Parachute Regiment, 2 Para, sailed from Portsmouth on *MV Norland* on the date noted. While Mike and his fellow correspondent, Tyler Landry, are fictional, Tony Banks is a real person currently living in Scotland and has contributed substantially to the writing of this book. Much of this chapter is taken from his excellent book, *Storming the Falklands,* and I am indebted to him for allowing me to take passages and incidents from that book, sometimes verbatim, in writing this novel. Leith Cullen is fictional.

CHAPTER 14

The crossing the Equator ceremony is a common rite of passage ritual that has been practiced for centuries in many navies. I've been unable to find a description of what exactly was done on the *MV Norland,* so I've made up this account.

CHAPTER 15

In writing the story of fictional character Army Gottara, I couldn't help thinking about James Garner's character in the film *The Americanization of Emily.* Such supply opportunists exist in every military establishment. The shipment of television sets to the Falklands, to be leased to the islanders, did take place, and the sets remained after the Argentines left and the owners had made only two payments.

CHAPTER 16

The first bombing of the airfield at Stanley took place as described here and the very expensive flight of the Vulcan bomber was the first of five such raids, but none of the subsequent raids achieved the success of the first raid in scoring a direct hit on the runway. The success of the British Harriers and their Aim-9L Sidewinder missiles on May 1, came as a shock to both the British and the Argentines. It did result in the shift in Argentine tactics to the Four Lessons Vice-Comodoro Lantana outlines here.

CHAPTER 17

The torpedo sinking of the *Belgrano* and the missile destruction of the *Sheffield* are well documented. The reaction of Captain Sam Salt (an historical figure) to the sinking of the *Belgrano* is purely my speculation, but I believe many within the military felt this dismay. As I have hinted, Captain Salt did go on to have a distinguished career and ended as a Rear Admiral. The Argentines initially claimed that over a thousand men had died when the *General Belgrano* went down, but this claim was later scaled back to the actual number of 368. Exaggerations of losses are common in wartime, but the Argentines tended to make highly excessive claims of both their losses and their victories. The *Sheffield* took the bodies of 19 sailors down with her.

The sunken wrecks of the *Belgrano* and *Sheffield* remain today designated war graves.

CHAPTER 18

The extreme stress on the town of Stanley and the failing municipal services caused by the Argentine over-population are well documented and taken from multiple sources. The stories of Drs. Daniel Haines and Alison Bleaney (both historical figures) are also well known, including Dr. Bleaney's celebrated technique for dealing with the Argentine leadership by breastfeeding in front of them. The infamous Major Patricio Dowling, the Argentine Chief of Police, was also a real character, much feared and hated.

Monsignor Spraggon, another historical figure, was one of the heroes of Stanley throughout the occupation and worked tirelessly on behalf of the residents. The decision to stay in Stanley or head out to the safety of the camp was agonizing for every resident. Roughly 400 people chose to leave the town when it became clear the British were coming, but many families stayed. Much of my recounting of what happened in Stanley is based on John Smith's book: *74 Days: An Islander's Diary of the Falkland's Occupation.* John Smith and his wife Ileen elected to stay in Stanley with their children: Jeremy 20, Martyn 19, Anya 16, and Tyssen 11.

CHAPTER 20

The raid on the Pebble Island airfield was a perfectly executed attack that made the Argentines fearful as much for the stealth of the raid as for the destruction. The SAS escape by helicopter, at night, in gale force winds could easily have been a disaster, but skill and courage won the day.

CHAPTER 21

The landing on the San Carlos beaches and the subsequent "Bomb Alley" period of the war have been thoroughly documented in many books and articles. I've tried to stay as close as possible to the actual events, including the heroics of the Argentine pilots. Lieutenant Crippa's flight is recounted just as it happened. The failure of the British-made bombs the Argentines were using to blow up upon contact remained a secret until late in the war when the Argentines subsequently made changes to their fusing. The loss of Staff Sergeant James Prescott and the destruction of *HMS Antelope* are recorded just as they happened. The bomb squads that deactivated bombs drew the highest respect from everyone and these heroes daily put their lives on the line to keep others safe. An unexploded bomb that had landed inside the First Aide Station at Ajax Bay gave an amazing demonstration of their courage. The bomb squad personnel determined that it could not be defused, but was safe if left alone. To show those working at the station that this was true, the bomb handlers slept next to the bomb at night.

CHAPTER 22

While the attack on Goose Green might not have been necessary from a strictly strategic point of view, it was absolutely critical in demonstrating to the Argentines the superiority of the British armed forces. The later success in overcoming the mountain strongholds on the path to Stanley, and the final capitulation of Stanley itself, was due to the growing awareness among the Argentines that they could not win. Goose Green gave them irrefutable proof that they were losing the war.

The Argentines also heard the BBC announcement that the British were about to attack Goose Green, but they did not take it seriously and did not reinforce the Goose Green garrison or make any special preparations for attack. They simply did not believe what they heard. What country would be foolish enough to broadcast their battle plans? It was absurd.

The suicidal charge up Darwin Hill by Col. H Jones, and his subsequent award of Britain's highest military honor, the Victoria Cross, remains controversial. Is it appropriate for the commander of an operation to risk his life in direct combat? Many would argue it is not. The incident did demonstrate the soundness of the British command structure and the thoroughness of their Sandhurst schooling. Chris Keeble seamlessly took command and the mission carried forward.

The incident with Platoon Commander James Barry and two other soldiers being killed while trying to negotiate a surrender is shrouded in the fog of war. I've told the incident from the point of view of Tony Banks as he described it in his book, *Storming the Falklands*. Other accounts differ from Tony's. Martin Middlebrook, in his book *Argentine Fight for the Falklands,* states that when James Barry met with the Argentine Second Lieutenant Gómez Centurión in front of the schoolhouse, Centurión expected the

British to surrender, not the other way around. He refused and gave the British soldiers two minutes to return to their lines, but before they could do so, British machine-gunners on Darwin Hill a mile away opened fire on the Argentines, not realizing that surrender negotiations were taking place. Enraged, the Argentines then opened fire killing Barry and his men. Middlebrook writes: "It was an unfortunate incident in which no one had done anything dishonorable."

When the war ended, two weeks after 2 Para recaptured Goose Green, seventeen-year-old Kevin Browning from Goose Green, moved to Britain and joined the Parachute Regiment. He was posted to 2 Para after his training.

CHAPTER 25

Forty-eight Army personnel and five civilians were killed on *Sir Galahad*. Among the survivors, fifty-eight Welsh Guardsmen were wounded, many badly burned. *Sir Tristram* was also bombed with the loss of three Army personnel and two Chinese sailors. It was the worst British disaster during the war.

The incident with the helicopters saving the life rafts reads like an author's invention, but I have related it pretty much as it happened.

The wreck of *Sir Galahad* was still burning two weeks after the Argentine surrender. It was finally hauled out to sea and torpedoed by submarine *Onyx* and became yet another war grave beneath the sea.

CHAPTER 27

By most military standards, the dropping of 6,000 high explosive shells on Wireless Ridge was excessive. But after 2 Para's attack on Goose Green, when a planned six-hour campaign had turned into a 36-hour siege, 2-Para's new commander, Lieutenant-Colonel David Chaundler, called for all the "softening up" artillery fire he could get. It had a devastating effect on the morale of the Argentines, but still, many of the defenders fought on bravely. Many others fled.

To my knowledge, there were no incidents of soldiers killing their commanding officers during the Falklands War, but such actions have certainly occurred in many other conflicts. I've included the killing of Corporal Cabruja incident for plotting purposes.

CHAPTER 28

In *Storming the Falklands,* author Tony Banks, who fought with 2 Para, states that the troops were ordered to take no prisoners during the assault on Wireless Ridge. I have found no corroboration for this in the other histories of the conflict that I've read, but it seems likely that such an order was given. In *Goodbye Darkness,* William Manchester states that in the Pacific Theater during World War II, standard procedure was to take no prisoners.

FINAL NOTES:

The British lost 222 men, two civilians working on Royal Navy ships, and three Falkland Islands civilians. Argentina lost 655 men.

In a reversal of the historic policy of burying their dead where they fell, the British government allowed the families of the deceased to determine if they wished the bodies of their loved ones to remain on the Falklands or be brought back home. Some who perished at sea could not, of course, be recovered. Only 16 of the British dead are buried on the Falklands.

The Argentine government did not allow the families of their dead to recover the bodies. The junta did not want the embarrassment of bringing home the dead from a disastrous war. A cemetery was set up near Darwin, they were given a military funeral with a Catholic service conducted by Monsignor Spraggon of Stanley.

ACKNOWLEDGMENTS

My deepest thanks to Tony Banks for both his willingness to appear in this book as a character and allowing me to use information, and in a few instances direct quotes, from his book *Storming the Falklands.*

I also wish to thank my editor, Cindy Rinaman Marsch, whose support and wise counsel are making me a better writer. And I am very grateful to my cover designer Bea Reis Custodio who did the cover, interior book design, and formatting.

If you enjoyed reading this, please leave a review on Amazon. I read every review and they help new readers discover my books.

Made in the USA
Middletown, DE
07 August 2022

70689799R00176